THE SENIOR MOVEMENT

References and Resources

Reference Publications on
American Social Movements

Irwin T. Sanders
Editor

THE SENIOR MOVEMENT
References and Resources

Steven P. Wallace
and
John B. Williamson
with Rita Gaston Lung

G.K. Hall & Co.
New York

Maxwell Macmillan Canada
Toronto

Maxwell Macmillan International
New York   Oxford   Singapore   Sydney

G.K. Hall & Co.   Maxwell Macmillan Canada, Inc.
Macmillan Publishing Company   1200 Eglinton Avenue East, Suite 200
866 Third Avenue   Don Mills, Ontario M3C 3N1
New York, NY 10022

Macmillan Publishing Company is part of the Maxwell Communication Group of Companies

Library of Congress Catalog Card Number: 91–40851

Printed in the United States of America

printing number
1 2 3 4 5 6 7 8 9 10

Library of Congress Cataloging-in-Publication Data
Wallace, Steven P.
    The senior movement : reference and resources / Steven P. Wallace,
John B. Williamson.
        p. cm. — (Reference publications on American social
movements)
    Includes bibliographical references and indexes.
    ISBN 0–8161–1841–8 (alk. paper)
    1. Senior power—United States—Bibliography.   2. Aged—United
States—Political activity—Bibliography.   I. Williamson, John B.
II. Title. III. Series.
Z7164.04W38   1992
[HQ1064.U5]
016.30526'0973—dc20
                                                    91–40851
                                                    CIP

The paper used in this publication meets the minimum requirements of American
National Standard for Information Sciences—Permanence of Paper for Printed Library
Materials. ANSI Z39.48-1984.   ∞ ™

Contents

Preface

The citations in this bibliography were generated from a broad range of sources. Computerized data bases were the most fruitful, especially Ageline. We also searched Medline, Dissertation Abstracts, Sociological Abstracts, and PAIS. Many of the citations, especially for older works, came from reference lists of more recent articles. We included them to guarantee that works that were useful in the research of other scholars are listed here. The abstracts in this volume are all original; we wrote them after reviewing material from the books and articles cited. We omitted unpublished interviews and other archival data that are difficult to obtain. We were pleasantly surprised, however, at the ability of the interlibrary loan system to obtain copies of articles and books that were not immediately available at our own libraries. Thus, every reference cited in this volume should be available to any person with access to an interlibrary loan service.

We would like to thank the University of Missouri–St. Louis Gerontology Program for its special assistance in the preparation of this volume. The personnel at the university library and also at the library of the University of California–Los Angeles provided professional and much-needed assistance. Genevieve Owens was especially helpful in devising data-base search strategies. Cory Craig provided essential reference assistance in the last phases of the project. Any errors or omissions are the sole responsibility of the authors.

Introduction: The Senior Movement in Historical Perspective

In this essay on the senior movement our goal is to discuss the major issues and debates in the literature, based on our review of over 800 books and articles that deal with aspects of the movement. These were drawn from the empirical, the theoretical, the policy, and the advocacy literature and a sample of the popular literature. Since our goal is to analyze the senior movement as a social movement, we begin with a discussion of the concept of social movement. Because of the variation among scholars in defining social movements, we review the full scope of definitions. We think this is important since our analysis of the senior movement encompasses the broadest conceptualization of the term and we did not want to rule out any alternatives. We follow this discussion of alternative conceptions of social movements with an overview of the different organizational forms the senior movement has taken. We then turn to a discussion of the issues that have driven the movement. Next, we delineate some of the most important resources the movement has drawn on and discuss some of the limitations to the growth and effectiveness of the movement. We conclude with an assessment of the senior movement's effectiveness in achieving its goals.

There is no commonly accepted definition of the term *social movement*. From a broad perspective, Marwell and Oliver (1984) identify two common elements of most definitions of this term. First, social movements involve promoting or resisting some type of social change. While an individual's participation in the movement can include an expressive component, the main purpose of the group is to achieve a specific end. Second, a social movement involves a scope of action that has potential ramifications beyond benefiting its immediate participants because social movements involve an aggregate of collective actions or events. Marwell and Oliver note that an isolated protest by dormitory residents over certain rules is not a social movement. From another conception, social movements are "unconventional groups that have varying degrees of formal organization and that attempt to produce or prevent radical or reformist types of change" (Wood and Jackson 1982:3). This definition, like many others, focuses on the importance of groups in social movements. Limiting the consideration to groups, however, eliminates attention to the actions of unaffiliated individuals and uncoordinated events such as those that characterize many riots, demonstrations, boycotts, and other actions found in some social movements (Oliver 1989; Piven and Cloward 1977).

An alternative conceptualization suggested by Gusfield (1981) stresses the ideas embodied in social movements and their relationship to broader social norms. He emphasizes the fluidity of social movements and the indirect consequences of formal goals. His approach is particularly well adapted to dealing with movements that involve no or weak organization and focus more on expressive outcomes. Examples are certain religious movements or counterculture movements.

Yet another alternative is to emphasize "the sustained challenge to state authorities in the name of populations having little formal power" (Tilly 1988:3). Tilly limits his definition to national challenges to the state so that he can develop generalizations about social movements and the contexts within which they occur. His conceptualization represents a resource mobilization theory of social movements. This theoretical framework typically limits its focus to movements that try to change the institutional framework of society and/or its distribution of social resources (Jenkins 1983).

Because of the diversity in definitions of social movements, we drew from the broadest possible base in this review of the senior movement literature. Our references include writings on organizations *of* the aged that work for social change, organizations that are advocates *for* the elderly, and mass movements *by* older persons as well as works that are important for explaining the context within which the senior movement has unfolded.

Organizational Forms

Some social movement theorists suggest that social movements experience a natural history of formalization and regularization (Mauss 1975). Williamson, Evans, and Powell (1982/30*) used this model to examine the history of the senior movement and found that it has indeed followed a route of increased formalization since the 1930s. Whether or not formalization has been a linear process, it is useful to observe the changing organizational forms in the senior movement: spontaneous mass activity, organizations with charismatic leaders, bureaucratized membership organizations, and organizations of professionals.

---

*The number following the slash refers to the entry number in this text. References with no slash/number are found only in the list at the end of this introduction.

Spontaneous Actions

While spontaneous actions may have occurred, we did not find evidence of the elderly engaged in unorganized mass action oriented toward aging issues. This type of activity is not unheard of in other social movements, which have involved spontaneous riots, strikes, demonstrations, and other unorganized actions (Piven and Cloward 1977; Tilly 1988). Also, we did not identify any studies that explain the lack of spontaneous collective action on the part of the aged.

Charismatic Leaders

Charismatic leaders have fostered much of the activity in the senior movement. Social movement theory often considers these individuals entrepreneurs because they are able to redefine existing grievances in such a way as to mobilize a group behind them. The entrepreneurs can either be genuinely concerned about the movement issue or can be opportunistically trying to increase their personal power or wealth. The literature on charismatic leaders in the senior movement has often portrayed their organizations as radical, perhaps because they generally operate as outsiders from the political system.

The desperate economic conditions of the Depression in the 1930s were the context for a variety of charismatic leaders. The most widely discussed of these is Francis E. Townsend, the leader of the Townsend movement. This movement attracted millions of followers, but was organized in an autocratic, top-down manner. It was directed out of a central office, which appointed the directors of state offices and local chapters. Information flowed from the top down, with appointed speakers and centrally produced literature being important vehicles for seeking new members and motivating existing followers (Holtzman 1963/91).

The Ham and Eggs movement of the 1930s in California was similarly led by several movement entrepreneurs who took a popular pension proposal and "marketed" it to the elderly. Putnam (1970/130) suggests that movement leaders were not disappointed when a state ballot measure to enact their plan was narrowly defeated as they retained an issue that would attract paying supporters.

Upton Sinclair's End Poverty in California (EPIC) movement was another example of a Depression-era senior movement with a charismatic leader. Unlike most other charismatic figures, Sinclair appeared to be motivated by utopian philosophy rather than personal gain (Pratt 1976/128; Putnam 1970/130). While EPIC operated directly in the political arena, successfully electing candidates to several state and local offices, it was treated by the dominant political parties and the mass media as a marginal organization.

Several of the observers of the pension movements writing during the 1930s imputed selfish economic motives and/or ignorance to the aged. The Townsend Plan and its followers in particular were held in contempt by most governmental and civic leaders (Altmeyer 1968/470). To discredit the proposals, however, writers often attacked the movement leaders rather than the plans or their followers. Sinclair was labeled a Bolshevik (Putnam 1970/130), the Ham and Eggs leaders were exposed as participants in shady business deals and the Townsend movement leadership was subjected to harsh congressional hearings (Holtzman 1963/91). Later analysts have concurred that the motives of some of the Townsend movement leaders were based on personal gain, although they generally conclude that Francis Townsend himself was not motivated solely by a desire for personal benefit (Pratt 1976/128; Putnam 1970/130).

While the 1930s provided a fertile ground for spawning charismatic leaders, the post–World War II years have proved less productive, probably because the slowly improving economic status of the aged and the growing visibility of government efforts to assist them. During the 1970s and 1980s the most significant leader to mobilize the elderly toward social activism was Maggie Kuhn, the founder of the Gray Panthers. She has differed from the leaders of the 1930s by appealing more to the general social conditions of the elderly than by proposing a specific popular program (Halamandaris 1986/39; Jacobs and Hess 1978/97). Her personal experience with age-based mandatory retirement led her to devote her "second career" to fighting ageism. She has worked to make the Gray Panthers intergenerational in focus and membership while retaining its character as a senior movement organization.

Movement entrepreneurs have founded only a few other groups in recent years. The son of Franklin Delano Roosevelt, James Roosevelt, founded the National Committee to Preserve Social Security and Medicare (NCSSS) in 1982 during the turmoil over the looming Social Security deficit. He used the popularity of FDR among the elderly to help develop a direct mail campaign to "save Social Security," gaining millions of members in the process (Day 1990/250). The organization had a resurgence during the agitation over the Medicare Catastrophic Coverage Act, with the NCSSS helping to lead the push to repeal the bill (Holstein and Minkler 1991/684; Roosevelt 1988/711; Rovner 1988/137). Using sophisticated marketing techniques, Roosevelt's organization mobilized millions of elderly who depended on or felt entitled to Social Security. Similarly, the organization focused on the social obligations to the aged and the issue of fairness when working for repeal of the Medicare Catastrophic Coverage Act. Like some of the pension advocacy groups of the 1930s, the NCSSS has earned the enmity of some politicians for its heavy-handed pressure tactics (Rovner 1988/137).

In 1974, a 27-year-old conservative, Curt Clinkscales, founded a direct-mail organization, the National Alliance of Senior Citizens, that claims several million members obtained through its mailings. While it sells its members an insurance plan, its major political activity is lobbying against most federal spending on the elderly as being against their long-term interests (Day 1990/250). In addition to national groups, there are local organizations, such as the Chicago Metro Seniors in Action (Reitzes and Reitzes 1991/133) and the movement of nursing home residents in Minnesota founded by Richard Burtis (Meyer 1991/115), that rely on the leadership of a strong central figure.

A different type of entrepreneur is the professional organizer. Perhaps the best-known group mobilized by professional organizers is the Tenderloin Senior Organizing Project (TSOP) in San Francisco. This project began as a university outreach program designed to improve the health of elderly single-room occupancy hotel residents. Using strategies adapted from such well-known working-class community organizers as Saul Alinsky and Paulo Freire, the project has worked to help empower the residents. The mobilization of the community continues to depend on the presence of university student volunteers and a small professional staff (Goldoftas 1988/184; Minkler 1991/118; Wechsler and Minkler 1986/155).

Other mobilizations using professional organizers include the Coalition of Advocates for the Rights of the Infirm Elderly (Alwang 1987/58), Minnesota Alliance of Health Care Consumers (Meyer 1991/115), Living Is for the Elderly (Kautzer 1988/99), and Citizens for Better Care in Nursing Homes (Jacobson 1977//190). These last organizations all work with institutionalized elderly. Given the constraints on residents in nursing homes and their limited resources, it is not surprising that outside organizers are needed to help the residents effect change.

Bureaucratic Membership Organizations

Most of the social activism that has directly involved the elderly has been channeled through formal organizations. An early one, the Grand Army of the Republic, was a central actor in the move to expand Civil War pensions (Glasson 1900/563, 1918/565). While it was an age-integrated group, its membership grew older as the years passed, and the group eventually advocated pensions for all veterans past a specified age.

Another age-integrated fraternal organization active in the early twentieth century was the Fraternal Order of Eagles, attracting members largely for the insurance it provided. A membership crisis in 1917 was caused by the failure of one of its insurance programs, so the organization began to work for old-age pensions as a way to attract members. The ideological shift was successful and membership grew rapidly, making the organization an active participant in state and local lobbying for pensions for the elderly (Leotta 1975/46; Quadagno 1989/131).

Bureaucratic membership organizations increased in importance after World War II with the decline of charismatic leaders. Much of the focus during the 1940s and 1950s was on the development of Golden Age clubs and other forums for recreation aimed specifically at the elderly (Graebner 1983/86; Schulze 1949/139). While nonpolitical in nature, these organizations provided a setting where many older persons could gather, share common grievances, and link their age status with political values (Trela 1971/149, 1972/150). They also provided a convenient place to recruit older persons to lobby for specific legislation (e.g., Cramer 1961/174). Some of the membership organizations, such as the golden ring clubs organized by the autoworkers, took an active role in supporting expanded public programs for the aged (Lichtenstein 1962/109).

In 1947 the kernel of the largest organization in the history of the senior movement was founded—the National Retired Teachers Association (NRTA). In 1955 Dr. Ethel Percy Andrus joined forces with New York insurance agent Leonard Davis to offer group life insurance to NRTA members. The insurance was so popular that the American Association of Retired Persons (AARP) was founded in 1958 as a way of offering it to retired people who were not former teachers. The combined organization was known as NRTA–AARP until 1982 when the NRTA became a division of the more general AARP (Minkler 1989/586). Andrus does not qualify as a movement entrepreneur as the organization did not voice grievances of the aged but rather served to market a service—insurance. In fact, the AARP conducted no government lobbying until 1967 because Andrus was committed to free-enterprise solutions to social problems (Mehlman and Scott 1977/113). Since the late 1970s, when the AARP's ties to the insurance company whose products it sold were cut, its lobbying positions have broadened to include advocacy for government support of programs that address a broad array of social issues affecting the aged.

Both organizations attract mostly middle-class and professional retirees. Many NRTA members join because of their interest in public policy that affects them, while most AARP members are attracted by general membership benefits (Franke 1984/85). Joining the organization is almost effortless; membership costs only $5 and involves no commitments. This ease of entry has helped the AARP grow to over 28 million members, second in size as a national club only to the American Automobile Association (Burek 1990/859). Two thirds of the operating budget for the organization comes from the revenues generated by advertising in its monthly magazine and commissions from the products it sells (life insurance, pharmacy products, vacation packages, etc.) (Day 1990/250). The political activities of the AARP during the 1980s led several studies to use local AARP membership as a proxy measure for the political organization of the elderly (Button and Rosenbaum 1989/230, 1990/231).

The National Council of Senior Citizens (NCSC) is the second largest membership group, with 4.5 million members (Burek 1990/859). It developed out of Seniors for Kennedy, established by the Democratic party and the United Auto Workers in 1960. Its initial purpose was to advocate the passage of the Medicare bill, but it became a general-focus organization after achieving this goal. The organization successfully developed a bureaucratic structure with ongoing financial and organizational help from the UAW (Binstock 1981/229). It maintains an active local base of clubs, especially in states with unionized heavy industry, that provide a ready source of elderly to work on political issues and give direction to the national organization (Lammers 1983/17). Officially nonpartisan, NCSC has been active in advocating policies more attuned to those of the Democratic party. It draws heavily from working-class retirees and is more participatory than the AARP, although like that organization, it has also adopted membership services such as a mail pharmacy and insurance to attract members.

Both the AARP and NCSC are sufficiently large and well established to be considered "insiders" by federal policymakers. This status provides them access to the multiple phases of policy development and implementation (Day 1990/250). The ability of these organizations to claim influence over public policy should also enhance their ability to attract members. The Harris Poll of 1975 found that about one third of the elderly in the United States reported that they would consider joining a group that was devoted to improving the social status and living conditions of older people. This finding suggests that a significant proportion of the aged population would find membership in such a senior movement organization attractive.

In addition to examining organizations, we can also analyze the elderly in the organizations by looking at membership and participation patterns. Membership of older people in organizations was described as early as 1953 by Havighurst and Albrecht (88). They found that membership in formal organizations rose with social class, while those from lower social-class backgrounds were more likely to be involved in informal (especially tavern) groups. Findings that social class was a more important predictor of group membership than age were repeated by Videbeck and Knox (1965/152) and Babchuk et al. (1979/61). Trela (1976/151), however, found no social-class differences in the likelihood that the elderly would belong to at least one organization, although wealthy elderly were more likely to belong to age-specific groups. Most studies have found that memberships are concentrated in organizations that meet immediate personal needs (churches, social groups, etc.) rather than groups with goals beyond membership itself (like political parties) (Babchuk et al. 1979/61). Although membership in a church or recreation club does not necessarily lead the elderly into social action, religious and social groups can be used as the basis for mobilization (cf. the involvement of the Catholic Church in abortion politics, the National Rifle Association in gun control, etc.).

At times bureaucratized organizations get ahead of the social movement. An example of this is the vocal opposition to the Medicare Catastrophic Coverage Care Act of 1988. As an organization, the AARP was an active supporter of the bill (Binstock 1990/636). Because many of its members are middle class and subject to the income tax surcharge, however, they were not convinced by the AARP publicity and remained opposed to the program (Holstein and Minkler 1991/684). One result was that 6,000 AARP members resigned in protest over the organization's position (Tolchin 1989). Despite the generally positive response to the bill by organizations for the elderly, there was little or no popular support or even awareness of the catastrophic measure (Rice, Desmond, and Gabel 1990/709). This disjuncture between the bureaucratic organizations and their members is not unique, as the major organizations for older people tend to advocate more public programs than their memberships favor (Day 1990/250).

Organizations of Professionals

The twentieth-century United States has been characterized in part by the growth of professional dominance in the society (Larson 1977). Professionals concerned with the elderly have exerted a conservative influence over the lives of the elderly according to several analysts (Estes 1979/411; Evans and Williamson 1984/490; Walker 1981/622; Williamson, Evans, and Powell 1982/30). This effect occurs when professionals individualize problems diverting attention from the social causes of these problems (Binney and Estes 1988/786; Wallace and Estes 1989/459). Many professional groups benefit from perpetuating an individual-centered problem focus because it provides them with jobs and authority (Cole 1991/750; Estes 1979/411). To the extent that the aged see their problems as individual, the potential for collective action is reduced and their dependency on others is increased.

On the other hand, many organizations made up largely of young professionals and other nonelderly are vigorous advocates for social change. National organizations include the National Citizens Coalition for Nursing Home Reform (Wells 1985/157), the Older Women's League (Lewis 1986/195; Rathbone 1985/706), and the Villers Foundations/Families USA (Allen 1984/57). Regional and local organizations include the Coalition of Advocates for the Rights of the Infirm Elderly (Alwang 1987/58), Highland Valley Empowerment Plan (Minkler 1988/117), and Citizens for Better Care (Jacobson 1977/190). Each of these organizations depends on the services of professional staffs and is supported by a variety of nonmembership funds. While each organization is devoted to social change for the benefit of the elderly, older people are more typically recipients of, rather than coalition partners with, the organization's professionally based actions. For example, much of the movement toward improved nursing home standards has come from professionals, while unorganized elderly patients may have the most to gain from improved care. Some see professionals as being in the strongest position to advance senior interests (Sainer 1982/443; Sanders 1973/138).

Another type of professional group is the organization of organizations. Even when their constituents are mass-membership groups, these associations typically involve only the executive leadership of each group. One important "insider" organization in Washington, DC is the Leadership Council of Aging Organizations (Crowley and Cloud 1979/176; Rosenberg 1985/136). The council includes officials of the largest mass membership organizations of the elderly, representatives of aging service and medical associations, and several academic and government agency organizations. The leaders of these groups, all organizational professionals, meet regularly to coordinate advocacy positions and activities. Similarly, thirty religious bodies have formed an interfaith council called the National Interfaith Coalition on Aging. Representing the largest network of voluntary community agencies in the country, this group has tried to foster intergenerational cooperation and advocacy for the elderly (Letzig 1987/194). Single-issue organizational coalitions have also come out of the senior movement. Save Our Security was formed in the early 1980s as a coalition of national organizations representing those with a concern about proposed Social Security reforms (Crowley and Cloud 1979/176; Light 1985/332; Walsh 1985/153). A coalition of Oregon organizations was formed to push for reform in the regulation of Medigap insurance (Wyden 1977/735).

This review of organizational forms within the senior movement suggests that they have no dominant type of structure. Notably absent has been the unorganized kind of collective action present in many other types of social movement. Wallace et al. (1991) suggest that avoiding this sort of typically disruptive protest contributes to the legitimacy of seniors in the eyes of a public that is wary of aggressive forms of social protest. The mix of organizations led by charismatic leaders, those that are bureaucratic, and those composed of professionals has changed over time. It is likely that professional organizations will continue to play an important role in the senior movement because of their resources and structural interest in senior policy. As they have the most to lose by radical social change, they promise to be the most conservative segment of the senior movement. Bureaucratic membership organizations currently have the largest following and appear to have the most influence over social policy within the movement. The incorporation of these organizations into the Washington, DC, policy process also means that the groups will be limited to working for incremental change if they hope to retain their insider status. While organizations led by charismatic figures are currently the least active in the senior movement, the success of the National Committee to Preserve Social Security and Medicare shows that social conditions still allow a movement entrepreneur to be successful.

Issues

With the exception of a few key works (Binstock 1972/289; Pratt 1976/128; Putnam 1970/130; Williamson, Evans, and Powell 1982/30), research has focused on specific elements of the senior movement rather than on the movement as a whole. The issue that has generated the most research and writing is pensions, especially Social Security. This is probably because Social Security was a signal legislative act in the U.S. welfare state's move toward an active federal role and was a centerpiece of Roosevelt's New Deal. Consequently, the issue of Social Security and its subsequent expansions have been studied by researchers from a variety of different perspectives, including that of those interested in the formation of welfare states and the containment of class conflict under capitalism (e.g., Domhoff 1986/87/487; Jenkins and Brents 1989/499; Quadagno 1988/516; Skocpol and Amenta 1985/523), those wanting to chronicle important events in history (Altmeyer 1968/470; Sundquist 1968/147; Witte 1962/528), partisans who are attacking or defending the system as it exists (Ball 1978/471; Kaplan 1985/501; Kingson, Hirshorn, and Cornman 1986/813; Longman 1987/818), and those concerned primarily with public policy and aging (Achenbaum 1983/389; Kleyman 1974/101; Lammers 1983/17; Light 1985/332; Williamson, Evans, and Powell 1982/30).

More recently, the central issue in the senior movement has been health care, especially the cost of long-term care. Among those age 45 and over surveyed in the late 1980s, long-term care funding was the most important policy issue reported and the only issue besides homelessness for which a majority favored increased federal spending (McConnell 1990/696). The rising cost of both acute medical care and long-term supportive care guarantees that government efforts to cut costs will continue and that the pressure on the pocketbooks of the elderly and their families will increase.

Pensions and Economic Security

Social movement activity around the issue of pensions and the elderly predates the Depression. The earliest "pension movement" that involved and benefited the aged dealt with military pensions. Glasson (1900/563, 1918/565) provides the most comprehensive histories of these pensions while Oliver (1915/595) offers additional documentation concerning the activities of organized groups in pushing for pension legislation. Veterans' pensions were established as early as the Revolutionary War to provide for veterans and their families in case of service-related death or disablement. They were viewed as an incentive for citizens to volunteer during a time of war and a just reward for their service afterward. Civil War pensions had a significant impact on the nation both because of the numbers of soldiers involved and because of the liberalization of benefits that followed the war. Economic growth and high import tariffs helped create federal budget surpluses, providing a context in which politicians and industries protected by high tariffs saw advantages in liberalizing veterans' pensions. By the 1890s, military pensions were the largest single item in the federal budget (Waite 1893/620). Other important advocates for military pensions included pension agents who were lawyers paid to assist with filing claims. Veterans' votes were also sought through a politicized pension administration, and an organization of veterans, the Grand Army of the Republic, became an effective voice in lobbying for broadened pensions (Glasson 1918/565; McMurry 1922/337; Oliver 1915/575).

While the military pensions were initially designed to compensate for war-related losses, by 1890 they were granted to all veterans (or their widows and dependents) who were no longer able to work. Eventually, provision was made for pensions that did not require any proof of disability for veterans age 62 and over. By the turn of the century, approximately one million veterans and surviving dependents were receiving military pensions. Some states, such as Kansas and Ohio, had as many as one pensioner for every forty residents (Glasson 1918/565).

After World War I came the Roaring Twenties and the emphasis shifted from military pensions to compulsory state- and local-level pensions. This movement was led by several key figures, including Abraham Epstein, who wrote several well-documented books showing the economic needs of the aged and arguing for public pensions (Epstein 1928/555, 1938/556, Leotta 1975/46; Lubove 1977/508). Several groups were involved in this lobbying effort, including the American Association for Labor Legislation, various labor unions, and the Grand Army of the Republic (Andrews 1923/532; Epstein 1928/555). Success was limited, however, as few states passed pension legislation and even fewer implemented their bills (Epstein 1928/555). Not until the economic collapse of the Depression were multiple social movements spawned that helped create a national pension system.

The most extensively documented pension movement of the Depression is the Townsend movement. Founded by an older, out-of-work physician, it advocated paying $200 per month to every retired citizen over age 60. It was to be financed by a national transaction tax and was promoted as a way to pump money back into the economy to counter the effects of the Depression (Brinton 1936/68; Dorman 1936/80). The movement attracted a large national following by promising to satisfy basic needs in a simple fashion while preserving individuals' self-esteem (Cantril 1941/70). Similarly, the Ham and Eggs movement became popular in California initially by promising $25 every Monday to the unemployed aged 50 and over. A statewide vote to implement the plan was narrowly defeated in 1938 (Putnam, 1970/130).

Contemporary accounts of the movements are highly partisan, either trying to discredit the pension proposals and their organizations' leaders (McWilliams 1949/112; Neuberger and Kelly 1973/122; *Tax Policy* 1939/54) or promoting the plans and attacking their detractors (Townsend 1943/53; Brinton 1936/68). They left an extensive, if biased, history in part because the sale of movement pamphlets and newspapers served as an important source of both information for members and revenue for the organizations, especially Townsend's (Putnam 1970/130).

While the passage of Social Security did not eliminate the popular movement toward adequate universal pensions, the earlier movements slowly died out. The primary pension issue quickly became the expansion of Social Security, except for George McLain's movement activity in California that focused on improving the welfare-based Old Age Assistance (McWilliams 1949/53; Putnam, 1970/130). Social Security was gradually expanded over the years to include more workers, their dependents, and the disabled. One of the most significant expansions occurred in 1972 when the state-run Old Age Assistance programs were transformed into the federally run Supplemental Security Income (SSI) program and Social Security benefits were raised substantially (Burke and Burke 1974/539).

While most social movement literature emphasizes the mobilization toward social change and improving the status of the groups involved, the most visible recent manifestations of the senior movement have been conservative in nature. During the 1980s the major issues involved "saving" Social Security (i.e., maintaining nearly status quo benefits) by stabilizing its long-term solvency and keeping Medicare based on a social insurance model (i.e., stopping the implementation of the Catastrophic Coverage Act's surcharge on the elderly). These general issues involve protecting the financial status of the aged, an issue that cuts across class and other divisions among older people (Smith and Martinson 1984/367).

Health Care

The problem of health care has long been an issue for the elderly. When older people were asked how they would spend the extra money promised by the

Townsend Plan in the 1930s, the largest number replied that they would spend it on medical and dental care (cited in Cantril 1941:202/70). A less partisan survey found that American families would nearly double their personal spending on medical care if the money were available (cited in Cantril 1941:175/70). While some professional groups advocated a national health plan during the 1930s (Chapman and Talmadge 1970/647; Starr 1982/723), no senior movement organizations included health as a central issue. The depth of the economic crisis in the 1930s apparently led them to concentrate on pension issues as the first order of business. The problem of paying for sufficient medical care led the Roosevelt administration to consider including a health care component in Social Security, but it was never proposed because of fear that opposition from the American Medical Association (AMA) could kill the entire Social Security bill (Altmeyer 1968/470; Starr 1982/723; Sundquist 1968/147). The lack of a ground swell of activism for such legislation probably also contributed to the absence of medical insurance in the initial Social Security proposal.

Health care became a senior movement issue during the 1950s as health care costs doubled and the rapid expansion of private insurance still failed to cover most retired workers (Fein 1986). Advocates of a national health insurance decided to scale back their ambitions after the defeat of President Truman's proposals in Congress and focus their efforts on advocating public health insurance for the aged (Starr 1982/723). Congressional hearings, state conferences, and academic studies publicized the problems facing older persons who were seeking medical care (Council of State Governments 1955/407). While the 1950s were a quiet time for mass membership senior organizations, professional organizations were active in establishing the groundwork for public health insurance for the aged.

The movement for national health insurance for the elderly received increased popular support when the National Council of Senior Citizens was formed with the assistance of the Democratic party and the United Auto Workers (Pratt 1976/25). The organization was initially founded as a single-issue group to mobilize the elderly to support the passage of Medicare. Popular support was also mobilized through other organizations such as golden ring clubs (Lichtenstein 1962/109). Most analysts conclude that the elderly played a relatively minor role in the passage of Medicare (Binstock 1972/289; Marmor 1973/695; Pratt 1976/25). Because of AMA opposition, however, it is unlikely that the prime movers of Medicare would have been successful had they not been able to invoke the special legitimacy of the elderly (Harootyan 1981/314; Skidmore 1970/366). In that sense, the public view of the elderly as an especially deserving group was a valuable senior movement resource that Medicare advocates used.

The problem of paying for medical care has not gone away because of Medicare, however. By the 1980s the elderly were spending the same proportion of their income on medical care as they were before Medicare (Kosterlitz 1986/575; Schrimper and Clark 1985/717). While most hospital care is now paid for through Medicare, long-term care has become the most costly component of the out-of-pocket expenses of the elderly. The lack of both public and private insurance for long-term care (except for the poor through Medicaid) makes it an important issue for the aged (Rice, Desmond, and Gabel 1990/708). There is a large and growing literature on the problems of paying for long-term care, but the only significant senior movement activity in the area was the attempt of several movement organizations to make long-term care a 1988 Presidential election issue (Smith 1988/145). The mismatch between professional and senior-organization activity may reflect a groundwork-building phase similar to the one that developed for Medicare during the 1950s. Or, the problems of paying for medical care may not yet have reached the level at which a movement entrepreneur can easily mobilize the aged around a targeted campaign.

The health care issue that *did* mobilize a significant number of elderly was the effort to repeal the Medicare Catastrophic Health Insurance Act. This mobilization, however, existed because of the increased taxes that were being levied on the middle class and wealthy elderly. The activism was not a rejection of broadened social health insurance for the aged but a reaction to its financing by the elderly themselves (Holstein and Minkler 1991/684; Rice, Desmond, and Gabel 1990/708).

Quality of Life and Symbolic Issues

The senior movement has also mobilized around quality-of-life issues such as improving nursing home care (Harrington 1991; Monk, Kaye, and Litwin 1984/200; Scott 1985/140; Weiss 1987/156), establishing senior-only communities (Anderson and Anderson 1978/59), and fighting ageism and powerlessness (Levin and Levin 1980/765). Several of those issues have generated durable movement organizations. The National Citizens Coalition for Nursing Home Reform (Brickfield et al. 1985/67) has a strong interest in health care quality; the Gray Panthers work to reduce negative stereotypes of the aged and to increase their power (Kuhn 1976/106).

It would be appropriate, however, to consider these quality-of-life concerns as second-tier issues in the senior movement. They are linked to the broader movement because their advocates often invoke the special social responsibility to the elderly. This special legitimacy of the aged is particularly useful in advocating legal exceptions to discrimination laws in housing or directing special attention to the conditions of institutions housing mostly elderly patients. Even those, like the Gray Panthers, fighting ageism and disenfranchisement by using an intergenerational strategy implicitly benefit from the public perception that the elderly "deserve better."

These issues in the senior movement are secondary in the sense that their advocates typically mobilize only a small number of elderly persons at any one time and/or involve more localized and transitory ends. The Gray Panthers, while a high-profile organization fighting ageism, is one of the smallest general membership organizations (Day 1990; Jacobs and Hess 1978; Wallace et al. 1991). Other efforts are even smaller and more localized. Senior mobilizations around quality-of-life issues appear to be most likely when the issue immediately affects the lives of older people in a local context, such as the Adults Only Movement (Anderson and Anderson 1978/29), Chicago's Metro Seniors (Reitzes and Reitzes 1991/133), and grass-roots activity around transportation (Perlman 1976/204).

Given the organizational forms and issues common to the senior movement, we could describe the movement as the combined (although rarely coordinated) efforts of a series of social organizations and professionals that have historically attempted to stabilize the economic security of the aged. The goals in the early years emphasized the provision of pensions, culminating in the passage and expansion of Social Security and private pensions. Even the shift in focus of the senior movement increasingly toward health care-related issues has primarily been concerned with the crippling *costs* of acute care (resulting in Medicare), and more recently with long-term care and catastrophic illness (Rice, Desmond, and Gabel 1990/708). Symbolic issues such as ageism and quality of life have generated only low levels of activism in comparison to the material issues. The potential for the future activity of seniors is therefore greatest around issues of material consequence to their lives. Given the rapidly escalating costs of health care (Kosterlitz 1986/575), this issue appears to have the highest chance of serving as a mobilizing cause in the coming years.

Movement Resources

The resource mobilization theory of social movements places as much importance on the way in which movements mobilize resources as they do people (Marwell and Oliver 1984). The theory typically classifies resources as tangible (e.g., money) and intangible (e.g., participant commitment and skills). Most of the research on the senior movement has focused on its intangible resources, some of which appear essential to the success of the movement.

The senior movement is notable for its generally nondisruptive tactics aimed at influencing government policy and social perceptions (Fischer 1979/306). The key to the viability and pressure tactics of many other social movements has been the willingness to disrupt the normal workings of social institutions through actions such as work strikes, withholding rent payments, occupying public or private spaces, or disrupting transportation (Piven and Cloward 1977; Tilly 1988). In contrast, the primary resource of the senior movement is the legitimacy accorded to the needs of the aged. The issue of "deservedness" has been a constant theme in the senior movement as far back as the Civil War, and it is this special resource that has been most under attack during the past fifteen years.

In addition to social legitimacy, two other characteristics of the elderly have been seen as resources by many writers. These include the group consciousness of older persons and their high voting rate. Group consciousness facilitates group mobilization, although it is not a necessary condition for bloc voting. Other resources used by the senior movement include alliances with other powerful interests and the use of mass communications.

Legitimacy

There were no public opinion polls during the Civil War era, but documentation from that time suggests that it was possible to extend pensions for non-service-related disabilities in large part because of the recipients' special status. In 1886, President Cleveland is cited (Glasson 1918:207/565) as announcing that he was favorably disposed toward extending veterans' pensions to those "who, having served their country long and well, are reduced to destitution and dependence, not as an incident of their service, but with advancing age or through sickness or misfortune." At this point in history, age was already a conditional criterion of deservedness.

Several social historians have examined the public image of the aged during the 1800s and have come to conflicting conclusions. Fischer (1977/11) found that old age was increasingly stigmatized during the nineteenth century as a result of changing values that increasingly emphasized achievement rather than traditional authority. Achenbaum (1974/738, 1985/739) found that the elderly were esteemed as "survivors" until the Civil War period, after which their status declined as public attention shifted more to the physical problems of old age. Range and Vinovskis (1981/776) take a middle ground, suggesting that the decline in the status of the aged had already begun by the Civil War but that it was not as severe as suggested by Fischer. There is a consensus, however, that physical deterioration was associated with aging, which would make unemployment in old age more politically and socially legitimate as an issue to be addressed through governmental assistance.

After the turn of the century, social reformers worked to increase the legitimacy of the aged independent of other criteria (like veteran status). This shift was accomplished by publicizing the poor economic conditions of the elderly who had worked hard all their lives (e.g., Epstein 1928/555; Gillin 1926/562; Leotta 1975/46; Squier 1912/616). The reformers' actions were often aimed at convincing policy elites in state legislatures of the worthiness of the elderly (Andrews 1923/532). These same reformers typically condemned the almshouse system of poor relief, pointing out the miserable conditions suffered by many destitute elderly. During the early 1900s the primary focus of the senior movement was directed at states, as the federal government was still without any clear constitutional power to provide social insurance benefits or regulation (Chapman and Talmadge 1970/647).

The Depression helped solidify the view that the elderly were poor through no fault of their own. The various mass membership organizations that developed during this time placed a strong emphasis on the hard work most elderly had done during their lives and how their current conditions were undeserved. Some of the movements, such as Upton Sinclair's End Poverty in California (EPIC), were oriented toward the general elimination of unnecessary human suffering (although EPIC's platform evolved into little more than a pension plan [Putnam 1970/130]). Other organizations, such as the Townsend movement and the Ham and Eggs movement, appealed specifically to the needs of the elderly (Pratt 1976/25; Putnam 1970/130). The Townsend movement not only built upon the legitimacy of the elderly as recipients of assistance but also claimed that the pensions would help end the Depression by boosting the demand for goods and services (Brinton 1936/68; Townsend 1943/53). In this argument, the elderly had already contributed to the growth and wealth of the society and would continue to contribute to the health of the economy by receiving and promptly spending their pensions.

The organizational structure of the senior movement returned to professional organizations during the 1950s as most of the mass membership organizations declined, but the key movement resource continued to be the image of the elderly as deserving. It seems that in each decade the legitimacy of the aged needs to be reinforced and redefined. During the 1950s there was a strong move by professionals and government officials to publicize the social and economic needs of the aged. In that decade the first national conference on aging, sponsored by the federal executive branch, was organized, and numerous state level committees were formed to study and publicize the needs of the aged (Pratt 1978/350; Tibbitts 1951/453). Pratt (1978/350) argues that these conferences and proceedings were only symbolic, but this symbolic content is what may have been most valuable. The early White House Conferences had little direct policy impact, but they were part of the senior movement's assertion of legitimacy of need (Roderick 1984/357; Vinyard 1983/458). Similarly, the establishment of committees in both the U.S. House and Senate were symbolic; they are unable to report bills directly to the floor (Vinyard 1983/458), but they provide a public and prestigious forum in which the grievances and problems of the aged are aired (Oriol 1984/438; Vinyard 1972/455).

The public image of the elderly has been a topic of research since the 1950s. Rosenfelt (1965/779) argued that this image was that of a group living in poverty, dependent on others, and physically incapacitated. While he claimed that this characterization was incorrect, it was supported by the dominant theoretical perspective of the time. Disengagement theory (Cumming and Henry 1961/4) fostered a view of the elderly as slowly declining and removing themselves from society. By helping perpetuate a sympathy-evoking image of this group, disengagement theory worked to sustain the popular legitimacy of the aged.

The continued legitimacy of the elderly during the 1970s is demonstrated by the 1975 Louis Harris poll, *The Myth and Reality of Aging in America*. A large national sample indicated that people of all ages supported the improvement of the status and conditions of the elderly. The follow-up 1981 Harris poll found most young and middle-aged persons felt that older people had "very serious problems" with finances, loneliness, crime, high costs of energy, and transportation. Health, housing, and jobs were seen as problems of the aged by over 40 percent of young and middle-aged respondents. In contrast, the elderly reported experiencing those problems personally at one half to one tenth of those rates. This mismatch suggests that many years of publicity focusing only on the problems of aging were reflected in public opinion. Studies of health professionals (Coe 1967/748), gerontologists (Cohen 1990/172), and members of Congress (Lubomudrov 1987/507) have found that typical beliefs of these professionals also fail to reflect accurately the true status of the elderly.

To some degree, support for programs for the elderly also reflects the self-interests of the younger generation. Younger adults want Social Security and other programs to exist for their old age after having paid for them during their working years (Flowers 1983/493; Goodwin and Tu 1975/495). They also do not want to be financially responsible for their older relatives (Crystal 1982/3) and do not believe that charity could replace government programs (Sheppard 1982/447).

Public support for spending on the elderly has been an enduring finding in the literature. Cook (1979/792) discovered that public opinion in Chicago favored public spending on the elderly, with support for the aged being higher than for any other group. Klemmack and Roff (1980/327, 1981/424) found general support for using age as a criterion for senior services in Alabama, based in part on the positive public image of the elderly as being needy because of circumstances beyond their control. Their study also showed spending on the aged to be the second priority among respondents after spending on national defense.

The construction of many programs for the elderly as social insurance rather than social welfare has helped to foster the public image of those programs as being for the deserving. The decision to call Social Security "insurance," even though it has historically been a "pay-as-you-go" program, was a conscious decision by program founders to make recipients believe they were receiving a return on their previous contributions (Altmeyer 1968/470; Ball 1978/630) Survey data support the validity of the assumption that the insurance metaphor increases the acceptance of Social Security (Goodwin and Tu 1975/495). This characterization also gives the politically important middle class a stake in the system by basing eligibility solely on previous work history and age (Quadagno 1991/517). Grounding the system in the American work ethic avoids the stigma of welfare as well. The result is that the public now views Social Security as a citizenship right and provides broad-based support for the program (Shapiro and Smith 1985/364).

Medicare built on the same perception, helping make support for Medicare consistent across all age groups (Tropman 1987/377). The Older Americans Act was established to provide for all elderly persons, once again avoiding the stigma associated with means tested programs (Cohen 1970/403). The lack of a tie to work history eliminates one source of legitimacy, and leaves support for the program only on the general sense that the aged are deserving.

Even during the height of tax revolt fever in the United States in the early 1980s, national surveys showed that over three quarters of younger adults aged 18 to 35 felt that the government was *not spending enough* on the elderly. About two thirds of middle-aged respondents felt similarly, and few of any age group felt too much was being spent (Day 1990/250). Polls showed that most people did not feel the private sector could assume governmental duties toward the aged (Sheppard 1982/447), and some local jurisdictions even voted to increase taxes to support programs for this group (Morgan and Smith 1988/340).

The strong belief in the deservedness and legitimacy of the elderly thus appears to be based on multiple elements. First, the public perceives that the elderly have serious needs that are not self-inflicted. Second, there is a public sense that because the elderly have already contributed to society, reciprocity is appropriate (Wynne 1991/837). Third, self-interest contributes to the support of younger adults for programs for the elderly. There is no other group in society that combines these attributes, giving the elderly an unusually solid base of legitimacy.

Group Cohesion

The power of the elderly will increase to the extent that they act and behave the same. Group cohesion would turn their demographic importance into a social and political force.

Group cohesion would be fostered if the elderly recognized the discrimination they face and attributed it to ageism. Confronting discrimination and ageism would raise consciousness of age and improve the cohesion of the elderly as a group. Barron (1953/740) provided one of the first analyses of the elderly as a minority group. He discovered that the elderly were increasingly behaving toward age discrimination in the same ways that racial minorities behaved toward racism. Arnold Rose extended this idea in an influential article arguing that the elderly were developing a distinct subculture that would serve to solidify group cohesion and mobilization (Rose 1965/359). He and several others concluded that the elderly would become more age conscious and therefore more politically active around aging issues (Bengtson and Cutler 1976/226; Cutler, Pierce, and Steckenrider 1984/246). Butler (1969/744, 1975/2), who coined the term *ageism* suggested that the common problems of the aged would provide the basis for future mobilization. Later authors have continued this line of analysis by showing how discrimination and prejudice (ageism) are providing the elderly a common grievance, similar to the problems faced by minority groups (Levin and Levin 1980/765).

It is likely that age-group consciousness has increased since the 1970s. The rapid growth of senior centers during the 1970s could be an influence since older persons belonging to age-segregated organizations are most aware that their social standing is a function of their age (Trela 1971/149; Ward 1977/381). Similarly, the growing use of chronological age as a criterion for public programs and in other laws has made the category of "elderly person" universally recognizable and has raised age consciousness among those who obtain senior benefits (Chudacoff 1989/747; Cutler, Pierce, and Steckenrider 1984/246). There is some empirical evidence to support the claim that the elderly have developed a group consciousness. Gurin, Miller, and Gurin

(1980/312) found that age identification was as strong as class identification and stronger than gender identification. The elderly were just as dissatisfied with their social power as a group as blacks and perceived less progress in empowerment. As political party identification continues to decline in the future and the number of elderly increases, the importance of age consciousness is likely to grow in the electoral arena (Bengtson and Cutler 1976/226; Cutler 1981/244).

Group cohesion among the elderly has frequently been defined as holding similar attitudes on key issues, regardless of behavior. The most influential early analysis of the political attitudes of the aged was by Crittenden (1962/239). He argued that people became more conservative as they aged and were more likely to become Republican regardless of income. Subsequent articles refute this conclusion, claiming that the conservatism of the aged is an effect of birth cohort rather than age (Cutler 1970/240; Glenn and Hefner 1972/260). Cutler (1974/241) also examined a nonaging policy area, foreign policy. As with domestic policy opinions, he found that stable views were more likely within birth cohorts over time than for a specific age. Cutler and Kaufman (1975/249) examined the tolerance of nonconformity to explain why the aged were reported to be less tolerant than the young. They found that this quality increased among all cohorts over a 20-year period, but at a faster rate among the younger generations. Thus, the variance in rate of change created the appearance that tolerance decreased with age when it actually increased.

Later research has shifted to examining the diversity of opinions of the aged. Day (1990/250) documents the variety of opinions among the elderly on the role of government in assisting older people. The aged who were most likely to feel that the government is not spending enough on the elderly had personal medical and financial problems, lower incomes, declining personal finances, and Democratic party affiliation. Similarly, Schreiber and Marsden (1972/716) found that the higher support among the aged for the establishment of Medicare in the 1950s and 1960s was a function of lower income rather than of age. Weaver's research (1976/382) led him to generalize that the aged will coalesce around issues of personal financial interest while remaining fragmented on other issues. In other words, the same types of personal problems that propelled millions of elderly into active participation in senior movement organizations during the 1930s continue to predict dissatisfaction with government efforts. The older population shares outlooks, but its cohesion is based less on chronological than on objective economic and health conditions, which are not necessarily age related.

The generally held view of the objective conditions of the elderly is more uniform than the elders' personal experience of problems. In the early 1980s (Louis Harris 1981/20), over half those 65 and over thought that all people their age faced very serious problems with finances, crime, and energy costs — two to three times the proportion of elderly who reported personal experience with those problems. The greatest discrepancies were between the experience of and the generalizations about poor housing, insufficient job opportunities, and inadequate medical care. Group cohesion could be fostered, nonetheless, by a sense among the elderly that other older people face pervasive problems that could also afflict them without warning—even if they are not currently confronting the problems personally.

Interest in the degree of uniformity of interests among the elderly shifted during the 1980s. One set of writers presented the elderly as all holding selfish interests to the detriment of society (Chakravarty and Weisman 1988/789; Longman 1985/816). To counter that image, another set of writers has provided survey data to show the diversity of the elderly and to demonstrate that they are no more likely to support spending on the aged than other groups. As an example that the elderly were not selfish, Ponza et al. (1988/823) reported that the elderly did not favor spending on older women more than on younger women with children when both groups were living in poverty.

The image of group cohesion is fostered by government-sponsored groups in which the elderly formulate *the* position of the aged on issues. One symbolic but politically visible forum is Silver-Haired Legislatures. These gatherings of elderly persons are mock state legislative sessions in which possible bills are debated and voted on (Ash 1983/60; Hamilton 1979/313; Smith and Martinson 1984/367). A more episodic forum is the gathering of senior advocacy and professional groups and community leaders in the White House Conferences on Aging. The 1981 White House Conference in particular was very politically active in pushing for measures for the aged (Dobelstein and Johnson 1985/297; Hubbard 1982/318; Johnson, Maddox, and Kaplan 1982/323), an activism that may have led President Bush to fail to call for a 1991 White House Conference.

The Senior Vote

Whether or not the elderly hold uniform opinions, there is a political concern with the "senior vote" (Pratt 1983/129). This attention comes in large part from the high voting rates of the elderly combined with their growing numbers. Politicians have been courting the senior vote for over a century, with some post–Civil War politicians actively seeking the support of aging veterans (Glasson 1918/565). Accounts of the formulation and passage of Social Security note that most congressmen were acutely aware of the popularity of the Townsend Plan and other "radical" redistributive plans (Altmeyer 1968/470; Pratt 1976/128). Several politicians successfully made one of the era's populist pension plans a key campaign issue, while others made symbolic gestures of support to gain votes (Putnam 1970/130).

Political concern with the senior vote moved from an issue orientation to a group orientation in 1960 when the Democratic party established Seniors for Kennedy (Pratt 1976/128). Given Kennedy's narrow victory, senior advocates were able to claim that their votes were critical (despite mixed data to support that claim [Pratt 1976/128; Sheppard 1962/365]). The Democrats have presented the party as a friend of the elderly as a political strategy to attract the older voter. They have associated themselves with popular programs like Social Security and Medicare to bolster their popularity with seniors and have established special campaign staffs to work on securing the support of this group of voters (Riemer and Binstock 1978/272). The perceived effectiveness of the Democratic strategy is suggested by Republican support for indexing Social Security benefits. Democratic Congresses had been voting for popular benefit increases before almost every election and taking the credit. Republicans saw automatic indexing as depoliticizing and limiting benefit increases (Burke and Burke 1974/539).

Social Security became "untouchable" in the 1980s after Republican congressional losses in the 1982 elections were attributed in part to their proposals to reduce or privatize Social Security (Light 1985/332; Light 1981/265). Members of both parties apparently feared the electoral power of the elderly when they quickly repealed the Medicare Catastrophic Coverage Act of 1988 in the face of the opposition of a group of vocal seniors (Holstein and Minkler 1991/684; Torres-Gil 1989/726). In both the Social Security reform and Medicare Catastrophic issues, members of Congress were impressed with the large volume of mail they received from seniors. While some of the volume came from preprinted postcards distributed by advocacy groups, much of it was handwritten—and congressional representatives count one handwritten letter as equivalent to numerous postcards (Light 1985/332; Rovner 1988/137).

The research on the voting power of the elderly has typically reported the *perception* of voting rather than documenting cases where the vote of the aged was swayed by a candidate and decided a contest. As with the legitimacy of the aged, however, perceptions are at least as important as factual data, as policymakers and the public act on their beliefs, regardless of how well those beliefs correspond to reality.

Coalition Partners

Williamson, Evans, and Powell (1982/30) argue that the senior movement succeeds primarily when it is allied with other powerful interests. Those range from organized labor in advocating Medicare, the blind and disabled in advocating Supplemental Security Income (SSI), and consumer groups in advocating improved nursing home regulation.

Estes (1979/411) provided an influential analysis of the vested interests of human service professionals and others who work with the elderly. She showed how the interests of professional groups are often at odds with those of the aged. Nonetheless, the presence of an aging network has been a resource in the senior movement to the extent that many human service professionals lobby government and the general population for remedies for some of the needs of the elderly.

The aging enterprise was useful in the 1950s in bringing public attention to the needs of the aged, helping to solidify the elderly's position as an especially deserving group. The National Committee on the Aging (1954/121), for example, brought together persons involved in nursing homes to discuss standards and procedures. The conclusion of the conference, however, was that professionals should become more active in publicizing the problems of the elderly to help create and maintain a "sound political situation." Congress was instrumental in building public support for the elderly through a series of public hearings around the country that documented the plight of the aged (Oriol 1984/438; Vinyard 1972/455). Organized labor was also a useful ally at the time in pushing for public acceptance of government assistance in medical care (Sundquist 1968/147).

The senior movement has also had a few important supporters within the government. The best-known advocate for the elderly was Claude Pepper, a longtime member of the House of Representatives from Florida (Sinclair 1984/52; Cardona 1986/35). He was a consistent and high-profile supporter of expanded benefits for the aged, and his visibility helped him mobilize both popular and legislative support for his positions (Rovner 1988/137). At the state level, legislators seldom specialize in aging issues. In Florida, Iowa, Michigan, and New Jersey, Browne and Ringquist (1985/397) found few if any legislators who had an interest and effectiveness in age-related legislation.

Mass Communications

While use of mass communications is not unique to the senior movement, these media are an essential resource, given the dispersed nature of the older population. Most early organizations and many later ones have been built on local chapters, in part to provide a local network to get information to members and to create a personal context for the organization. Similarly, these locally organized movements have generally held regular national conferences to gather the faithful for inspiration and education. This type of face-to-face communication, however, is expensive and difficult to sustain on a national level. The most common form of regular mass communication with followers has been movement newspapers, pamphlets, and magazines. These become particularly critical when the mainstream media attack an organization. When the Townsend movement began to generate a steady stream of negative press and editorials in major newspapers, the *Townsend Weekly* and Townsend pamphlets provided an alternative communication network that answered its critics and went on its own attack against detractors (Cantril 1941/70; Putnam 1970/130). The Ham and Eggs movement was unusual in its effective use of a popular radio program to promote its program (Moore and Moore 1939/119; Putnam 1970/130). Every successful organization has in its control some type of communication link to its members.

Recently, some organizations have taken a lesson from the direct mail marketing of retailers and politicians. At least two organizations, the National Committee to Preserve Social Security and Medicare and the National Alliance of Senior Citizens, depend on direct mail for their membership and activities (Day 1990/250). And while no senior movement organizations have yet followed the lead of religious groups into television evangelism, there is no reason that a charismatic leader could not use that medium to mobilize the elderly in the senior movement.

Although movement newsletters can shape the ideas of the faithful, generating broad public support for movement goals depends on the mainstream media. Several of the "how-to" books of the 1970s described ways to organize events and generate information that would attract media coverage (Kerschner 1976/191). Professionals and their organizations have been particularly important in providing the mass media with images of the elderly that sustain a public sympathy for the aged. When a business-funded organization (Americans for Generational Equity [AGE]) was founded to generate media coverage *against* the legitimacy of the aged (Quadagno 1989/131), the largest national society of academic and professional gerontologists (The Gerontological Society of America) responded by sponsoring a book and other publicity to counter the attack (Kingson, Hirshorn, and Cornman 1986/813). Both groups targeted their efforts at the mass media and at information sources that would reach policy elites. The importance of the mass media is reflected in the relative success of the small group, AGE, to make intergenerational equity a potent public issue during the 1980s (Binney and Estes 1988/662; Minkler 1986/197; Quadagno 1991/517).

Limitations of the Movement

With the senior movement's large variety of stable organizations, the saliency of several key issues for the elderly, and its high level of legitimacy and other resources, we need to ask why the movement is not more visible and active currently. This issue rests in part on its limitations. These involve both movement resources and the environment within which the movement operates. The key resource, legitimacy, has been attacked by those trying to foster intergenerational conflict, and the level of group consciousness and cohesion may not be strong as some researchers claim. The social and political environment constantly confronts the senior movement with attempts at cooptation and the resistance of competing interests.

Intergenerational Conflict
There has long been a discussion of the existence of a "generation gap." This debate has often focused on the differences between the younger and older generations, and the conflict created by youth in society. Given the youth-dominated social movements and unrest of the 1960s, one can understand why the focus was on the youth side of the generation gap (Rosenfelt 1965/779; U.S. President's Science Advisory Committee 1973/835; Yankelovich 1969/795). Foner's (1972/255) analysis of the elderly in the polity, for example, addressed the rebelliousness of youth against established authority in looking at generational conflict. Starting in the 1970s, however, the critical focus turned toward the other side of the generation gap. Some researchers began warning about the possibility of conflict caused by the elderly (Neugarten 1972/702; Ragan 1977/827; Schram 1979/445). Others began to write about

the existence of conflict as a result of the demands of the elderly on national resources (e.g., Affeldt 1975/390; Oriol 1970/821; Stewart 1970/832). Even sympathetic observers were beginning to warn that the improving economic and health status of the aged could combine with increasing program costs to create pressure against spending on the elderly (Hudson 1978/319). The generation gap had become "intergenerational conflict," with the protagonists now the elderly rather than youth (Cooper 1985/36).

Many authors during the 1980s called for reducing public benefits for the aged, arguing that the elderly were already receiving more than their "fair share." Most of those articles examined government spending on social security and to a lesser extent Medicare to argue that the elderly were greedy and/or (regardless of motive) depriving younger generations of needed assistance. The arguments were found in the full range of publications, including business journals (Chakravarty 1988/789; Flint 1980/755; Smith 1987/831), news and popular publications (Borger 1986/473; DeMott 1985/483; Longman 1985/816; Schiffres 1984/830), popular/trade books (Longman 1987/818), and the academic press (Callahan 1986/643; Preston 1984/864). Much of the publicity that made intergenerational conflict a visible topic was generated by the nonmembership group, Americans for Generational Equity (Quadagno 1988/516). The intellectual justification for attacking programs for the elderly also came from conservative think tanks such as the Heritage Foundation and the Cato Institute (Ferrera 1988/492).

The senior movement responded to defend its legitimacy. As noted above, the professional organizations were among the most active in publicly defending programs for the elderly (Kingson, Hirshorn, and Cornman 1986/813). Academics attacked both the motives and facts used by those claiming that the elderly received too much (Binney and Estes 1988/662; Binstock 1984/742; Minkler 1986/197). They argued that only government could meet the needs of the aged, and that social insurance was a right of citizenship (Hudson 1987/421, 1988/422). While refuting many of the arguments about intergenerational conflict, the level of defensive activity by senior movement supporters demonstrates how significantly the conflict debate was perceived as affecting policymakers and public opinion.

The theme of pensioners as greedy and imperiling the economic strength of the nation is not a new one. Glasson (1900/563) presents a strongly worded account of the "avarice" of those who did not have war injuries who sought Civil War pensions. He implies that the advocates were making a raid on the national treasury beyond all limits of fairness or necessity. These same themes of undeservedness and national economic peril were repeated in the 1980s, although under a context of fiscal austerity (Estes 1986/304, 1988/659) rather than the nineteenth century's fiscal surplus.

The impact on public opinion of the academic and media debates over the deservedness of the elderly may be more apparent than real. In the early 1980s, no more than 9 percent of respondents felt the government spent too much on the elderly. The elderly themselves were most likely to report that the government spent too much; the youngest group of respondents, (age 18–35) were the least likely to hold this view (Day 1990/250). Data from the late 1980s provide a similar picture (McConnell 1990/696). While public opinion may not have been much affected by the conflict debate, there is some evidence that policy elites have been influenced. Quadagno (1989/131) suggests that the debate pushed Congress to make the Medicare Catastrophic Coverage Act funded solely by the aged (a feature that soon led to the act's repeal). Other proposals in the late 1980s to expand programs for the aged significantly have not met with wide support in Congress (Rovner 1988/137). The needs and legitimacy of the elderly may no longer be assumed by lawmakers, or, at a minimum, their needs have been made second to budgetary concerns (Estes 1989/660).

Group Consciousness

Many authors have theorized that the elderly would develop an increased group consciousness and cohesion, but empirical data also point to group fragmentation, especially along economic and ideological lines. The actual level of current group consciousness and its future potential is highly contested in the literature. The case against the significance of group consciousness includes the diversity of the elderly, their lack of minority group status, and the gap between perceived and experienced problems among this group.

The most common critique of the presence and/or significance of a group consciousness is the diversity among the aged (Binstock 1972/289; Dobson 1983/252). Class divisions that existed during working years largely continue during old age (Streib 1976/372; Wallace et al. 1991/29), as do racial and ethnic differences (Ragan and Davis 1978/352). Several studies that examine differences in public opinion by age find that age ceases to be a significant factor after accounting for income (Day 1990/250; Schreiber and Marsden 1972/716). For example, to the extent that people develop a common consciousness only around problems they face immediately, the generally good health of most elderly persons will also limit their group consciousness of long-term health care issues (Harootyan 1981/314).

Riley (1971/354) predicted that over time cohort experiences would become more important, and that the elderly would be the most likely to cohere around cohorts because of their lifelong commonalities of experience. Pampel (1981/24) argues the opposite, that period effects and changes in popular values work to fragment cohorts as they age, making the elderly the least likely to have a strong sense of solidarity. This issue has interested public opinion poll analysts, with the general conclusion that the elderly are not a single unified block (Ragan and Davis 1978/352; Streib 1976/372, 1985/373; Ward 1977/381).

Most authors also argue against the concept that the elderly are similar to minority groups, which develop a group consciousness. Palmore (1978/773) concludes that while the aged suffer from prejudice and discrimination, it is not a status they are born into. He sees society becoming increasingly age irrelevant, making age even less likely to serve as a common identity. Ward (1977/381) concludes that the limited group consciousness that exists is a result of reference group comparisons rather than membership in a normative subculture, making mobilization around age issues unlikely. Miller et al. (1981/267) find that the elderly do not behave as either a subordinate (minority) group or a dominant group.

Several authors find that the common beliefs about the problems of the aged held by the elderly themselves are inaccurate. O'Gorman (1980/343) and Day (1990/250) find that the elderly overestimate the problems of the aged, attributing many problems to the elderly in general that they do not face themselves. This phenomenon suggests that the elderly may have a conception of common problems, but that this group consciousness will not be very effective in mobilizing the aged because the problems are actually felt by only a small proportion of the group. Thus there is a potential for a split in the senior movement that leaves the poor and disenfranchised out (Demkovich 1976/78; Wallace et al. 1991/29). Those most likely to be facing the greatest problems are also the least active in local (Dobson and St. Angelo 1980/178) and national politics (U.S. Bureau of the Census 1990). Smeeding (1986/615) argues that there are actually three different interest groups among the aged: the poor, who benefit from welfare programs, the wealthy, who benefit from tax breaks, and the near-poor "Tweeners," who, though needing government benefits, cannot qualify for them.

Many of the early (e.g., Rose 1965/358) and later (e.g., Binstock 1981/229) researchers have asked whether the elderly are capable of developing a group consciousness and uniting in the future to dominate social policy. While the findings are mixed, the question would be quite different if set in a resource mobilization framework. It is not a critical problem that the aged have a generally low sense of collective membership, low identification of being "aged," and only average propensity to support benefits for the aged. Social movements research has shown that disorganized collectivities such as the elderly are capable of creating a strong social movement when an entrepreneur arises who is able to redefine existing grievances and unify and direct institutional resources (McCarthy and Zald 1973).

Cooptation and Social Control

The political and social systems have been generally successful in blunting the force of a variety of social movements by changing just enough to reduce the urgency felt by many movement supporters (Pratt 1976/25). These measures are often more symbolic than real, however, leaving supporters in much the same position as before (Binstock, Levin, and Weatherly 1985/291; Lowi 1979; Odell 1962/269). Tibbitts (1962/217) warned that the proliferation of programs and service organizations would prevent a unified movement from occurring. Estes (1979/411, 1986/304) argues that current public programs work to individualize problems, making it difficult for the elderly to see any common social causes of their condition. Even the way in which Social Security is designed provides a conservatizing force on the aged (Williamson, Evans, and Powell 1982/30; Williamson, Shindul, and Evans 1985/462).

Competing Interests

The senior movement has often faced organized groups with interests counter to theirs. Perhaps the clearest example of a competing interest that blunted the impact of the senior movement is the opposition of the American Medical Association to any type of government-financed health care program. Despite general public support and senior movement advocacy for government assistance in providing health care, especially to the aged, legislation to enact such a program has been blocked for decades by the AMA (Marmor 1973/695; Harris 1966/683; Starr 1982/723). Sundquist (1968/147) feels that the AMA has actually overplayed the issue and created a backlash of support for the aged.

At the local level, advocates for the aging have found it difficult to increase state-level regulation of industries that affect the elderly. In Oregon, a well-organized effort to increase the regulations on Medigap insurance was only partly successful as a result of the power of the insurance industry over the regulatory agency (Wyden 1977/735). Efforts to improve the quality of nursing home care have met a similar fate, with attempts to improve the oversight of care moving slowly in the face of industry resistance (Jacobson 1977/190; Litwin, Kaye, and Monk 1984/196; Scott 1985/140). Vested interests in housing (Pynoos 1984/351), social services (Cutler 1984/408; Estes 1979/411), and consumer products (Minkler 1989/586) also frequently push a policy agenda that benefits their interests at the expense of the elderly. The relative power of these interests means that they are more likely than the elderly to prevail in policy-making (Browne 1989/396).

Effectiveness

Many of the issues that the senior movement has been involved in have led to social change that has benefited the elderly. The question remains, however, if the extent to which the senior movement has been responsible for those social changes. Few if any issues have been advanced solely by the elderly. While coalition-building is a strength, it creates difficulty in disentangling the relative contributions of all the actors.

There are several instances in which the senior movement may have had an impact. There is little controversy over the importance of the Townsend movement in the *discussions* about Social Security. Supporters, detractors, and later academics all agree that government officials were very concerned with the popularity of the Townsend movement (Altmeyer 1968/470; Dorman 1936/80; Neuberger and Loe 1936/122). The question is whether the movement changed the scope of the final Social Security program. Labor, business, and southern agricultural interests had more power than the elderly to determine the final content and implementation of Social Security (Quadagno 1988/516; Domhoff 1986, 1987/487). The final Social Security program looked nothing like the Townsend proposal, but the existence of the Townsend Plan (and other populist proposals) raised public awareness and provided strong pressure to pass some type of national pension plan (Carlie 1969/71; Mason 1954/111; Pratt 1976/25).

The success of the senior movement in fostering social change since World War II is more difficult to document. While seniors were involved in advocating Medicare, they appear to have been more of a side player compared to other interests (Feingold 1966/666; Marmor 1973/695; Sundquist 1968/147). Similarly, benefit increases in Social Security, its indexing, and the broadening of Medicare, the Older Americans Act, and other programs do not appear to be a direct outcome of senior activism (Burke and Burke 1974/539; Estes 1979/411; Freeman and Adams 1982/494; Kingson 1984/502). The major successes that can be directly attributed to the senior movement over the past 40 years have been conservative in nature—protecting programs and preventing the imposition of new taxes.

While there is limited evidence that senior activism was responsible for the growth of Social Security during the 1970s, it was unmistakably key in the protection of Social Security during the 1980s. Proposals during the early 1980s to reduce Social Security benefits and change eligibility evoked a storm of protest by seniors. This unexpectedly vehement reaction led the U.S. Senate to vote unanimously for a resolution asking newly elected President Reagan not even to submit his proposal for changing Social Security (Ferrara 1988/492). The Democrats used the Social Security issue to their benefit in the 1982 elections by claiming that Republican proposals would hurt the elderly (Light 1985/332). The volatility of the issue has made Social Security "off limits" in discussions of cutting the federal deficit, and has even led to public pronouncements by President Bush that he will not "mess around with Social Security" (Bush 1990).

Besides protecting Social Security, the senior movement was effective in overturning the Medicare Catastrophic Coverage Act. Those most active in the movement to repeal the legislation represented primarily the middle- and upper-income elderly (Crystal 1990/650; Ferrara 1989/667; Holstein and Minkler 1991/684; Longman 1989/694; Wallace et al. 1991/29). Congress was impressed by the quantity of mail its members received on the topic, and television images of seniors heckling congressmen over their votes provided a powerful image (Torres-Gil 1989/726). The strength of the senior movement in recent years has been greatest in blocking change, not moving it forward. This observation has led some to suggest that the future power of the movement will rest primarily in protecting its past gains rather than moving ahead (Binstock, Levin, and Weatherly 1985/291).

Most of the literature on the effectiveness of the senior movement has focused on efforts at the national level. Research at the local level has been more limited and mixed. Research in Florida has generally found the elderly to be little involved in local politics, despite their large numbers in that state.

Local studies have found that Florida's officials do *not* generally respond to the preferences that they perceive to be the primary concerns of the elderly. Indeed, these studies suggest that the elderly are not organized or active enough to have a direct policy impact, even when they are visibly and actively involved in local politics (Button and Rosenbaum 1990/231; Dobson and St. Angelo 1980/178; Franke 1985/417; Rosenbaum and Button 1989/230).

These results do not mean that the elderly are incapable of having an impact. Scattered examples of senior movement successes are well documented. In Arizona, the power of older persons united around the issue of senior-only housing developments had a strong influence on legalization of such developments by the state legislature (Anderson and Anderson 1978/59; Streib, Folts, and LaGreca 1985/374). In Oregon, the elderly lobbied for stricter control over Medigap insurance policies (Wyden 1977/735). Dobson and St. Angelo (1980/178) document an atypical county in Florida that had a high concentration of politically organized senior high-rise apartment buildings. The large number of votes that the apartment association could mobilize became an important factor in several local races. In San Francisco, when single-room-occupancy hotel residents organized, they were able to gain the political attention needed to increase police protection and tenants' rights. This group also turned to self-help strategies of establishing food co-ops and support groups (Minkler 1985/116, 1991/118). Even relatively powerless nursing home residents have been able to organize (with the help of those outside the homes) to improve their quality of life (Kautzer 1988/99; Meyer 1991/115). These are scattered examples of effective action, but no one has yet examined the common threads in these cases that could help us predict the possible success of future local actions.

While there are few clear examples of the elderly defining policies at the national level, the large national membership organizations have achieved a sufficient level of respect from policymakers that they are involved in policy debates. Several authors (Coombs 1985/250; Day 1990/405; Rosenberg 1985/136) conclude that national organizations such as the AARP and NCSC have become so well established in Washington power circles that they have achieved insider status and access, reflecting the regularization and bureaucratization of social movements discussed by Williamson et al. (1982/30). This type of power is typically "quieter" and less visible to outsiders as it is often exercised behind closed doors.

Overall, there is substantial literature documenting the existence of a senior movement in terms of organizational capacity, issues, and resources. The effectiveness of the movement is a subject of debate, but there are a few clear examples of its shaping social policy and society. Recently, it has been most effective in blocking social policy that would negatively affect some of the elderly. The rise of the debate over intergenerational equity poses the greatest risk to the senior movement by attacking its most valuable resource; legitimacy. We have seen that older persons *can* be mobilized. The future success of the senior movement will depend on whether the conditions exist to activate the elderly sufficiently and whether they can marshal their resources to overcome the resistance to their demands for social change.

REFERENCES

BUSH, GEORGE. 1990. State of the Union Address. *Congressional Quarterly,* 48 (February 3):349.

FEIN, RASHI. 1986. *Medical Care, Medical Costs.* Cambridge, MA: Harvard University Press.

GUSFIELD, JOSEPH. 1981. "Social Movements and Social Change: Perspectives of Linearity and Fluidity." *Research in Social Movements, Conflict and Change,* 4:317–339.

HARRINGTON, CHARLENE. 1991. "The Nursing Home Industry: A Structural Analysis." In *Critical Perspectives on Aging,* Meredith Minkler and Carroll L. Estes, 135–150. Amityville, NY: Baywood.

JENKINS, J. CRAIG. 1983. "Resource Mobilization Theory and the Study of Social Movements." *Annual Review of Sociology,* 9:527–553.

LARSON, MAGALI SARFATTI. 1977. *The Rise of Professionalism.* Berkeley: University of California Press.

LOWI, THEODORE. 1979. *The End of Liberalism.* New York: Norton.

MARWELL, GERALD, and OLIVER, PAMELA. 1984. "Collective Action Theory and Social Movements Research." *Research in Social Movements, Conflict and Change,* 7:1–27.

MAUSS, ARMAND L. 1975. *Social Problems as Social Movements.* Philadelphia: Lippincott.

MCCARTHY, JOHN D., and ZALD, MAYER N. 1973. *The Trend of Social Movements.* Morristown, NJ: General Learning.

OLIVER, PAMELA E. 1989. "Bringing the Crowd Back In: The Nonorganizational Elements of Social Movements." *Research in Social Movements, Conflict and Change,* 11:1–30.

PIVEN, FRANCIS F., and CLOWARD, RICHARD. 1977. *Poor People's Movements.* New York: Pantheon.

TILLY, CHARLES. 1988. "Social Movements, Old and New." *Research in Social Movements, Conflict and Change,* 10:1–18.

TOLCHIN, M. 1989. "How The New Medicine Law Fell on Hard Times in a Hurry." *New York Times.* October 9, pp. A1, A10.

U.S. Bureau of the Census. 1990. *Voting and Registration in the Election of November 1988.* Current population reports, P-20, #444. Washington, DC: U.S. Government Printing Office.

WOOD, JAMES L., and JACKSON, MAURICE. 1982. *Social Movements: Development, Participation and Dynamics.* Belmont, CA: Wadsworth.

1

General Works

1   BROWNE, WILLIAM P., and OLSON, LAURA KATZ (Eds.). 1983. *Aging and Public Policy: The Politics of Growing Old in America*. Westport, CT: Greenwood Press. 266 pp.
> Presents a collection of essays by widely cited authors designed to stimulate the political interest and expand the literacy of those concerned with gerontology. The introduction provides an extensive bibliography on a variety of policy issues. The text offers chapters on women's issues, national interest groups, rural inequities, congressional practices, and the economics of aging. Offers extensive bibliography and chapter notes.

2   BUTLER, ROBERT N. 1975. *Why Survive? Being Old in America*. New York: Harper & Row. 496 pp.
> Describes the social, psychological, and economic difficulties plaguing the elderly. An oft-cited classic, the problems and issues addressed are still relevant. Asserting that pacification has been the goal of public policy, the author calls for increased political activism by the elderly. Offers 15 policy goals that emphasize elimination of poverty and malnutrition. Well documented with large bibliography.

3   CRYSTAL, STEPHEN. 1982. *America's Old Age Crisis: Public Policy and the Two Worlds of Aging*. New York: Basic Books. 232 pp.
> Views public policy as a major contributing factor in the tremendous gap between the best-off and worst-off elderly during a period when their benefits command an increasingly large budget share. Recommendations include changes in retirement income and health care systems and expanded flexibility in addressing long-term care needs.

4   CUMMING, ELAINE, and HENRY, WILLIAM E. 1961. *Growing Old: The Process of Disengagement*. New York: Basic Books. 293 pp.
> Firmly establishes disengagement theory. The research for this

classic study is based on a random survey of 172 noninstitutionalized native-born whites aged 50 to 70 in Kansas City, and a quasi sample of 107 aged 70 to 90. The authors find disengagement to be an inevitable process of severing many of the ties between individuals and society and altering the remaining ties. Disengagement softens intergenerational tensions and helps keep society in equilibrium.

5   DAVIS, RICHARD H. (Ed.). 1982. *Aging: Prospects and Issues.* Los Angeles: University of Southern California Press. 477 pp.

Presents a broad selection of papers dealing with adult development and aging. Chapters 14–18 deal with social policy issues including congressional responsiveness, advocacy, retirement, and employment. Chapters 5–8 analyze ethnic, family, and community service aspects of aging.

6   DOWD, JAMES J. 1975. "Aging as Exchange: A Preface to Theory." *Journal of Gerontology*, 30(5):584–594.

Reviews the major concepts of the social-psychological theory of exchange. Dowd uses the work of Blau and Emerson to develop a view of aging as exchange, with the problems of aging being seen as problems of declining power resources. The relative power of the elderly compared with their exchange partners deteriorates and the aged are forced to exchange compliance for their continued sustenance. Retirement is utilized to illustrate the phenomenon.

7   ———. 1980. *Stratification among the Aged*. Monterey, CA: Brooks/ Cole. 153 pp.

Examines the stigma and relative powerlessness of the elderly using social exchange theory. Dowd shows the importance of class differences in the ability of the aged to obtain desired outcomes from interaction. He describes the sources of power and how they are used in social interaction, arguing that social policy is paternalistic.

8   EISELE, FREDERICK R. (Ed.). 1974. *Annals of the American Academy of Political and Social Science: The Political Consequences of Aging*, 45(211).

Reviews policy analyses from a variety of paradigms. The issue contains articles with "perspectives [that] are long range, attempting to situate and analyze their broader, historical context." Topics include income issues, federal policies, pensions and retirement, long-term care, black aged, women's issues, and the future impact of aging interest groups.

9   ESTES, CARROLL L. 1978. "Political Gerontology: The Politics of Aging." *Society*, 15(5):43–49.

Analyzes dominant perspectives in political gerontology. Estes identifies two basic orientations of research and theories of power and politics: "social control" and "partisan" perspectives. She recommends that the concept of senior power be expanded to include those who may not be chronologically old but identify with and act as advocates for old-age issues. She also predicts future research objectives and techniques.

10 ———; SWAN, JAMES H.; and GERARD, LENORE E. 1982. "Dominant and Competing Paradigms in Gerontology: Towards a Political Economy of Ageing." *Ageing and Society*, 2(2):151–164.

Critiques the emphasis in gerontological theory on individual level explanations and the limited research on how the political and economic structure of the nation affects the elderly. The authors challenge the concept that the aged are a separate, distinct class, and propose a political economy approach to the problems of the aged and others in society.

11 FISCHER, DAVID HACKETT. 1977. *Growing Old in America*. New York: Oxford University Press. 242 pp.

Widely cited history of aging in the United States. Fischer traces four periods in history: 1607–1820, when the elderly were held in high esteem and had considerable social power; 1770–1820, when age relations were in flux; 1770–1970, when old age was stigmatized; and 1909–1970 when aging was defined as a social problem. Power of and respect for the elderly in the first period were rooted in religion, reinforced by the knowledge and property resources of the old. The decline in respect for the aged occurred before industrialization, caused by ideas of liberty and equality embraced by the French and American revolutions. National economic problems led to the identification of old age as a social problem.

12 FOWLES, DONALD. 1984. "Numbers Game: Four New Reports on Aging and Older Persons." *Aging*, 347:48–49.

Reviews four reports that provide statistical portraits of the older population: the 1983 Senate Special Committee on Aging, "Developments in Aging," covers income and poverty, health, social, and other general demographic characteristics; a joint publication of the Senate Special Committee on Aging and the AARP, "Aging America: Trends and Projections," contains 75 multicolored charts; "Demographic and Socioeconomic Aspects of Aging in the United States" from the Bureau of the Census; and a brochure, "A Profile of Older Americans: 1984," by the Administration on Aging and the AARP.

13 GELFAND, DONALD E. 1988. *The Aging Network*. New York: Springer. 341 pp.

Provides an introductory overview of the full variety of public programs for the elderly, including income, employment, housing, transportation, nutrition, social services, and health programs. Each section includes a brief historical overview that stresses the legislative rationale for every program. Includes the complete text of the Older Americans Act of 1965 as amended in 1987.

14 HENDRICKS, JON, and HENDRICKS, C. DAVIS. 1986. *Aging in Mass Society: Myths and Realities* (3rd ed.). Boston: Little, Brown. 539 pp.

Links the study of aging with the historical and social currents that affect it. Initial chapters discuss demographic and cross-cultural patterns of aging. The social and physiological theories that provide the framework for the study of aging are identified. Included in the discussion are questions of health, finances, retirement, politics and minority aging. The book concludes with a focus on the future of aging.

15 ——, and LEEDHAM, CYNTHIA A. 1991. "Dependency or Empowerment? Toward a Moral and Political Economy of Aging." In *Critical Perspectives on Aging*, edited by Meredith Minkler and Carroll L. Estes, 51–64. Amityville, NY: Baywood.

Presents a theoretical framework, moral economy based on use values, that demonstrates the links between personal troubles and public issues in aging. The authors provide the grounding for models of social organization that allow for the emancipation of the aged and young alike.

16 HUDSON, ROBERT B. (Ed.). 1984. "Politics of Aging." *Generations*, 9(1): 1–56.

Presents various perspectives on aging policy in 14 articles. Hudson addresses the cost pressures of Medicare, Medicaid, and federal housing programs. Advocacy, the lobbying efforts by the elderly at the state level, and the role of aging issues in elections are among other topics considered. Problems confronting policymakers and the elderly and strategies for use by the elderly and their advocates are delineated.

17 LAMMERS, WILLIAM W. 1983. *Public Policy and the Aging*. Washington DC: C.Q. Press. 265 pp.

Presents a picture of a heterogeneous elderly population with diverse and complex needs. Lammers examines policy issues in the areas of Social Security, Supplemental Security Income, pension regulation, retirement, Medicare, Medicaid, long-term care, and social services. He considers shifts in federal and state government roles, the tension between means and income tests in existing and future programs, the plight of older women, the hospice movement, the aged as consumers, and the consequences of inflation. He examines the impact of the large aging based organizations on policy decisions.

18 LANDIS, JUDSON T. 1946. "Old-Age Movements in the United States." In *Social Adjustment in Old Age: A Research Planning Report*, edited by Ernest W. Burgess, Clark Tibbetts, and Robert J. Havighurst, 64–66. New York: Social Science Research Council.

Outlines possible research agendas, including studies of the

Townsend movement, the changing status of the aged, and their political behavior. References are included.

19 LOUIS HARRIS and ASSOCIATES, INC. 1975. *The Myth and Reality of Aging in America*. Washington, DC: National Council on the Aging. 245 pp.

Widely cited study of the opinions about elderly persons. The report is based on a national sample of 1,457 adults age 18 to 64, and 2,797 aged 65 and over, with an oversample of blacks. It examines public attitudes and expectations toward the aged; the social, economic, and health status and experiences of the elderly; and the politics of old age. It concludes that most people of all ages would support a movement to improve the conditions and social status of the elderly. About one third said they would join an organized group toward that end.

20 ———. 1981. *Aging in the Eighties. America in Transition*. Washington, DC: National Council on the Aging. 245 pp.

Widely cited national survey that follows up on the 1975 survey. Most younger and middle-aged persons believed the elderly had "very serious problems" with finances, loneliness, crime, energy costs, and transportation. Forty percent thought health, housing, and jobs were serious problems. The elderly reported experiencing these problems at one third to one tenth of those rates, while similarly overestimating the extent of problems reported by other elders.

21 MANNHEIM, KARL. 1952 [1928]. "The Problem of Generations." In *Essays on the Sociology of Knowledge*, edited by Paul Kecskemeti, 276–320. New York: Oxford University Press.

Classic article analyzing the importance of generations in social change. Generations are based on an awareness of social positions and expectations, an awareness that creates the potential for collective action. The point at which individuals enter the historical experience (i.e., their generation) is one such social position. The greatest impact of generations is in the political realm.

22 MORRIS, ROBERT. 1966. "Viewpoint: Gerontological Research and Social Policy." *Gerontologist*, 6(1):2–3.

Calls for gerontological research to investigate topics that have direct relevance to current policy areas.

23 OLSON, LAURA KATZ. 1982. *The Political Economy of Aging: The State, Private Power and Social Welfare*. New York: Columbia University Press. 252 pp.

Contends that the plight of disadvantaged elders stems from market and class relationships, along with racist and sexist institutions. Olson challenges basic assumptions underlying aging issues and policies and encourages greater recognition of factors linking the interests of younger workers with those of elders.

24   PAMPEL, FRED C. 1981. *Social Change and the Aged*. Lexington, MA: Lexington Books. 212 pp.

 Analyzes national survey and census data from 1952 to 1978 to determine the causes of the changes in the social position of the aged. Cohort and composition changes explain little of the social changes, with period changes having the largest effect. Pampel suggests that cohort cohesion will decline over time as a result. He finds that the financial status of the aged has improved and that increases in the rates of retirement at every age are a result of normative demand for leisure.

25   PRATT, HENRY J. 1976. *The Gray Lobby*. Chicago: University of Chicago Press. 250 pp.

 The most widely cited book on the senior movement. Pratt examines the changing effectiveness of the symbols used by and the leadership of the senior movement to explain its changing effectiveness from the 1920s to the 1970s. He finds that pension movements (especially Epstein's) were important in establishing Social Security, but that sustained senior power has existed only since the 1960s. He also looks at the shift from charismatically led senior organizations to more durable bureaucratically structured organizations. The decline of age based movements in the 1940s allowed a hiatus in government policy initiatives. The reactivation of senior activism in the 1950s came from professionals who worked with the aged. Pratt reviews the structure and function of Senior Citizens for Kennedy and shows how the 1971 White House Conference on Aging increased the access of senior organizations to the government policy-making process. He discusses how political constraints will prevent the granting of "unwarranted and dangerous levels of political power" to the elderly, concluding that a distinct old-age policy system has emerged in the federal government that includes the major senior organizations.

26   RICH, BENNET M., and BAUM, MARTHA. 1984. *The Aging: A Guide to Public Policy*. Pittsburgh: University of Pittsburgh Press. 275 pp.

 Discusses the major federal programs for older Americans. In the context of a brief historical overview, the authors outline the objectives, administration, and operation of these programs. They discuss the role of major interest groups representing the elderly and provisions of the Older Americans Act. The book covers retirement, the economics of public and private pension plans, transportation, housing, health care programs, age discrimination in the workplace, and the needs of aged American veterans. The authors note the incremental nature of policy enactment and highlight the rapid growth of the old-old population and its vulnerability.

27   U.S. SENATE SPECIAL COMMITTEE ON AGING. 1991. *Developments in Aging: 1990*. Vol. 1. Washington, DC: U.S. Government Printing Office. 474 pp.

 Annual volume that reviews all the federal program areas that affect the elderly, including social security, private pensions, taxes, employment, supplemental security income, food stamps, health care, research, housing, energy assistance, Older Americans Act, community services, and general budget issues. The book describes programs and discusses recent issues such as the passage and later repeal of the Medicare Catastrophic Care Act.

28   VAN TASSEL, DONALD, and STEARNS, PHILLIP N. (Eds.). 1986. *Old Age in a Bureaucratic Society: The Elderly, the Experts and the State in American History*. Westport, CT: Greenwood Press. 259 pp.
      Provides a collection of views on aging policy in light of old-age history. The authors review and critique old-age security programs. An essay by Brian Gratton reviews new interpretations of historical influences on the elderly. The book contains excellent references. (See also entry 468.)

29   WALLACE, STEVEN P.; WILLIAMSON, JOHN B.; LUNG, RITA GASTON; and POWELL, LAWRENCE A. 1991. "A Lamb in Wolf's Clothing? The Reality of Senior Power and Social Policy." In *Critical Perspectives on Aging*, edited by Meredith Minkler and Carroll L. Estes, 95–114. Amityville, NY: Baywood.
      Examines three types of power exerted by the elderly: electoral, organizational, and societal. The authors argue that the electoral power of the aged has only a limited impact, that the power of senior organizations is greater than the elderly's electoral influence but not always used for their best interests, and that the societal power of the aged has the greatest potential for social change. They note that minority and poor elderly have little power of any type. They believe that the possibility for fragmentation of senior power is greater than the possibility of its further consolidation.

30   WILLIAMSON, JOHN B.; EVANS, LINDA; and POWELL, LAWRENCE A. 1982. *The Politics of Aging: Power and Policy*. Springfield, IL: Charles C Thomas. 331 pp.
      Examines the power relations of the elderly in three areas: the conditions under which the elderly have had power and those in which they have not, the political power of the elderly especially as it relates to social security and the pension movement, and finally the issue of power in terms of interpersonal relations. Social security is viewed as a potent force for the elderly but at the social cost of dependence on the government. The authors anticipate a marked increase in the political influence of the elderly through a coalition of interests. (See also entry 384.)

2

The Movement

The Leaders

31   • 1979. "Working the System: An Interview with Norm Schut." *Aging*, 297–298(July–August):6–13.

Presents an interview with Norm Schut, the creator of the Senior Citizens Lobby. The article describes how he organized a coalition of senior groups, his efforts at target lobbying, and his feelings about professionals acting as advocates for the elderly.

32   • 1985. "Ollie A. Randall: Greatest Single American to Help the Elderly's Cause." *Perspective on Aging*, 9(1): 4–5+.

Profiles the accomplishments of Ollie A. Randall, founder of the National Council on Aging (NCOA).

33   ARIEFF, IRWIN B. 1981. "Claude Pepper: Champion of the Aged." *Congressional Quarterly Weekly Report*, 39(48):2342.

Brief discussion of Claude Pepper's efforts to establish and support political programs for the elderly.

34   BRADEN, ANNE. 1985. "The Long View of Elder Activists: Their Vision of a More Just Society Keeps Them Going." *Southern Exposure*, 13(2–3):34–39.

Provides brief profiles of a dozen elderly activists from various states in the South. All of the activists expressed concern with the problems of the young.

35   CARDONA, IVAN. 1986. "Aging in America: A Propositional Analysis of Selected Congressional Speeches of Representative Claude Pepper." Ph.D. dissertation, Southern Illinois University. 522 pp.

Analyzes the floor speeches of Claude Pepper to categorize the themes and rhetorical styles he used in Congress.

36 COOPER, ANN. 1985. "Generation Gap." *National Journal*, 17(8):440.
    Describes the views of Paul Hewitt, founder of Americans for Generational Equity (AGE), who asserts that the elderly have wealth and numbers to plead their case while welfare, nutrition, and other poverty programs for children are declining. Cooper concludes that Hewitt has stirred discussions about generational inequity, but there are not likely to be major policy changes regarding Social Security.

37 ELDRIDGE, MARY (Ed.). 1985. "Older, Wiser, Stronger." Southern Exposure, 13(2–3):1–152.
    Profiles southern elders and describes federal programs benefiting the elderly. Eldridge describes elder activists, including a Gray Panther leader from Austin, Texas; a leader of the National Council of Senior Citizens in Knoxville, Tennessee; and the grass-roots advocacy network in West Virginia. An annotated list of publications and organizations to assist the elderly is included.

38 FISHER, JAN. 1986. "Maggie Kuhn's Vision: Young and Old Together." *50 Plus*, 26(7):22–23+.
    Profiles the remarkable life of the founder of the Gray Panthers organization, Maggie Kuhn, emphasizing her dedication to intergenerational unity.

39 HALAMANDARIS, VAL J. 1986. "Compassionate Revolutionary, A Tribute to Maggie Kuhn." *Caring*, 5(2):34–36+.
    Provides a brief biography of Maggie Kuhn from her childhood through the founding of the Gray Panthers.

40 HESSEL, DIETER T. 1977. *Maggie Kuhn on Aging*. Philadelphia: Westminster Press. 140 pp.
    Edited transcript of a seminary workshop conducted by Maggie Kuhn. Hessel provides insights into Kuhn's views on ageism, mandatory retirement, changing life-styles, social activism, and the role of the church.

41 JONES, ROCHELLE; MEYER, ANN; and BREO, DENNIS. 1986. "Advocates." *Mature Outlook*, 3(5):51–63.
    Profiles the involvement in aging issues of three older American advocates for the elderly: Esther Peterson, former assistant secretary of labor under Kennedy; Reverend Leon Sullivan, an advocate for civil rights; and Dr. Robert Butler, a widely read author and former head of the National Institute on Aging.

42 KIESTER, EDWIN, JR. 1988. "Stand Up and Fight." *Fifty-Plus*, 28(6):22–26.
    Discusses the contributions to nursing home reform of Pat McGinnis, director and co-founder of the Bay Area Advocates for Nursing Home Reform (BANHR) based in San Francisco.

43 LAWRENCE, KEN, and HARGER, DICK. 1985. "Persistence is the Key." *Southern Exposure,* 13(2–3):120–124.

Profiles the activities of activist Eddie Sandifer. He is involved in gay rights as well as a founding organizer of the Jackson, Mississippi, Gray Panthers. The Panthers currently focus on housing and health issues. He was involved in placing consumer advocates on the new Health Systems Agency in 1975, and has helped organize successful phone trees and demonstrations that include numerous elders in wheelchairs.

44 LAYNG, KRISTIN, and SZAKOS, JOE. 1985. "The Older I Get, the Closer I Get to the Ground: An Interview with Everett Akers." *Southern Exposure,* 13(2–3):68–71.

The opinions of senior activist Everett Akers about the problems caused by strip mining of coal in Eastern Kentucky. The article reviews his efforts to help individuals whose land is endangered by strip mining.

45 LEHMAN, HARVEY C. 1953. *Age and Achievement.* Princeton, NJ: Princeton University Press. 359 pp.

Provides data on the age of attainment to a variety of political and organizational offices, as well as ages of achievement in a number of literary and scientific fields. Lehman finds that the elderly have been dominant in the quest for political power, with less success in other fields. The median age of leaders in all fields has become older over time.

46 LEOTTA, LOUIS. 1975. "Abraham Epstein and the Movement for Old Age Security." *Labor History,* 16(3):359–377.

See entry 107.

47 McCARTHY, REBECCA. 1985. "We're All Going to Get Old, So We Better Learn to Deal with It." *Southern Exposure,* 13(2–3):7.

Brief profile of the community contributions of Josephine Matthews, a black woman named the 1974 Outstanding Older American for South Carolina and a retired midwife.

48 NEELY, JACK. 1985. "Tennesseans Fight for Social Justice: Grassroots Power." *Southern Exposure,* 13(2–3):40–45.

Describes the work of two organizations led by senior activist Lucille Thornburgh that work on issues of concern to seniors and low-income persons, including utility rates, health-care cuts, and taxation. The National Council of Senior Citizens has been a key ally.

49 PINNER, FRANK A.; JACOBS, PAUL; and SELZNICK, PHILIP. 1959. *Old Age and Political Behavior.* Los Angeles: University of California Press. 341 pp.

Focuses on George McClain. See entry 125.

50 PUTNAM, JACKSON K. 1970. *Old-Age Politics in California.* Stanford: Stanford University Press. 211 pp.

See entry 130.

51 QUAM, JEAN K. 1985. "The Almonership of Ollie A. Randall: Affording Temporary Relief to Unobtrusive Suffering." *Gerontologist*, 25(2):116–118.

Describes the work of senior advocate Ollie Randall in distributing small cash grants to needy elderly in New York City for the Havens Relief Fund Society. The author suggests that Randall's contact with these elderly, who were not well served by the social welfare system, contributed to her motivation to improve the status of the elderly.

52 SINCLAIR, MOLLY. 1984. "Keeping up with Claude." *50 Plus*, 24(10):23–27.

Profiles the life of the late congressman, Claude Pepper. The interview highlights his crusade for the rights of the elderly.

53 TOWNSEND, FRANCIS. 1943. *New Horizons*. Chicago: J. L. Publishing. 246 pp.

Autobiography by the charismatic leader of the Townsend movement beginning with his childhood on a farm. Townsend describes influences on his life including medical school, World War I, and the Depression. The book details his involvement in the Townsend movement.

The Organizations

54 • 1939. "Threat of Pension Pressure Groups." *Tax Policy*, 7(1):1–7.

Warns against crackpot pension schemes and outlines a plan for providing financial relief to the elderly. The article discusses problems with the Ham and Eggs movement and the Ohio Pension Plan, examining the political climates that led to their popularity as well as the manipulation of the elderly by pension promoters.

55 • 1988. "Public Policy Agenda 1988–1989 of the National Council on the Aging, Inc." *Perspective on Aging*, 17(2):1–40.

Presents the public policy statements of the National Council on the Aging and its eight membership units for 1988–1989. The agenda emphasizes the need for action by the private sector and identifies issues that demand federal action.

56 ADLER, MARJORIE. 1958. "History of Gerontological Society, Inc." *Journal of Gerontology*, 13(1):94–102.

Provides the history, organization, and purposes of the Gerontological Society, which was established by the Club for Research on Aging, initial funding for which was provided by Josiah Macy, Jr. Foundation. Adler describes activities of society members and the formation and development of the Society's publication, *Journal of Gerontology*. She lists affiliate organizations and provides membership totals for the years 1946–1957.

57 ALLEN, ANNE. 1984. "Problems That Won't Go Away." *Foundation News*, 25(4):54–59.

Examines a recent trend on the part of foundations to assist the elderly, especially the elderly poor. The Villers Foundation, established in 1982, has allocated $40 million in assets to improving quality of life for the elderly. Several other major foundations and their programs and activities are summarized.

58 ALWANG, JENNIFER. 1987. "Voice for the Frail Elderly." *Aging*, 355:10–13.

Reviews the work of the Coalition of Advocates for the Rights of the Infirm Elderly (CARIE). Developed in Philadelphia in 1977, the organization provides advocacy for individuals, organized community advocacy, and advocacy for policy change. It runs a nursing home ombudsman program, conducts community education, and lobbies for public policy changes.

59 ANDERSON, WILLIAM A., and ANDERSON, NORMA D. 1978. "The Politics of Age Exclusion: The Adults Only Movement in Arizona." *Gerontologist*, 18(1):6–12.

Describes the success of Arizona's Adults Only Movement (AOM) in legalizing discrimination against families and younger adults in housing. A coalition organization, Adult Action, coordinated 26 homeowner and community association groups in working for legislation to overturn a court case allowing a family with children in an adults-only community. The Andersons describe AOM ideology and efforts in implementing the new law.

60 ASH, GENEVIEVE M. 1983. "Silver-Haired Lawmakers Aim to Educate Older Voters." *Perspective on Aging*, 13:9, 28.

Outlines the activities of the Massachusetts Silver-Haired Legislature to educate seniors with regard to the legislative process, lobbying, and community organizations. Activities represent grass-roots activities by senior volunteers.

61 BABCHUK, NICHOLAS; PETERS, GEORGE R.; HOYT, DANNY R.; and KAISER, MARVIN A. 1979. "The Voluntary Associations of the Aged." *Journal of Gerontology*, 34(4):579–587.

Analyzes membership and participation in voluntary organizations by individuals aged 65 and older. Data were based on a random sampling of a small nonmetropolitan midwest community. Findings show the elderly are more active in organizations than is usually assumed. After-church, fraternal-sororal organizations, and age-based organizations were most common. Women were more active than men in general and were as likely as men to be affiliated with multiple organizations. Reasons for involvement are discussed.

62 BINSTOCK, ROBERT H. 1972. "Interest Group Liberalism and the Politics of Aging." *Gerontologist*. 12(3):265–280.

See entry 289.

63 BLAIKIE, ANDREW. 1990. "Emerging Political Power of the Elderly in Britain 1908–1948." *Ageing and Society*, 10(1):17–39.

History of the public pressure for pensions in Britain. Blaikie contrasts the two main organizations involved—one a professional group and one a mass membership group—and compares the success of these two groups in pension policy with the failure of other organizations in welfare policy.

64 BOETHEL, MARTHA. 1985. "Attacking Elder Abuse." *Southern Exposure*, 13(2–3):46–49.

Describes the efforts of the Gray Panthers in Texas to document the problem of elderly abuse and work with the legislature to pass remedial laws. The Panthers wanted adult protective legislation but found the legislature willing to pass laws concerning only targeted groups like the elderly and disabled.

65 BORCHARDT, MARJORIE. 1962. "Personal Expression Organizations." In *Politics of Age*, edited by Wilma Donahue and Clark Tibbitts, 154–155. Ann Arbor: University of Michigan Press.

Brief description of the Senior Citizens Association of Los Angeles County, established 1955, including its work to reduce local transit fares for the retired.

66 BRICKFIELD, CYRIL F. 1985. "American Association of Retired Persons, 'Voice of the Nation's Older Consumers." *American Health Care Association Journal*, 11(5):5–6, 10.

Executive director of the AARP briefly explains the purpose and programs of the organization.

67 BRICKFIELD, CYRIL F.; HOLDER, ELMA L.; OSSOFSKY, JACK; MASTALISH, RAYMOND; and QUIRK, DANIEL. 1985. "Talking Consumer Interests." *American Health Care Association Journal*, 11(5):5–18.

Series profiling the goals and activities of six major organizations for the aging from the viewpoint of the elder as consumer. The organizations presented include the American Association of Retired Persons (AARP), the National Citizens Coalition for Nursing Home Reform (NCCNHR), the National Council on Aging (NOCA), the National Association of Area Agencies on Aging (NAAAA), the National Association of State Units on Aging (NASUA), and the National Council of Senior Citizens (NCSC).

68 BRINTON, J. W. 1936. *The Townsend National Recovery Plan* (3rd ed.). Chicago: Townsend National Weekly. 96 pp.

Explains the Townsend Plan of providing a flat pension of $200 per month to every retired citizen over age 60. Much time is devoted to explaining the transaction tax and trust fund proposed for financing the pensions. Brinton attacks the motives and conclusions of Townsend

Plan critics and tells why industrialization makes such a pension necessary to reduce the labor force. Booklets such as these were sold through Townsend Clubs to raise funds.

69 CANTERBURY, JOHN B. 1938. "'Ham and Eggs' in California." *Nation*, 147(17):408–410.

Describes the Ham and Eggs movement and its 1935 referendum on the California ballot. Canterbury outlines the growth of public support for the movement and discusses the objectives and economic implications of the pension plan.

70 CANTRIL, HADLEY. 1941. "The Townsend Plan." In *The Psychology of Social Movements*, 169–209. New York: Wiley.

Explains the social and psychological context of American society that made the Townsend Plan so popular. Cantril outlines the plan and the course of the movement since its inception. He reviews data showing the low incomes, maldistribution of wealth, and unmet human needs present in the 1930s. Opinion data from 1939 show supporters are older and have lower incomes. The author presents three case histories of average supporters and suggests the plan is popular because it would satisfy basic needs, appears to be simple, fits social norms, and preserves self-regard.

71 CARLIE, MICHAEL K. 1969. "The Politics of Age: Interest Group or Social Movement?" *Gerontologist*, 9(4):259–263.

Questions whether income-maintenance legislation came about as a result of actions by old-age political organizations or was the product of nonage-based social movements. Carlie contrasts Cottrell's and Tibbitts's social movement perspective with that of Holtzman, who adopts an interest group interpretation. He concludes that if old-age political organizations prior to 1935 were evaluated on their direct influence on legislation, they failed. If, however, their effectiveness is measured by their ability to concern others with the plight of the elderly, they succeeded.

72 CLARK, TIMOTHY B. 1983. "Congress Avoiding Political Abyss by Approving Social Security Changes." *National Journal*, 19(March):611–615.

See entry 479.

73 CLOWES, PHILIP J. 1962. "Older People Observe Their Organizational Roles." In *Politics of Age*, edited by Wilma Donahue and Clark Tibbitts, 146–150. Ann Arbor: University of Michigan Press.

Describes the activities of the United Steelworkers of America in advocating private and public benefits for the aged and in establishing senior clubs and services.

74 COLLINS, WANDA R.; FLANAGAN, JEAN M.; and DONNELLY, TERRENCE M. 1972. "The Senior Citizens Project of California Rural Legal Assistance: An Ac-

tion Arm of the National Senior Citizens Law Center." *Clearinghouse Review*, 6(4–5):220–221.

Outlines the Senior Citizens Project plan to develop a national program to train seniors as paralegals. Training was to be provided to individuals with backgrounds in health and social agencies, legal aid, or senior groups. Its aim was to make elderly participants familiar with government programs and advocacy techniques.

75 COSTA, CYNTHIA. 1971. "Why a National Caucus on the Black Aged?" *Harvest Years*, 11(November):13–18.

Describes the problems of poverty, racial discrimination, and health of black elderly and the positions of the one-year-old National Caucus on the Black Aged on those issues.

76 CUTLER, STEPHEN J. 1976. "Age Profiles of Membership in Sixteen Types of Voluntary Associations." *Journal of Gerontology*, 31(4):462–470.

Identifies trends such as increased leisure time resulting from early retirement, improvements in health and economic security, and better education as reasons that future cohorts of elderly may belong to and participate in voluntary associations more than current cohorts. Cutler uses data from the 1965 and 1975 NORC General Social Surveys of 2,974 adults. A rank order of the types of associations older persons were likely to belong to is compared with data from a 1955 survey. Older persons were more likely than younger people to belong to fraternal and church-affiliated groups while younger persons were more likely to belong to sports groups. Gender differences are discussed.

77 ———. 1977. "Aging and Voluntary Association Participation." *Gerontologist*, 32(4):470–479.

Longitudinal analysis of two samples (n = 374 and 104) of middle-aged and older persons examining their involvement in voluntary associations. Cutler finds very high levels of association membership and participation that do not change over time and concludes that age differences are therefore generational in origin.

78 DEMKOVICH, LINDA E. 1976. "There's a New Kick in the Step of the Senior Citizen Lobbies." *National Journal*, 8(40):1382–1389.

Examines the power and potential of advocacy groups for the aging in federal policy. Demkovich claims the elderly have had a presence in policy-making for only five years (since the early 1970s), primarily from the American Association of Retired Persons (AARP) and the National Council of Senior Citizens (NCSC). Strengths of these advocacy organizations include their expertise, staff work, large memberships, and ability to mobilize their members. The article describes the organizations' lobbying for housing programs. Shortcomings of the advocacy group include the ties of the AARP to the insurance industry and the NCSC to organized labor and their lack of attention to the problems of the poor and minorities.

79 DIETRICH, T. STANTON. 1971. "Politics in the Golden Age Clubs." *Research in Review: Florida State University*, 2(4):5–6.

Discusses the growing number of elderly in Florida, their marginal economic status, and their potential for political action via senior clubs.

80 DORMAN, MORGAN J. 1936. *Age before Booty, An Explanation of the Townsend Plan*. New York: Putnam's. 102 pp.

A popularly written account of the financial problems of old age and the failure of existing government programs to provide relief. Dorman argues that industry can afford to produce enough to satisfy the needs of the elderly and explains how the Townsend plan would accomplish that. Foreword by Francis Townsend.

81 EDELMAN, JOHN W. 1967. "National Council of Senior Citizens, Inc." *Senior Citizen*, 13(3):15–18.

History, goals, and membership incentives of the National Council of Senior Citizens are described by its president. The article describes the work of the council's founding president, Congressman Aime Forand, and its work on Medicare and Social Security issues.

82 EHRLICH, PHYLLIS. 1983. "Elderly Health Advocacy Group: An Integrative Planning Model of Elderly Consumers and Service Deliverers." *Gerontologist*, 23(6):569–572.

Outlines the development of the Elderly Health Advocacy Group, a citizen-oriented structure in which elderly consumers (over 51% of membership) and health care providers participate in health services planning, review, evaluation, and change. The model was tested in Union County, Illinois, and sponsored by the Illinois Department of Health. Outcomes indicate that the model provided for grass-roots consumer participation.

83 ELDER, CHARLES D., and COBB, ROGER W. 1984. "Agenda-Building and the Politics of Aging." *Policy Studies Journal*, 13:115–129.

See entry 299.

84 FESSLER, PAMELA. 1984. "Tactics of New Elderly Lobby Ruffle Congressional Feathers." *Congressional Quarterly Weekly Report*, 42(22): 1310–1313.

Summarizes congressional complaints about the tactics of the National Committee to Preserve Social Security and Medicare. The problems cited include the committee's late hiring of a lobbyist, reportedly misleading scare tactics about the impending bankruptcy of Social Security being used to solicit members, and questions about the use of committee funds. Fessler concludes that the group, led by James Roosevelt, the son of Franklin D. Roosevelt, will have some impact on Congress.

85 FRANKE, JAMES L. 1984. "Representation in Age-Based Interest Groups." *Research on Aging*, 6(3):346–371.

Analyzes the National Retired Teachers Association (NRTA) and the

American Association of Retired Persons (AARP). Franke notes that while the two are frequently viewed as a single entity, their memberships are quite different. Members of both groups are well educated, retired professionals who are financially independent. Survey data from group members and leaders found NRTA members more interested in public policy affecting themselves while AARP members were more interested in membership benefits. Franke questions whether these groups will work for legislation that affects less-affluent elderly.

86 GRAEBNER, WILLIAM. 1983. "The Golden Age Clubs." *Social Service Review*, 57(3):416–428.

Describes the origin and functions of the Golden Age Clubs in Cleveland, Ohio. Founded in 1940, the organization grew to 15 local clubs with 500 members by late 1944, reaching about 2,000 elderly through 35 clubs in 1952. Biographies are used to analyze the clubs as the product of democratic social control. The social theories of John Dewey and others provided the roots of the organization. The clubs provided entertainment and recreation to a socially isolated population. They represented an effort to secure social stability. Cleveland's social service community utilized the city's history of philanthropy and volunteerism to accomplish its objectives.

87 HARRIS, HERBERT. 1936. "Dr. Townsend's Marching Soldiers." *Current History*, 43(5):455–462.

Describes the objectives and proposed financing of the Townsend Plan. Public acceptance of the plan is based in three beliefs: that society should provide for the elderly, that purchasing power should be used to redistribute wealth, and that resources are abundant in the United States. Harris discusses the characteristics and effects of the Townsend Plan political platform.

88 HAVIGHURST, ROBERT J., and ALBRECHT, RUTH. 1953. *Older People*. New York: Longmans. 415 pp.

Describes the community associations of the elderly in a small midwestern town. The elderly held almost none of the leading offices in 130 adult-centered organizations. Many dropped memberships as they became elderly. Lower-status elderly men were least likely to be in formal organizations, but were more involved in informal (tavern) groups. The authors conclude that mixed-age associations are not attractive to the elderly; they advocate the formation of special organizations for the aged.

89 HENRETTA, JOHN C. 1974. "Political Protest by the Elderly: An Organizational Study." Ph.D. dissertation, Harvard University. 193 pp.

Examines a senior advocacy organization, the Legislative Council, to determine how it was able to maintain long-term political involvement. Henretta focuses on the charismatic leadership of Frank Manning, the member commitment that is more social than political, and the group's ability to mount sporadic protest activities.

90 HOBMAN, DAVID. 1988. "The Role of the Charitable and Voluntary Orga-
    nizations." In *The Ageing Population: Burden or Challenge*, edited by
    Nicholas Wells and Charles Freer, 131–142. London: Macmillan.
        Reviews the charity and advocacy work of organizations in England.
    Hobman describes U.S. advocacy organizations to show that no compa-
    rable English organizations exist.

91 HOLTZMAN, ABRAHAM. 1963. *The Townsend Movement: A Political Study*.
    New York: Octagon. 256 pp.
        A widely cited book that analyzes the plan advanced in the 1930s
    as a solution to the economic depression. A $200-a-month pension
    for the elderly and full employment were key features of the pro-
    posal. The work examines the social, political, and economic factors
    that led to an increased political consciousness among the aged. The
    importance of the organization and leadership of the movement are
    outlined. Efforts on the part of the Townsend lobby to elect and con-
    trol sympathetic congressmen are reviewed and the failures are ana-
    lyzed. A congressional investigation of the Townsend movement in
    1936 led to changes in its political behavior and organizational struc-
    ture. Activities of the movement within political parties and at the
    state level are reviewed. Many reasons for the ultimate failure of the
    movement are offered and its influence on modern society is dis-
    cussed.

92 HORNBLOWER, MARGOT. 1988. "Gray Power!" *Time*, 131(January 4):36–
    37.
        Focuses on the political power utilized by the Gray Lobby in the
    1988 presidential elections. Spending millions, the American Associa-
    tion of Retired Persons launched an extensive media blitz. The major
    topics of the campaign were long-term care issues and the sanctity of
    Social Security. Other organizations involved in the political activity
    were the National Council of Senior Citizens and the National Commit-
    tee to Preserve Social Security.

93 HUBBARD, LINDA. 1983. "Turning the Heat on Energy." *Modern Maturity*,
    26(1):35–37.
        Calls for a national energy policy to address the issue of rising en-
    ergy costs. Hubbard describes the formation of the Energy and Aging
    Consortium in 1980 by the American Association of Retired Persons to
    pioneer energy projects to help the elderly. The consortium includes
    members from energy industry associations, federal agencies, aging or-
    ganizations, and utility and petroleum companies.

94 JACKSON, HOBART C. 1971. "National Caucus on the Black Aged: A Prog-
    ress Report." *Aging and Human Development*, 2:226–231.
        Reviews the history of the National Caucus on the Black Aged, the
    issues it is working on, and other groups it is cooperating with.

95 JACKSON, JACQUELYNE JOHNSON. 1974. "NCBA, Black Aged and Politics."
    Annals of the American Academy of Political and Social Sciences,
    415(September):138–159.

    Provides background on the National Caucus on the Black Aged
    (NCBA), providing data to support the existence of a policy-oriented
    organization separate from other minority groups. Demographic data
    show that older blacks are in a worse condition than Spanish-surnamed
    or white elderly on a number of variables. Black elderly are more likely
    to vote than other minority elderly, but less likely than older whites.
    Jackson concludes that little is known overall about the political behav-
    ior of older blacks.

96 JACOBS, RUTH H. 1980. "Portrait of a Phenomenon—the Gray Panthers:
    Do They Have a Long-Run Future?" In *Public Policies for an Aging Pop-
    ulation*, edited by Elizabeth W. Markson and Gretchen R. Batra, 93–103.
    Lexington, MA: D.C. Heath.

    Examines membership, activities, and organizational structure of
    the Gray Panthers. The organization has a diverse membership, includ-
    ing some young people, representing a wide range of political interests
    and inclinations. The focus is on local grass-roots activities, although
    some national conventions are held. Structural changes and initiation of
    fund-raising activities have led to greater organizational control. Jacobs
    suggests that a wider and stable membership base, greater diversity
    among members, leadership as effective and charismatic as that pro-
    vided by founder Maggie Kuhn, and greater consensus among members
    will be necessary to enact social change in the future.

97 JACOBS, RUTH H., and HESS, BETH B. 1978. "Panther Power: Symbol and
    Substance." *Long Term Care and Health Services Administration
    Quarterly*, 2(3):238–244.

    Describes the history of the Gray Panthers, noting the advantages
    and problems it has had in pursuing a nonhierarchical, locally based,
    loose structure. The organization has modified the most radical social
    positions of some organizers to retain its unity, but continues to oppose
    nuclear weapons, racism, sexism, and other issues that transcend old
    age. It also tends to use more radical tactics than the mainstream aging
    organizations.

98 JOHNSON, ELIZABETH R. 1972. "National Senior Citizens Law Center."
    Clearinghouse Review, 6(4–5):189–191.

    Describes the organizational structure and functions of the Na-
    tional Senior Citizens Law Center, a nationwide organization that pro-
    vides legal services to low-income elderly and drafts legislation dealing
    with issues of concern to the aging.

99 KAUTZER, KATHLEEN. 1988. "Empowering Nursing Home Residents: A
    Case Study of 'Living Is for the Elderly,' an Activist Nursing Home Orga-

nization." In *Qualitative Gerontology*, edited by Shulamit Reinhardz and Graham Rowles, 163–183. New York: Springer.

Strengths and weaknesses of the Living Is for the Elderly (LIFE) program are evaluated. LIFE was founded in 1972 to promote self-help and protected activism for nursing home residents. Emphasis is on devising strategies to improve the self-image of nursing home residents by strengthening their social ties and empowering them to exert control over their lives.

100   KENT, DONALD P. 1978. "The How and Why of Senior Centers." *Aging* (283–284):22–23.

Describes the functions and benefits of senior centers. Kent lists various organizational concepts around which senior centers can be designed. He discusses the types of services provided and federal funding for programs.

101   KLEYMAN, PAUL. 1974. *Senior Power. Growing Old Rebelliously*. San Francisco: Glide Publications. 177 pp.

Anecdotes from a local senior power movement, including civil rights rallies and struggles for increased social security benefits. Kleyman focuses on an energetic group of seniors at San Francisco's Glide Memorial Methodist Church whose activities gave birth to the California Legislative Council of Older Americans in 1970.

102   KOSTERLITZ, JULIE. 1987. "Mailouts to the Elderly Raise Alarms." *National Journal*, 19(7):378–379.

Focuses on mail solicitations of the elderly, specifically the fundraising activities of the National Committee to Preserve Social Security and Medicare. Founded by James Roosevelt, son of President Franklin D. Roosevelt, the committee has garnered 4.5 million members since 1982, urging them to contribute $10 to fight threats to Social Security and Medicare.

103   ———. 1987. "Test of Strength." *National Journal*, 19(43):2652–2657.

Describes the American Association of Retired Persons (AARP) and its membership and services for senior citizens. Founded in 1958 as a self-help group, it was criticized in the 1970s for its association with an insurance broker. Its membership has increased rapidly and it has proved to be a powerful advocate for its constituents. The effectiveness of the marketing and lobbying efforts of the AARP is a major strength. The new executive director, Jack Carlson, is profiled.

104   KROUT, JOHN A. 1983. "Correlates of Senior Center Utilization." *Research on Aging*, 5(3):339–352.

Reports on the types of elderly using senior centers, based on interviews with 250 elders in a small urban area. Krout found the center users to have relatively low income and education levels. He suggests that attendees have a greater than average need for social activity and contact.

105 KROUT, JOHN A.; CUTLER, STEPHEN J.; and COWARD, RAYMOND T. 1990.
     "Correlates of Senior Center Participation: A National Analysis." *Geron-*
     tologist, 30(1):72–79.
        Analyzes data from a national sample of 13,737 elders from the
     1984 National Health Interview Survey. Utilization of centers was related
     to higher levels of social interaction, decreasing income, living alone,
     fewer activity-of-daily-living impairments, being female, and living in
     suburbs and rural nonfarm areas, as had been found in previous studies.
     Race, self-reported health status, and residence in urban and rural farm
     areas were not significantly related to center use.

106 KUHN, MAGGIE. 1979. "Advocacy in This New Age." *Aging*, 297–298:2–5.
        Focusing on public transportation as an example, Kuhn outlines the
     12 steps recommended by the Gray Panthers for use in the advocacy pro-
     cess. Some of these steps are documenting the problem, bringing together
     those affected and increasing their understanding of the causes of the
     problem, organizing the group for support and empowerment, finding al-
     lies within the community, planning media campaigns, drafting legislative
     or legal action, and evaluating and celebrating successes.

107 LEOTTA, LOUIS. 1975. "Abraham Epstein and the Movement for Old Age
     Security." *Labor History*, 16(3):359–377.
        Examines the efforts of the Fraternal Order of Eagles, while Epstein
     worked for them, in lobbying at the state level for pensions for the aged.
     State laws enacted in the 1920s were largely ineffective, but the efforts of
     the Eagles raised public awareness of the problems of almshouses and
     the need for pensions. Epstein helped found the American Association
     for Old Age Security (AAOAS) in 1927 but failed to obtain support from
     the Eagles because they opposed the contributory insurance he fa-
     vored. The AAOAS worked with a small budget but generated much
     press coverage and developed numerous coalitions. The author de-
     scribes the association's behind-the-scenes lobbying in states and Con-
     gress.

108 LEVINE, HARRY A. 1952. "Community Programs for the Elderly." *Annals of*
     the American Academy of Political and Social Science, 279(Janu-
     ary):164–170.
        Discusses government responsibility to provide recreational activi-
     ties for the elderly. Levine describes golden age clubs, day care centers
     for retired workers, and the importance of social interaction for the el-
     derly.

109 LICHTENSTEIN, ZALMEN J. 1962. "Direct Political Pressure Groups." In *Pol-*
     itics of Age, edited by Wilma Donahue and Clark Tibbitts, 150–153. Ann
     Arbor: University of Michigan Press.
        Describes some of the mass social action activities of the Golden
     Ring Clubs to celebrate the twenty-fifth anniversary of Social Security
     and to push for health insurance for the aged.

110   MAGANN, ALLENE. 1983. "NCOA Urges Elders to Spearhead Voter Drives at Local Levels." *Perspective on Aging*, 12(5):20–24.

Outlines activities suggested by National Council on Aging (NCOA) executive director, Jack Ossofsky, to encourage grass roots-level voter registration and education. Coalition efforts of more than 50 organizations in New York are described. Magann urges elders to get involved as educators and registrars of younger persons.

111   MASON, BRUCE. 1954. "The Townsend Movement." *Southwestern Social Science Quarterly*, 35(1):36–47.

Describes the establishment, growth, and political effects of the Townsend movement. The political climate and large elderly population in 1930s California contributed to popular support for the movement. Efforts to establish federal pensions based on the Townsend Plan were weakened by financing problems. The Townsend movement failed to win the political support of either Democrats or Republicans but probably contributed to the passage of the Social Security Act of 1935.

112   MCWILLIAMS, CAREY. 1949. "Pension Politics in California." *Nation*, 169(14):320–322.

Early discussion of pension politics in California and the problems inherent in the representation of a large group of elderly by a small group of nonelderly. McWilliams describes Townsend, Ham and Eggs, and Citizens Committee for Old-Age Pensions (CCOAP), focusing on the political activities of George McLain, founder of CCOAP. He discusses incidents of profiteering and the growing political power of McLain.

113   MEHLMAN, STEVE, and SCOTT, DUNCAN. 1977. "The Advocacy Role of NRTA–AARP." In *Handbook of American Aging Programs*, edited by Lorin A. Baumhover and Joan Dechow Jones, 161–177. Westport, CT: Greenwood Press.

Briefly reviews old age movements of the 1930s and the history of the American Association of Retired Persons (AARP). The founder advocated free-enterprise solutions to social problems, so the organization avoided governmental lobbying until 1967. The authors describe organizational structure and membership, policy goals, and the low profile advocacy methods. They contrast AARP with the National Council of Senior Citizens.

114   MESSINGER, SHELDON L. 1955. "Organizational Tra[n]sformation: A Case Study of a Declining Social Movement." *American Sociological Review*, 20(1):3–10.

Discusses factors that contributed to the decline of the Townsend movement despite growing public support for old-age pensions. Emphasis on economic reconstruction and the tendency to link pension plans with Depression issues resulted in the loss of popular support and inability to recruit new members. Loss of support for the values of the organization has resulted in an inability to maintain the organization's structure.

115   MEYER, MADONNA HARRINGTON. 1991. "Organizing the Frail Elderly." In *Growing Old in America*, 4th ed., edited by Beth B. Hess and Elizabeth W. Markson, 363–376. New Brunswick, NJ: Transaction.

Case study of the Minnesota Alliance of Health Care Consumers (MAHCC), an advocacy organization of nursing home residents. Meyer describes the history of the organization and its funding, administration, and actions. It worked successfully in the state legislature for an increased personal needs allowance for nursing home residents and for state funding for the organization. Tactics included lobbying, media outreach, and even a sit-in at the governor's office. Professional organizers played a key role.

116   MINKLER, MEREDITH. 1985. "Building Supportive Ties and Sense of Community among the Inner-City Elderly: The Tenderloin Senior Outreach Project." *Health Education Quarterly*, 12(4):303–314.

Describes the history of the Tenderloin Senior Outreach Project (TSOP) from its inception as a grass-roots organization through its bureaucratization. The original purpose was to increase social networks and develop a sense of community among single-room occupancy hotel residents. Residents took control of the project when it addressed the problem of crime by developing safe houses and obtaining increased police protection. After the group incorporated and began to receive outside funding it developed mobile minimarkets to serve the hotels to improve the nutrition of the residents. Minkler reviews problems with trying to implement Freire's community organizing methods in this context.

117   ———. 1988. "Community-Based Initiatives to Reduce Isolation and Enhance Empowerment of the Elderly: Case Studies from the U.S." *Danish Medical Bulletin, Special Supplement Series on Gerontology*, 6:52–56.

Examines four different programs designed to improve the social support and social interaction of the elderly: Tenderloin Senior Organizing Project, On Lok, Highland Valley Empowerment Plan, and Alzheimer's Disease and Related Disorders Association (ADRDA) support groups. Each adopts a different strategy to help empower the elderly, and their families confront their problems.

118   ———. 1991. "Community Organizing among the Elderly Poor in the U.S.: A Case Study." *International Journal of Health Services*. In press.

Reviews the past 10 years' work of the Tenderloin Senior Organizing Project (TSOP). Minkler shows how the project has made progress in the areas of crime and safety, nutrition, and tenants' rights. She reviews the problems of funding, evaluation, and volunteer burnout.

119   MOORE, WINSTON, and MOORE, MARIAN. 1939. *Out of the Frying Pan*. Los
      Angeles: DeVorss. 185 pp.
         An unflattering journalistic account of the rise and popularity of the
      Ham and Eggs pension movement in California. The authors describe
      the importance of the movement's radio show in starting and sustaining
      the movement. They detail leadership conflicts, political scandals, and the
      ways in which the leaders enriched themselves from the movement,
      showing how the movement was autocratically run.

120   MORGAN, ELMER JOY. 1955. "Our First Issue, Editorial." *Senior Citizen*,
      1(1):3–4.
         Outlines the mission of a new organization, Senior Citizens of
      America, which is a nonpartisan, nonsectarian membership organiza-
      tion of persons age 40 and over. Its monthly magazine contains many
      short general interest articles.

121   NATIONAL COMMITTEE ON THE AGING. 1954. *Standards of Care for
      Older People in Institutions. Section III. Bridging the Gap between
      Existing Practices and Desirable Goals in Homes for the Aged and
      Nursing Homes*. Washington, DC: National Committee on the Aging.
      112 pp.
         Provides the keynote addresses and summaries of workshops held
      during a series of regional conferences involving state officials, nursing
      home administrators, and nonprofit councils involved with the elderly.
      Insight is provided into the aging network at its infancy. Section III in-
      cludes recommendations that professionals become more active in pub-
      licizing the problems of the elderly to "create and maintain a sound po-
      litical situation."

122   NEUBERGER, RICHARD L., and LOE, KELLY. 1936. "The Old People's Cru-
      sade: The Townsend Plan and Its Astonishing Growth." *Harper's*,
      172(March):426–438.
         Growth and political power of the Townsend movement is de-
      scribed. The almost religious fervor of the movement's founder and its
      supporters made rapid development possible and captured the atten-
      tion of national politicians. Allegations of corruption and future political
      impact of the movement are described.

123   ———. 1973. *An Army of the Aged: A History and Analysis of the
      Townsend Old Age Pension Plan*. New York: Da Capo. 329 pp.
         An unflattering contemporary account (original edition was printed
      in 1936) of the rise of the Townsend movement. Based on movement
      documents, media reports, interviews, and observation, the movement
      leaders are portrayed as interested primarily in personal gain and
      power. Francis Townsend is described as a mediocre, colorless country
      doctor who came to lead a national movement by chance. His associate,
      Robert Clements, was a shrewd real estate agent who assumed the daily
      management of the movement and exerted autocratic control. Elderly

followers are portrayed as ignorant of the (un)feasibility of the economics of the plan, self-centered in their quest of government money, but also honest in their belief that the plan would end the Depression. The National Townsend Weekly paper had a peak circulation of 250,000 and was a demagogic propaganda tool. The movement alienated natural allies in the labor and left movements by its conservative positions and endorsements. The authors describe the club system of organization, Townsend Plan conventions, the financial operations of the movement, leadership conflicts, the political strategy in Washington, D.C., and congressional investigations aimed at discrediting the movement.

124   NEWALD, JANE. 1986. "Medicare Group Spreads the Word: Appeal." *Hospitals*, 60(18):92.
      Profiles the activities of an advocacy program established by John Whitman and Associates of Philadelphia in their successful appeal of Medicare denials of skilled nursing facility claims. The author urges advocacy coalitions between physicians, health care providers, patients, and state governments.

125   PINNER, FRANK A.; JACOBS, PAUL; and SELZNICK, PHILIP. 1959. *Old Age and Political Behavior*. Los Angeles: University of California Press. 341 pp.
      Widely cited study of the California Institute of Social Welfare (CISW), a political activist group composed of recipients of Old Age Assistance. The authors describe the charismatic, energetic leadership of George McLain. Comprising 65,000–75,000 persons at the time of the study, CISW sought a federally funded annuity or pension for all U.S. citizens over age 55. The authors discuss reasons that aging movements in the late 1930s through the early 1950s were likely to form in California. They analyze in great detail the institute, its leader, and its members. They liken CISW to other emerging and dependent social groups, noting that the aged have unique interests and problems but tend to rely on outside sources of leadership.

126   POLNER, WALTER. 1962. "The Aged in Politics: A Successful Example of the NPA and the Passage of the Railroad Retirement Act of 1934." *Gerontologist*, 2:207–215.
      Presents the history of the Railroad Retirement Act of 1934 to show a rare case of legislation for the aged that was enacted as proposed by its advocates. Demands for pensions came from skilled workers rather than the unskilled workers whose jobs were less secure and who were nonunion. Agitation came from junior workers who were blocked by older workers from advancing into better paying jobs as a result of declining growth in the industry and seniority rules. Unions were more interested in organizing, so the National Pension Association (NPA) was founded as a single-issue group. The most important lobbying of the NPA was directed at the national railroad unions to adopt the call for a federal railroad pension system.

127 PRATT, HENRY J. 1974. "Old Age Associations in National Politics." *Annals of the American Academy of Political and Social Science*, 415:106–119.

Details the goals, resources, and organizational growth of the National Council of Senior Citizens (NCSC), the National Retired Teachers Association (NRTA)/American Association of Retired Persons (AARP), and the National Association of Retired Federal Employees (NARFE). Pratt shows how they have found funding in addition to membership dues and have utilized organized senior power through increased lobbying and internal managerial skills to promote their goals. The importance of a positive social climate for old age activity has been pivotal for their success.

128 ———. 1976. *The Gray Lobby.* Chicago: University of Chicago Press. 250 pp.

The classic book in the field. See entry 25.

129 ———. 1983. "National Interest Groups among the Elderly: Consolidation and Constraint." In *Aging and Public Policy: The Politics of Growing Old in America,* edited by William Browne and Laura Katz Olson, 145–179. Westport, CT: Greenwood Press.

Begins with the Townsend movement of the 1930s and traces the history and evolution of senior organizations such as the Gray Panthers, the National Council of Senior Citizens (NCSC), and the American Association of Retired Persons (AARP). Pratt shows that a common political purpose, active local chapters, and direct member service provide groups with stability. He notes the difference in social class composition of membership among the groups and compares successes of lobbying efforts by aged groups with those of the American Legion and the National Rifle Association. The absence of a single federal agency to administer aging programs is seen as a major impediment to the realization of the political potential of senior groups.

130 PUTNAM, JACKSON K. 1970. *Old-Age Politics in California.* Stanford: Stanford University Press. 211 pp.

Respected history of pension and old-age assistance movements and legislation in California from the turn of the century. Putnam explains how Upton Sinclair's broadbased EPIC (End Poverty in California) movement elected its own members to state offices but became primarily focused on state pension issues. He describes the Townsend movement as an autocratic national organization that influenced legislation and generated substantial income. He characterizes the Ham and Eggs movement as completely centralized and dictatorial, providing large profits to some of its leaders. It advocated the issuing of special scrip to all unemployed Californians over age 50, had influence over state office elections, and almost won a state initiative to institute its proposal. Putnam portrays the career of George McClain as an organizer of the el-

derly who had realistic aims in improving legislation rather than demagogic, unworkable plans.

131 QUADAGNO, JILL S. 1989. "Generational Equity and the Politics of the Welfare State." *Politics and Society*, 17(3):353–376.

Details the development of Americans for Generational Equity
(AGE) and their work to foster intergenerational conflict in public policy. Funded by private corporations, AGE strived to reframe the debate
about social security to one based on intergenerational transfers. The
organization advocated the transformation of Social Security into a welfare program, undoing the socialization of most income support for the
elderly. While support for Social Security remains high, AGE's efforts
supported the reliance of Medicare's Catastrophic Coverage proposal
entirely on taxes of the aged.

132 QUADAGNO, JILL S., and MEYER, MADONNA HARRINGTON. 1989. "Organized
Labor, State Structures, and Social Policy Development: A Case Study of
Old Age Assistance in Ohio, 1916–1940." *Social Problems*, 36(2):181–196.

Compares the power of class theory and state-centered theory to
explain the struggle over establishing an old-age pension in Ohio. Early
advocacy for old age pensions by the American Federation of Labor
(AFL) and the United Mine Workers (UMW) was unsuccessful, leading
to a coalition with the Fraternal Order of Eagles. The unions worked to
put supporters in office and finally passed a pension by popular vote.
Pensions were administered under a patronage system in which Eagle
or AFL members often held key posts. Patronage administration continued through the 1930s as the federal government was building administrative capacity. Both class and state theory are needed to understand
this process.

133 REITZES, DONALD C., and REITZES, DIETRICH C. 1991. "Metro Seniors in
Action: A Case Study of a Citywide Senior Organization." *Gerontologist*,
31(2):256–262.

A historical case study of a Chicago coalition of senior organizations that shows how it attempted to meet both its own organizational
needs and represent the aged. Over time the organization changed
from a coalition of senior groups with a clear focus to a membership
organization with a diffuse focus. The authors show that the aged are
able to establish citywide networks, create a broad coalition, and act as
advocates for senior issues. They also show the problems with person-
alistic leadership.

134 RILEY, MATILDA WHITE, and FONER, ANNE. 1968. "Voluntary Associations."
In *Aging and Society*, vol. 1, 501–510. New York: Russell Sage Foundation.

Summary data from existing research on the continuity of membership rates over the life span, the tendency of joiners to be of higher
socioeconomic status, and the types of organizations to which the aged
belong.

135 ROSE, ARNOLD M. 1960. "The Impact of Aging on Voluntary Associations." In *Handbook of Social Gerontology*, edited by Clark Tibbitts, 666–697. Chicago: University of Chicago Press.

An overview of organizations that are age-integrated but involve large numbers of aged, those organized by and for the elderly, and aging advocacy/service organizations with nonaged members. The author notes that few age-related organizations existed before the 1930s and discusses factors that contribute to the attractiveness of voluntary organizations for the aged as well as factors that discourage their membership. More voluntary associations have been formed for the aged than by them. Rose reviews the activities of a wide variety of voluntary organizations with, by, and for the aged.

136 ROSENBERG, CHARLOTTE. 1985. "How You'll Feel Their Political Muscle." *Medical Economics*, 62(9):50–53+.

Describes the functions and composition of the Leadership Council of Aging Organizations. The potential political strength of the elderly and its impact on physicians are emphasized. Threats to social security benefits and increasing health care costs are the central focus of concern of organizations for the aging.

137 ROVNER, JULIE. 1988. "Catastrophic Costs Irked by Lobbying Assaults." *Congressional Quarterly Weekly Report*, 46(13):777, 780.

Brief discussion of legislation that would protect Medicare beneficiaries from catastrophic medical expenses. Rovner describes the lobbying activities of the National Committee to Preserve Social Security and Medicare, which opposes the bill, and the Pharmaceutical and Manufacturers Association, which supports it.

138 SANDERS, DANIEL S. 1973. *The Impact of Reform Movements on Social Policy Change*. Fairlawn, NJ: R. E. Burdick. 205 pp.

Examines the activities of the labor movement, Townsend movement, and women's groups such as the League of Women Voters, the Women's Trade Union League, and the Women's Joint Congressional Committee and the roles each played in the passage of Social Security. Sanders concludes that social workers need to serve as advocates for the poor and disenfranchised.

139 SCHULZE, OSKAR. 1949. "Recreation for the Aged." *Journal of Gerontology*, 4(3):310–313.

Describes establishment of the first Golden Age Club, an organization that plans recreational programs for the elderly. The author lists prerequisites for running a successful program.

140 SCOTT, HOWARD I., JR. 1985. "Tennessee's 'Real People' Organize for Fair Health Care." *Southern Exposure,* 13(2-3):88–93.

Describes the efforts of the Real People's Coalition to improve health care conditions. The organization's members are mostly elderly.

Real People grew out of a coalition of 30 community groups in Nashville that fought to redirect Community Development Block Grant funds from the downtown to poor neighborhoods. The parent organization has worked to make Medicaid facility reimbursement records public, make the health department conduct annual unannounced inspections of nursing homes, and provide increased weatherization funds to the elderly and handicapped. Their tactics include both lobbying and public confrontations. The organization faces a powerful hospital lobby in the state.

141 SCOTT, W. RICHARD. 1981. "Reform Movements and Organizations: The Case of Aging." In *Aging: Social Change*, edited by Sara Kiesler, James N. Morgan, and Valerie Kincade Oppenheimer, 331–345. New York: Academic Press.

Examines rationalization tendencies in society that act to differentiate the elderly and institutionalize their needs for assistance and protection. General features and conditions that shaped this societal process are discussed. Scott notes the trend toward creating new organizations and the use of planning rather than direct services to satisfy public demands.

142 SENIOR CITIZENS OF AMERICA BOARD OF TRUSTEES. 1966. "Senior Citizen to Become a Quarterly." *Senior Citizen*, 12(10):17–18.

Gives a brief history of the Senior Citizens of America, explaining that the growth of other membership organizations of the elderly has eroded their member base. The journal was published for only one more year after 1966.

143 SINCLAIR, UPTON. 1934. *Immediate EPIC: The Final Statement of the Plan*. Los Angeles: End Poverty League. 43 pp.

An intellectual summary of Sinclair's End Poverty In California (EPIC) plan to increase production in the state. Sinclair explains that pensions for the aged, blind, disabled, and widowed mothers are one of the three program planks, but suggests waiting to see what federal action occurs first. The book lists movement headquarters and secretaries statewide.

144 ———. 1934. *EPIC Answers: How to End Poverty in California*. Los Angeles: End Poverty League. 32 pp.

A discussion of how Sinclair's End Poverty In California (EPIC) program would affect each type of worker in the state (e.g., teachers, salesmen). The author presents public pensions as a benefit to be provided to assist those at the end of their work lives.

145 SMITH, LEE. 1988. "World According to AARP." *Fortune*, 117(5):96–98.

Analyzes the political power of the 28 million member American Association of Retired Persons (AARP). With expansion in Medicare a priority goal, AARP has moved from advocating a private-enterprise solution to long-term care problems to suggesting that federal programs be developed to provide funding.

146 SOMMERS, TISH. 1987. "Old Woman." In *Handbook of Applied Gerontology*, edited by Lesnoff Caravaglia, 369–377. New York: Humana Services Press.

Examines the function of the Older Women's League in its role as advocate for older women. Sommers discusses negative images provided by the media that contribute to the older woman's sense of powerlessness and deals with women's issues of widowhood, poverty, and illness.

147 SUNDQUIST, JAMES L. 1968. "For the Old, Health Care." In *Politics and Policy: The Eisenhower, Kennedy, and Johnson Years*, 287–321. Washington, DC: The Brookings Institution.

Provides a detailed account of the congressional and White House efforts around the formulation and passage of Medicare. Sundquist presents the Republican strategy of keeping all insurance private versus the Democratic strategy of adding health insurance to Social Security. Grass-roots support rose quickly in the late 1950s, partly in response to labor movement support, American Medical Association opposition, and congressional hearings. The National Council of Senior Citizens was formed in the process, subsidized by the Democratic party and the AFL–CIO. The 1964 Democratic landslide was the key factor in Medicare's passage.

148 TARR, CLARENCE M. 1967. "Champion of Retired Federal Employees." *Senior Citizen*, 13(2):23–26.

Brief history and goals of the National Association of Retired Civil Employees by its president. The work lists names of all national officers, describes publications and other membership incentives, and summarizes legislative issues the organization claims to have influenced.

149 TRELA, JAMES E. 1971. "Some Political Consequences of Senior Center and Other Old Age Group Memberships." *Gerontologist*, 11(Summer, Part 1):118–123.

Compares the political orientations of 256 older persons belonging to a senior center and/or other organizations with 64 elders who are not members of any organizations. The elders with no memberships were the least likely to engage in any political activity. Those belonging to senior organizations and centers were most likely to say that they would be willing to join an organization that advocated government benefits for the aged. Those only in mixed age groups were less likely to be politically active, along with those without any memberships. The author suggests that senior organizations provide a reference group that socializes their members to senior concerns.

150   TRELA, JAMES E. 1972. "Age Structure of Voluntary Associations and
      Political Self-Interest Among the Aged." *Sociological Quarterly*,
      13:244–252.
          Examines the relationship between the age structure of voluntary
      associations and the political sentiments of their members. Age-graded
      voluntary associations were found to facilitate the linkage of age status
      and political values. The elderly with a negative view of aging who were
      not members of associations desired political change the most.

151   ———. 1976. "Social Class and Association Membership: An Analysis of
      Age-Graded and Non-Age-Graded Voluntary Participation." *Journal of
      Gerontology*, 31(2):198–203.
          Finds that there is no significant social class difference in the ten-
      dency for older persons to hold at least one voluntary association
      membership. Most memberships are not age graded, but wealthier
      elderly are more likely than poor elders to be in age-graded groups.
      Social class did not affect the likelihood that new senior center mem-
      bers near Cleveland, Ohio, would retain their membership during six
      years.

152   VIDEBECK, RICHARD, and KNOX, ALAN B. 1965. "Alternative Participatory
      Responses to Aging." In *Older People and Their Social World*, edited by
      Arnold M. Rose and Warren A. Peterson, 37–48. Philadelphia: F. A.
      Davis.
          Analyzes data from 1,500 adults in Nebraska concerning their level
      of involvement in voluntary, political, and church organizations, and the
      extent of their reading. Findings show continuity throughout life in level
      of participation, with age-associated declines a function of social cir-
      cumstances rather than age.

153   WALSH, KENNETH T. 1985. "Graying Armies March to Defend Social Secu-
      rity." *U.S. News and World Report*, 101(3):25–26.
          Discusses activities by the elderly and their advocates concerning
      proposed legislation to limit cost-of-living increases for Social Security.
      Walsh describes the loose coalition of the American Association of Re-
      tired Persons, the National Council for Senior Citizens, and Save Our
      Security (a group of more than 100 organizations representing the el-
      derly, disabled, and labor unions).

154   WEBBER, IRVING L. 1954. "The Organized Social Life of the Retired: Two
      Florida Communities." *American Journal of Sociology*, 59:340–346.
          Describes the organizational involvement of a sample of 474 retired
      persons in West Palm Beach and Orlando, Florida. Webber found no
      relationship between age and organizational involvement. Involvement
      is lower for lower socioeconomic background elders and women. About
      half of memberships were with churches and 17 percent were with fra-
      ternal organizations.

155   WECHSLER, ROBIN, and MINKLER, MEREDITH. 1986. "A Community Ori-
      ented Approach to Health Promotion: The Tenderloin Senior Outreach
      Project." In *Wellness and Health Promotion for the Elderly*, edited by
      Ken Dychtwald, 301–311. Rockville MD: Aspen.

      Describes a community-oriented health promotion program that
      builds supportive relationships among elderly hotel residents and fos-
      ters broader community action. The authors discuss how the project
      follows from social support theory and Paulo's "education for a critical
      consciousness" ideas. They describe how the project moved from one
      centered around outside organizers to a grass-roots organization, and
      finally to a formal organization with the hiring of paid staff.

156   WEISS, HERBERT P. 1987. "Trade Groups, Consumer Advocates Seek
      Common Ground." *Contemporary Long-Term Care*, 10(3)·19–20+

      Discusses joint efforts by the American Health Care Association
      (AHCA), an organization representing nursing homes, and the National
      Citizens' Coalition for Nursing Home Reform (NCCNHR), a national
      consumer advocacy group addressing the issue of quality of care in
      nursing homes. The legislative timing of their proposed nursing home
      reform resulted in failure, but continued lobbying by these groups may
      have an impact in the future.

157   WELLS, JANET. 1985. "Citizens' Coalition for Nursing Home Reform: An
      Interview with Elma Holder." *Southern Exposure*, 13(2–3):116–119.

      Describes the efforts of the Citizens' Coalition for Nursing Home
      reform, a network of over 278 state and local organizations. The group's
      primary focus is quality of care and nursing home financing. Many of
      their activities involve local nursing home ombudsmen.

158   ———. 1985. "It's in the Doing That You Get Your Strength." *Southern
      Exposure*, 13(2–3):24–31.

      Profiles the Bethlehem Area Community Association, a grass-roots
      community-based organization led primarily by older persons in Au-
      gusta, Georgia. Their most significant activities have been to try to ob-
      tain a share of Community Development Block Grant money for the
      poor black Bethlehem area and to develop an employment co-op focus-
      ing on domestic, janitorial, and garden services.

159   ZINSSER, JOHN. 1986. "Gray Panthers: Fighting the Good Fight for 15
      Years." *Fifty Plus*, 26(3):12–13.

      Reviews the accomplishments of the Gray Panthers since its found-
      ing in the early 1970s. These include successful lobbying to increase the
      mandatory retirement age, publication of directories of physicians ac-
      cepting Medicare assignment, and efforts to preserve social security
      cost-of-living adjustments. The author discusses the group's crisis in fu-
      ture leadership.

Advocacy

160 • 1981. "Public Access to Nursing Home Records." *Nursing Home Law Letter* (48):1–23.

Provides information for use by advocates to assist them in utilizing publicly available records. Three sources include federal legislation, state legislation, and provider litigation. Procedures for requesting records along with disclosures required by federal law are summarized.

161 • 1985. "Now They've Got to Treat Folks Right." *Southern Exposure*, 13(2–3):113–115.

Reviews the unionization efforts at Beverly Enterprises, a national nursing home chain. In two years, 58 of 82 elections at facilities were in favor of unionization. A primary bargaining issue is quality of care, which relied on community support. The article also outlines the corporate campaign against Beverly enterprises that led the company to stop its anti-union activities.

162 AMIDEI, NANCY. 1982. "How to Be an Advocate in Bad Times." *Public Welfare* (Summer):37–42.

Outlines a strategy to be used by advocates. Amidei emphasizes use of the media and the importance of political power, noting the success of the elderly. She recommends coalition formation and persistence.

163 BARNARD, JESSIE. 1974. "Age, Sex and Feminism." *Annals of the American Academy of Political and Social Sciences*, 415(September):120–137.

Analysis of the role of age in the orientation to feminism. Older men favor the women's movement more than older women, while younger women are more favorable than younger men. Since voting is more common among older men and younger women, this should encourage feminist policies. Traditional values are also associated with education. The author defends the feminist movement against charges that it ignores older women and the poor.

164 BASS, SCOTT A.; KUTZA, ELIZABETH A.; and TORRES-GIL, FERNANDO (Eds.). 1989. *Diversity in Aging: Challenges Facing the White House Conference on Aging*. Glenview, IL: Scott, Foresman. 187 pp.

Examines diversity among the elderly and the implications of this for public policy and providers. The authors provide a demographic profile of the elderly population and consider whether advocacy groups such as AARP can respond effectively to the entire aged community, especially the most vulnerable. They outline the challenges involved in providing for a diverse elderly community and discuss the consequences of both meeting and failing to meet these challenges. The authors identify four myths of aging that must be dispelled in order to plan effectively for future generations of elderly.

165   BORKMAN, THOMASINA. 1982. "Where Are Older Persons in Mutual Self-Help Groups?" In *Aging*, edited by Aliza Kolker and Paul Ahmed, 257–284. New York: Elsevier.

Reports a literature search that yields only two areas in which there are clear-cut cases of mutual self-help groups of the elderly: the Gray Panthers and certain groups for older alcoholics. Borkman asserts that gerontologists are unfamiliar with mutual self-help approaches and may indeed hold negative attitudes about the ability of the elderly to pursue such independent self-determining behaviors.

166   BRODSKY, RUTHAN. 1987. "As Much to Gain as Give." *Modern Maturity*, 30(2):46–48+.

Discusses the positive impact of volunteerism on the elderly and includes various volunteer opportunities available to them. The Volunteer Talent Bank operated by the American Association of Retired Persons functions to match potential volunteer skills with opportunities within the AARP and other organizations. A program funded by ACTION, the Retired Senior Volunteer Program, provides referral and placement services for those 60 and over. The article includes tips on tax deductibility of volunteer-related expenses as well as hints for successful volunteering.

167   BROWN, ARNOLD. 1985. "Grassroots Advocacy for the Elderly in Small Rural Communities." *Gerontologist*, 25(4):417–423.

Utilizes grounded theory methodology to examine the processes of developing services for the rural elderly. Service programs such as senior citizens centers, nutrition programs, and transportation arose not as a result of formal planning or efforts by network professionals but rather out of a grass-roots model of advocacy. The commonalities of the advocacy model included common motivational, needs-defining, goal-setting, and organizational processes. Recommendations for study to determine the existence of and/or potential for grass-roots advocacy in urban areas are offered.

168   BUTLER, ROBERT N. 1980. "The Alliance of Advocacy with Science: Kent Lecture—1979." *Gerontologist*, 20(2):154–162.

Discusses the competition between aging advocates and researchers during the emerging era of limited funds. The author recounts his efforts in both advocacy and scientific research and calls for a coalition of the two groups to influence aging policy.

169   BUTLER, ROBERT N. 1986. "Advocacy for the Elderly." In *Advocacy in Health Care: The Power of a Silent Constituency*, edited by Joan H. Marks, 61–65. Clifton, NJ: Humana Press.

Stresses the struggle that continues in providing economically for

an aging population. Butler condemns the "victim blaming" that is occurring and suggests a more positive focus in health care management
of the elderly. He emphasizes the need for expanded curricula in
schools of medicine, nursing, and social work to better prepare gradu-
ates to manage the demands of health care of an aging population.

170   CARLIE, MICHAEL K. 1969. "The Politics of Age: Interest Group or Social
      Movement?" *Gerontologist*, 9(4):259–263.
          See entry 71.

171   CHAMPLIN, LESLIE. 1982. "Militant Elderly: The Wave of the Present." *Ger-
      iatrics*, 37(9):125-130.
          Assesses the effectiveness of the elderly lobby. Champlin suggests
      that the diversity of ages and backgrounds of the activists enhances
      their appeal to the special interest groups they join on legislative issues.
      The major organizations of the aging purposely generate an appearance
      of grass-roots activity. She points to Medicare and Social Security as ex-
      amples of successful lobbying by the elderly and concludes that contin-
      ued legislative power will depend on the popular activity the major or-
      ganizations can generate.

172   COHEN, ELIAS S. 1990. "The Elderly Mystique: Impediment to Advocacy
      and Empowerment." *Generations*, 14(Supplement):13–16.
          Examines how the language of geriatrics and gerontology perpetu-
      ates the inaccurate idea that continued growth, development, and en-
      gagement are not possible when an elderly person suffers a physical dis-
      ability. Cohen suggests that the elderly and their advocates work for a
      "right to flourish" and provides policy suggestions to implement that
      right.

173   COTTIN, LOU. 1979. *Elders in Rebellion: A Guide to Senior Activism*. Gar-
      den City, NY: Anchor. 224 pp.
          A newspaper columnist's overview of the problems of income,
      housing, health, and public image for the elderly. Cottin calls on the
      elderly to become active in overcoming those problems, suggesting spe-
      cific actions that seniors can take on a variety of issues.

174   CRAMER, WILLIAM C. 1961. "Senior Citizens in Politics." *Congressional Re-
      cord*, 107(24):5554–5555.
          Text of a Florida newspaper column. It provides a conservative per-
      spective on the elderly's options for political participation.

175   CRITTENDEN, BETH. 1985. "West Virginia Elders Make a Difference."
      Southern Exposure (March–June):52–56.
          Describes the local grass-roots advocacy of the elderly. The Area
      Agencies on Aging assist by providing technical support and contacts
      with local elites. Key issues identified by the elderly included the cost of
      utilities, availability of transportation, and health care access and cost.
      The author describes both the statewide and local senior organizations
      that worked to influence legislation, including a generic drug bill. While

it passed, the bill was not enforced until seniors pressured the Department of Health and local pharmacies. Seniors also helped prevent the elimination of homemaker services in 1982. A senior action phone tree was one of their more effective pressure tools.

176 CROWLEY, DAVID C., and CLOUD, DEBORAH. 1979. "Aging Advocacy at the National Level." *Aging* (297–298):13–17.
Describes unification of advocacy groups to obtain more political power. The authors briefly discuss the history of advocacy for the elderly and list 22 advocacy groups. They describe the achievements of advocacy organizations and conclude with a statement of the policy objectives of advocacy groups and a discussion of future directions for advocacy.

177 CUSHING, MAUREEN. 1984. "Wronged Rights in Nursing Homes." *American Journal of Nursing*, 84(10):1213+.
Suggests guidelines for nurses to use in acting as advocates and protectors for nursing home patients. Cushing reviews Massachusetts and Minnesota laws regarding abuse and supportive care of the terminally ill.

178 DOBSON, DOUGLAS, and ST. ANGELO, DOUGLAS. 1980. *Politics and Senior Citizens: Advocacy and Policy Formation in a Local Context.* De Kalb, IL: Center for Governmental Studies, Northern Illinois University. 255 pp.
Examines the extent to which local government is responsive to the policy concerns of the aged by studying 10 Florida counties. The focus is on policy development, community perceptions of seniors, community leadership support for government programs for the aged, accuracy of leadership perceptions of senior preferences, and extent of leadership representation on senior issues. The authors found that seniors most in favor of public sector programs are least politically involved. Community opinions varied by socioeconomic status and party affiliations. Area Agencies on Aging (AAAs) did not play an advocacy role, and local governments generally provided the aged with little assistance.

179 ERWIN, WILLIAM SHAFER. 1974. "Consumer Participation in Aging Planning." *Gerontologist*, 14(3):245–248.
Describes the planning process used by the Northern Arizona Council of Governments to produce Arizona's first Aging Plan. Senior participation is identified as the most important factor in developing a plan that identifies specific needs of the local elderly community rather than general aging issues.

180 ESTES, CARROLL L. 1973. "Barriers to Effective Community Planning for the Elderly." *Gerontologist*, 13(3):178–183.
Examines the organizational, political, and professional barriers

that impede effective community planning for the elderly. Estes states that unless broad social change replaces the band-aid services approach to problem solving, the elderly will remain peripheral in decisions directly effecting them.

181 ———. 1981. "Public Policy and Aging in the 1980s." In *Empowering Ministry in an Ageist Society*, edited by Dieter Hessel, 23–38. Atlanta: United Presbyterian Church.

Discusses how gerontologists justify the policy focus on individuals rather than on the social causes of the problems of the elderly. The author shows how policies are bifurcated into those for the "deserving" elderly (the upper and middle classes) and those for the "undeserving" (the poor). She sees the uncertainty created by the fiscal crisis, decentralization, and interest group conflict as creating the conditions under which the powerful interests in society can be challenged.

182 FELDMAN, ALBERT G., and FELDMAN, FRANCES LOMAS. 1974. "Community Strategies and the Aged." In *Professional Obligations and Approaches to the Aged*, edited by Arthur Schwartz and Ivan Mensh, 157–197. Springfield, IL: Charles C Thomas.

Discusses the role of social movements in changing both the stereotype and actuality of old age as a time of loneliness and poverty. Community organization is defined and five models of community organization are described. The social planning model emphasizes recognition of community needs and cooperation between government and interest groups. The social action model targets influential decision makers. The advocacy model relies on identification with and willingness to take action on behalf of the group being served. Developing problem-solving skills and learning to use outside resources characterize the self-help model. The educational model focuses on dissemination of knowledge. For these models to be effective goals must be identified, and community organizers must be knowledgeable about their community.

183 FRITZ, DAN. 1979. "The Administration on Aging as an Advocate: Progress, Problems and Perspectives." *Gerontologist*, 19(2):141–150.

Asserts that the Administration on Aging's overwhelming program responsibilities may hamper its function as an advocate for the elderly. Fritz recommends dividing advocacy tasks with other federal units and more appropriate use of research findings.

184 GOLDOFTAS, BARBARA. 1988. "Organizing in a Gray Ghetto: The Tenderloin Senior Organizing Project." *Dollars and Sense*, 133(January–February):18–19.

Provides a brief history of the Tenderloin Senior Organizing Project (TSOP) in San Francisco. Initially established to improve the health status and reduce the social isolation among single-room occupancy hotel residents, it now facilitates tenant organizing. The author provides an example of a successful tenant action.

185 HANNA, WILLIAM J. 1981. "Advocacy and the Elderly." In *Aging: Prospects and Issues*, edited by Richard Davis, 297–310. Los Angeles: University of Southern California Press.

Defines advocacy, identifies how it is done, and emphasizes participation of older persons in various capacities including coalitions, county and state commissions, and national organizations. The author identifies issues that demand action by advocates.

186 HAPGOOD, DAVID. 1978. "The Aging Are Doing Better." In *The New Old: Struggling for Decent Aging*, edited by Ronald Gross, Beatrice Gross, and Sylvia Seidman, 345–363. Garden City, NY: Anchor Books.

Finds that organized advocacy and active public support on aging issues are responsible for legislative successes by the elderly. The problems of enforced retirement and age discrimination in the workplace are serious problems still to be addressed. Positive programs in housing and nursing home reform are highlighted.

187 HEALTH LAW PROJECT, UNIVERSITY OF PENNSYLVANIA LAW SCHOOL. 1972. "Legal Problems Inherent in Organizing Nursing Home Occupants." *Clearinghouse Review*, 6(4–5):203–211.

Proposes that nursing home patients do not receive adequate care and should be organized into self-governing groups. The authors outline the steps necessary to accomplish this and discuss problems that might be encountered because of opposition from nursing home administrators as well as their legal remedies.

188 HESS, CLINTON W., and KERSCHNER, PAUL A. 1978. *The Silver Lobby: A Guide to Advocacy for Older Persons*. Los Angeles: University of Southern California Press. 53 pp.

Designed as a training manual for senior movement leaders. The authors provide a workbook-style guide to identifying issues, building a case, and planning and conducting an advocacy campaign.

189 JACKSON, JACQUELYNE JOHNSON. 1976. "Aged Blacks: A Potpourri in the Direction of the Reduction of Inequities." In *Growing Old in America*, edited by Beth Hess, 390–416. New Brunswick, NJ: Transaction Books.

Recommends reducing the minimum age-eligibility requirements for Old-Age, Survivors, Disability and Health Insurance (OASDHI) in the social security system. The work of the National Caucus on the Black Aged is discussed. The author notes the disparities in life expectancy rates between blacks and white to support arguments.

190 JACOBSON, SOLOMON G. 1977. "Consumer Advocacy." In *Handbook of American Aging Programs*, edited by Lorin A. Baumhover and Joan Dechow Jones, 119–131. Westport, CT: Greenwood Press.

Describes the history and activities of the Citizens for Better Care

(CBC) in nursing homes, homes for the aged, and other after-care facilities. Founded in 1969 through the efforts of the Detroit Department of Health to establish a citizen's advocacy group to address quality problems in nursing homes, the CBC has membership consisting mostly of retired members of the autoworkers union and younger professionals. The organization served as advocate for nursing home residents as a class through successful law suits to open nursing home inspection results. It worked for individuals through its ombudsman program. It also conducted numerous studies, relying heavily on student interns. Organization funding was primarily from contracts, limited donations (mostly from churches), and very limited membership income.

191   KERSCHNER, PAUL A. (Ed.). 1976. *Advocacy and Age: Issues, Experiences, Strategies.* Los Angeles: University of Southern California Press. 162 pp.
      Provides a three-part examination of the advocacy efforts of and for the elderly. Kerschner begins with an analysis of the historical and philosophical approaches to advocacy. He employs pluralist theory to discuss partisan political activities of the elderly. The first section concludes with discussions of major organizational and policy problems involved in aging advocacy. Part two details three case studies of advocacy by and for the elderly. Part three suggests tools and methods for implementing advocacy efforts. A bibliography on advocacy is included.

192   KOLLAR, NATHAN. 1988. "Interfaith Coalitions and the Crisis of the Elderly: A Practical Solution." *Journal of Aging and Judaism*, 2(4):221–236.
      Explains "the crisis" involving the religiosity of the elderly in terms of their need for service providers to be aware of the religious needs of their clients and the variety of needs and resources of the elderly. Kollar suggests interfaith coalitions for and with the elderly to establish programs.

193   KUHN, MARGARET E. 1976. "What Old People Want for Themselves and Others in Society." In *Advocacy and Age*, edited by Paul A. Kerschner, 87–96. Los Angeles: University of Southern California Press.
      Founder of the Gray Panthers describes the disenfranchisement of the aged from important decisions. She describes 10 steps in preparing the elderly for advocacy and discusses the roles of advocate, social critic, testers of new models, and public citizen.

194   LETZIG, BETTY J. 1987. "Church as Advocate in Aging." *Journal of Religion and Aging*, 2(4):1–11.
      Emphasizes the increasing role of the church as an advocate for the elderly. Because churches are the largest single network of voluntary community organizations, they are equipped to act as advocates in legislative and public policy areas as well as in supportive services and education. Letzig suggests that the church congregation provides a natural base for intergenerational cooperation. One example of church advo-

cacy for the aged is the National Interfaith Coalition on Aging (NICA), which represents 30 Protestant, Roman Catholic, Jewish, and Orthodox national religious bodies.

195   LEWIS, MYRNA I. 1986. "Advocacy Issues for Older Women." In *Advocacy in Health Care: The Power of a Silent Constituency*, edited by Joan Marks, 67–76. Clifton, NJ: Humana Press.

Addresses women's unique health issues. Lewis points up the potential of organizations for older women (Older Women's League) in that growing numbers of women are becoming politically active and holding public office. Their political power is significant by virtue of their number and high voter participation. She notes on the other hand that their increased longevity over men makes them the predominant users of long-term care. The positive and negative financial impact of long life on women is also addressed.

196   LITWIN, HOWARD; KAYE, LENARD W.; and MONK, ABRAHAM. 1984. "Conflicting Orientations to Patient Advocacy in Long-term Care." *Gerontologist*, 24(3):275–279.

Analyzes national survey data on nursing home ombudsman programs to demonstrate disparity in perceptions of patient advocacy. The position held within the long-term care delivery network determined the focus held. Providers held an individualized developmentally focused viewpoint, commissioners of health had an individualized/patient rights focus, and ombudsmen and citizen organizations held a facility/patient rights focus. Programs to align conflicting perspectives are needed.

197   MINKLER, MEREDITH. 1986. "Building Support Networks from Social Isolation." *Generations* (Summer):46–49.

Briefly describes the philosophy and operation of the Tenderloin Senior Outreach Project. The author also describes some of the challenges in organizing an isolated, poor, and often unhealthy group of seniors.

198   ———. 1990. "Improving Health through Community Organization." In *Health Behavior and Health Education: Theory, Research and Practice*, edited by K. Glanz, F.M. Lewis, and B.K. Rimer, 257–287. San Francisco: Jossey-Bass.

Reviews the concept of community organizing, identifying as key elements empowerment, community competence, starting where the people are, and identifying issues. The article provides brief descriptions of the Tenderloin Senior Organizing Project and the Minnesota Heart Health Program as case studies of two different approaches.

199   MONK, ABRAHAM, and KAYE, LENARD W. 1982. "The Ombudsman Volunteer in the Nursing Home: Differential Role Perceptions of Patient Rep-

resentatives for the Institutionalized Aged." *Gerontologist*, 22(2):194–199.

Examines the roles assumed by volunteer nursing ombudsmen in New York City, showing that they frequently take a therapeutic, supportive role rather than an advocacy or mediating role. This role is what is perceived as the proper role by long-term care providers as well. The authors found that ombudsmen and nonprofit nursing homes feel that ombudsmen need more power.

200   MONK, ABRAHAM; KAYE, LENARD W.; and LITWIN, HOWARD. 1984. *Resolving Grievances in the Nursing Home: A Study of the Ombudsman Program*. New York: Columbia University Press. 247 pp.

Reports research from 1979 to 1981 on the effectiveness of the Nursing Home Ombudsman Program in New York City and nationally. The authors describe the different models used by various states that varied on a collaborate-contest continuum. Rather than mediating and advocating, most ombudsmen are found to adopt a more therapeutic role. Long-term care providers prefer the therapeutic model while aging interest groups prefer the advocacy orientation. The program has low visibility among nursing home residents but was found to be moderately successful overall. The authors also provide a review of the historical, philosophical, and political antecedents of the program.

201   MOORE, MICHAEL D. 1985. "Old People's Day: There's Power in Us A-Comin' Together." *Southern Exposure*, 13(2–3):14–18.

Describes the history and present practice of Old People's Day in a small Arkansas town. Begun as a way to diminish factionalism in the town's church in 1932, it remains the most important public occasion in the town.

202   NETTING, F. ELLEN, and HINDS, HOWARD N. 1984. "Volunteer Advocates in Long-Term Care: Local Implementation of a Federal Mandate." *Gerontologist*, 24(1):13–15.

Describes the ombudsman program as developed in eastern Tennessee. Volunteers are recruited by local area agencies on aging and tend to be elderly. The program emphasizes both helping individual residents and pursuing legislative action.

203   OSSOFSKY, JACK. 1988. "Connecting the Networks: Aging and Lifelong Disabilities." *Educational Gerontology*, 14(5):389–397.

Emphasizes the importance of shared networks for those with developmental disabilities (DD) and the aging. The joint problems of the aging and the DD, such as fragmentation and inaccessibility of services, increased attention on caregivers, and the need to focus on the individual are highlighted. A coalition between the groups is suggested to demand resources and national policy changes.

204 PERLMAN, JANICE E. 1976. "Grassrooting the System." *Social Policy* (September–October):4–20.

Describes the grass-roots associations of the 1970s involving local people mobilized on their own behalf around concrete issues of importance in their communities. The author details activities by seniors in Rhode Island, Chicago, and Arkansas that affected public transportation in their areas.

205 ———. 1979. "Grassroot Empowerment and Government Response." *Social Policy* (September–October):16–21.

Discusses the neighborhood movement of the 1970s as an emerging social force that may serve to bridge the gap between the individual and local, state, and federal governments.

206 PERRY, RALPH B. 1942. *Plea for an Age Movement*. New York: Vanguard. 23 pp.

Lecture delivered at the forty-fifth reunion of the Princeton class of 1896. Perry laments the decline in the status and power of the elderly in the family and society; he calls on the aged to reclaim their status by asserting the positive elements of old age.

207 PRATT, HENRY J. 1976. *The Gray Lobby*. Chicago: University of Chicago Press. 250 pp.

The classic book in the field. See entry 25.

208 ———. 1983. "Politics in Aging." In *Hoffman's Daily Needs and Interests of Older People*, edited by Woodrow Morris, Iva Bader, and Adeline Hoffman, 39–52. Springfield, IL: Charles C Thomas.

Explores the contradiction in the popular stereotype that seniors withdraw from political and community activities upon retirement. The authors utilize the Townsend movement to illustrate how effective organization to promote self-interest can be. A direct relationship between societal perception of the elderly and public policy formation exists. The future of the elderly is closely linked to the ability of their leaders and the effectiveness and cooperation of senior citizen organizations.

209 RALSTON, PENNY A. 1981. "Educational Needs and Activities of Older Adults: Their Relationship to Senior Center Programs." *Educational Gerontology*, 7(2–3):231–244.

Analyzes a survey of 110 elderly homeowners and five senior centers in Champaign-Urbana, Illinois, to determine the congruence between educational needs and services. Black respondents were more likely than whites to say they wanted to learn more about how to become an advocate for the elderly and more about the Gray Panthers. Senior centers' offerings need strengthening to meet diverse education needs.

210 RANDALL, OLLIE. 1977. "Aging in America Today—New Aspects in Aging." *Gerontologist*, 17(1):6–11.

Stresses the necessity for creating the opportunity for the elderly to enjoy a quality of life consonant with the individual's wishes.

211 REGAN, JOHN J. 1977. "When Nursing Home Patients Complain: The Ombudsman or the Patient Advocate?" *Georgetown Law Journal*, 65:691–738.

Reviews the legal basis and operation of ombudsmen and advocacy programs as means for assuring nursing home quality. Quality assurance has depended on licensing and certification standards, funding formulas, and physician peer review. These have been inadequate and also fail to have patient involvement. Regan reviews the ombudsman demonstration projects of the 1970s, most of which established non-adverserial facilitators for complaints. Most programs were limited because they had no special statutory authority. Nursing home advocates take a more adversarial role. The author reviews legal remedies available to patients via tort, contract, and civil rights actions.

212 ROEBUCK, JANET. 1983. "Grandma as Revolutionary: Elderly Women and Some Modern Patterns of Social Change." *International Journal of Aging and Human Development*, 17(4):249–266.

Describes successful coping tactics of aging women who have experienced significant social and personal changes and who subsist on limited material resources. The author suggests that greater study of female aging might provide insights and models for coping by future generations.

213 ROSE, ARNOLD M. 1962. "Organizations for the Elderly: Political Implications." In *Politics of Age*, edited by Wilma Donahue and Clark Tibbitts, 135–145. Ann Arbor: University of Michigan Press.

Describes five forms of political activity by the aged: age-integrated pressure groups, age-segregated pressure groups, political parties, age-specific party subgroups, and voting. Increasing age consciousness has created a "diffused social movement." Rose predicts increasing age consciousness that will be blunted by public programs to satisfy the greatest unmet needs.

214 SHEINMAN, ALLEN J. 1987. "TV Goes Gray at the Grass Roots." *Fifty Plus*, 27(9):24–27+.

Promotes the potential of cable television as an effective resource for service agencies in communicating with the elderly. Sheinman notes that 1,400 cable channels provide programming produced by and for seniors. The American Association of Retired Persons offers a cable program called Modern Maturity. While individuals over 50 are underrepresented on prime time television, cable television can provide an important format for presentation of senior issues.

215 SICKER, MARTIN. 1979. "The AoA Advocacy Assistance Program: Origins and Directions." *Aging*, (297–298):18–21.

Gives 1975 AoA Task Force assessments of both the Nursing Home Ombudsman Demonstration Program (NHODP) and the need for development of an AoA legal services program. The author describes the functions and activities of NHODP and proposed services of the legal program. These programs were merged in 1978 and renamed the AoA Advocacy Assistance Program. Sicker concludes with 1978 Reassessment of NHODP and legal services identifying new areas of focus.

216 ST. ANGELO, DOUGLAS. 1982. "Aging Advocacy: The Cozy Triangle's Hesitant Angle." *Journal of Applied Gerontology*, 1:115–125.

Employs the Cobb and Elder format of agenda formation to examine how local program administrators serve the older citizens in ten local Florida governments. The author emphasizes the conditions of scope, visibility, and intensity as the key to successful advocacy. Study findings show that scope and visibility are adequate but intensity of advocacy efforts by aging-services administrators is a weak link.

217 TIBBITTS, CLARK. 1962. "Politics of Aging: Pressure for Change." In *Politics of Age*, edited by Wilma Donahue and Clark Tibbitts, 16–25. Ann Arbor: University of Michigan Press.

Briefly reviews the beginning of senior activism in the late 1920s around pension issues. Tibbitts finds the aged weakly attached to existing senior organizations. The increasing number of organizations working for the aged and the expansion of government programs will prevent any unified movement from occurring.

218 TORRES-GIL, FERNANDO. 1988. "Interest Group Politics: Empowerment of the Ancianos." In *Hispanic Elderly in Transition*, edited by Steven R. Applewhite, 75–93. Westport, CT: Greenwood Press.

Discusses the marginal role of Hispanic elderly in U.S. politics. The traditional sources of political power for Hispanic aged have declined. Mass membership groups for the aging have generally ignored minorities, while Hispanic political leaders and organizations have ignored the aged. The only activity has been advocacy by human service professionals. The author suggests that activism by Hispanic elderly should and will increase in the future.

219 WALLER, CHARLES H., JR. 1977. "The Michigan Ombudsman Program." In *Handbook of American Aging Programs*, edited by Lorin A. Baumhover and Joan Dechow Jones, 140–160. Westport, CT: Greenwood Press.

Describes Michigan's demonstration ombudsman program, which is operated independently from government sponsorship. Organization, staffing, and goals are described. Program issues include the ineffective enforcement system, inadequate nurse aide training, staffing levels, and patients' bill of rights. The program has been active in mediating individual complaints as well as in legislative lobbying and other advocacy.

220   Zischka, Pauline C., and Jones, Irene. 1984. "Volunteer Community Rep-
      resentatives as Ombudsman for the Elderly in Long-Term Care Facili-
      ties." *Gerontologist*, 24(1):9–12.
           Outlines a program in Rockland County, New York, to train volun-
      teers to act as advocates on behalf of long-term care facility residents.

221   Zola, Irving K. 1988. "Aging and Disability: Toward a Unifying Agenda."
      Educational Gerontology, 14(5):365–387.
           Cites the increase of disabling illnesses, the effect of technology
      and the medicalization of care, and the shift to home care as phenom-
      ena shared by the aging and the disabled. Zola suggests that these
      groups should be afforded the same rights as other minorities in free-
      dom from discrimination and allotment of government and private ben-
      efits.

Electoral Strategy and Behavior

222   • 1981. "The Aging of Broward and Palm Beach." *Congressional
      Quarterly Weekly Report*, 39(48):2383.
           Brief discussion of the political power of retirees in Palm Beach,
      Florida, and the attention the area's congressional representative pays
      to his older constituents.

223   Abramson, Paul R. 1974. "Generational Change in American Electoral
      Behavior." *American Political Science Review*, 68(1):93–112.
           Examines the declining relationship between social class and parti-
      san choice since World War II, a shift that resulted from generational
      change. Data from six presidential election surveys (1948–1968) are ex-
      amined for white voters. Results show older voters exhibit a strong rela-
      tionship between social class and partisan choice; this relationship is
      much weaker among younger voters. The author concludes that this is
      due to different social composition and liberal policy preferences of
      younger middle-class voters.

224   ———. 1976. "Generational Change and the Decline of Party Identifi-
      cation in America." *American Political Science Review*, 70(2):469–
      478.
           Analyzes the postwar decline in party loyalties as a function of dif-
      ferences in the formative socialization of voters entering the electorate
      after World War II, based on national survey data. Abramson shows how
      this decline in party identity results from generational change. He
      groups white voters according to strong or weak party identification and
      concludes that weak party identity of younger voters is due to differ-
      ences in their socialization. He briefly discusses the implications of
      weak party affiliation on political stability.

225 AGNELLO, THOMAS J. 1973. "Aging and the Sense of Political Powerlessness." *Public Opinion Quarterly*, 37:251–259.

Notes the changing voter participation levels between the young and the old. Agnello states that political response is dependent on the role the individual has been allocated in society and his or her interpretation of that role. The author utilizes data from presidential elections in 1952, 1960, and 1968 to measure the feelings of powerlessness among various age groups and relate this to each cohort's voting behavior. He concludes that while older cohorts have a continued high level of voting, they experience an increasing sense of powerlessness.

226 BENGTSON, VERN L., and CUTLER, NEAL E. 1976. "Generations and Intergenerational Relations: Perspectives on Age Groups and Social Change." In *Handbook of Aging and the Social Sciences*, edited by Robert H. Binstock and Ethel Shanas, 130–159. New York: Van Nostrand.

Discusses different conceptualizations of generations. The authors argue that changes attributed to age are commonly generational in origin, including party identification, political alienation, and social policy attitudes. They found intergenerational solidarity within families to be high and suggest that conditions in the future will lead to increased age consciousness and political mobilization.

227 BENGTSON, VERN L.; CUTLER, NEAL E.; MANGEN, DAVID J.; and MARSHALL, VICTOR W. 1985. "Generations, Cohorts, and Relations between Age Groups." In *Handbook of Aging and the Social Sciences* (2nd ed.), edited by Robert H. Binstock and Ethel Shanas, 304–338. New York: Van Nostrand.

Reviews the evidence concerning generational differences in creating political behavior, family relationships, and social conflict. When cohort and period are controlled, aging is found to correlate with increased support for government medical aid programs. Party identification is associated more with cohort than age. The authors note that explaining differences between elections also requires examining macrolevel demographic shifts. They review the factors that could both increase and decrease generational conflict.

228 BINSTOCK, ROBERT H. 1974. "Aging and the Future of American Politics." *Annals of the American Academy of Political and Social Science*, 415(September):199–212.

Forecasts little change in senior power as a result of a cohesive voting pattern by the elderly. Binstock fails to see the elderly gaining much power and suggests that government's adequate and appropriate response to the needs of the rapidly growing elderly population will be the critical issue.

229 ———. 1981. "The Aging as a Political Force: Images and Resources." In *Aging: Challenge to Science and Social Policy. Volume II: Medicine and Social Science*, edited by A. J. J. Gilmore, A. Svanberg, M. Rarois,

W. M. Beattie, and J. Piotrowski, 390–396. London: Oxford University Press.

Essay critiquing the popular images of the elderly as a powerful voting bloc with politically powerful organizations. The author notes that most generalizations are made on very limited evidence. He describes the political access that aging organizations have, but argues that their actual power is limited. He warns of a possible backlash if the elderly continue to be seen as a powerful, monolithic group.

230 BUTTON, JAMES W., and ROSENBAUM, WALTER A. 1989. "Seeing Gray: School Bond Issues and the Aging in Florida." *Research on Aging*, 11(2):158–173.

Tests the assumption that the elderly oppose local school bond issues because they receive no direct benefits from them. The results of Florida school bond referenda from 1969 to 1988 are analyzed. Of the nine variables only the presence of an American Association of Retired Persons (AARP) chapter and the growth of the aging population significantly correlated with affirmative votes. The authors speculate that the presence of an AARP chapter indicate political organization, and activity and increasing growth rate indicate an influx of predominantly middle-class elderly. These factors contribute to a social environment supportive of increased funds for local education.

231 ———. 1990. "Gray Power, Gray Peril, or Gray Myth?: The Political Impact of the Aging in Local Sunbelt Politics." *Social Science Quarterly*, 71(1):25–38.

Examines county government budgets in Florida between 1973 and 1986 to determine whether the elderly population influences taxes, types of programs, or spending on education. The size of the older population, its rate of growth, and/or the presence of a local AARP chapter are significant in about half of the issues in at least one year. Overall, the elderly appear to have a limited impact on taxing and spending differences.

232 CAMERON, SANDRA W. 1974. "The Politics of the Elderly." *Midwest Quarterly*, 15(2):141–153.

Asserts that the elderly have organized into political interest groups and that their efforts to secure benefits have been successful. Most problems of the elderly result from health care issues or inadequate income. These include social disengagement as a result of forced retirement and a youth-oriented culture, psychological difficulties, dependency, inadequate housing, and poverty. Efforts of the various advocacy organizations to deal with these problems are described. Political influence of the elderly has resulted in substantial improvements, largely through lobbying activities of these special interest groups.

233 CAMPBELL, ANGUS. 1962. "Social and Psychological Determinants of Voting Behavior." In *Politics of Age*, edited by Wilma Donahue and Clark Tibbitts, 87–100. Ann Arbor: University of Michigan Press.

Reviews the reasons some groups are strongly identified with one political party. Campbell argues that age will not become an organizing feature of group political consciousness because of heterogeneity, geographical dispersion, and traditional party habit that would be hard to break.

234 CAMPBELL, ANGUS. 1971. "Politics through the Life Cycle." *Gerontologist*, 11(1):112–117.

Presents data from Survey Research Center's Surveys of National Electorate in 1960, 1964, and 1968 to examine voting behaviors of different age groups in national elections. Campbell concludes that great heterogeneity exists across age groups and predicts that the elderly are not likely to become a strong political force in the near future as they lack size, cohesion, and organization.

235 CAMPBELL, JOHN CREIGHTON, and STRATE, JOHN M. 1981. "Are Old People Conservative?" *Gerontologist*, 21(6):580–591.

Utilizes data from the 14 American National Election Studies conducted by the University of Michigan from 1952 to 1980 to learn whether the elderly are more politically conservative than the middle aged. Issues of conceptualization of conservatism, identification with ideological groups, voting behavior and party identification, opinions regarding issues, and policy priorities are examined. The authors conclude that simple knowledge that a voter is old will not serve to predict how conservative he or she is.

236 CLAGGETT, WILLIAM. 1980. "The Life Cycle and Generational Models of the Development of Partisanship: A Test Based on the Delayed Enfranchisement of Women." *Social Science Quarterly*, 60(4):643–650.

Finds more support for a generational than a maturational effect on the strength of party affiliation of women in public opinion data from 1952 to 1964.

237 CLEMENTE, FRANK. 1975. "Age and the Perception of National Priorities." *Gerontologist*, 15(1):61–63.

Utilizes a national sample of 1,504 adults divided into three cohorts: young (18–39), middle aged (40–59), and elderly (60 plus). Clements presents questions regarding expenditures to solve national problems of health, the environment, drugs, defense, and education. His findings indicate that the elderly group was significantly more conservative than younger respondents with regard to proposed spending, even in areas such as health programs from which they would directly benefit.

238 COTTRELL, FRED. 1966. "Aging and the Political System." In *Aging and Social Policy*, edited by John C. McKinney and Frank T. de Vyver, 77–112. New York: Appleton-Century-Crofts.

Discusses the distribution of power in society as it will affect the likelihood that the aged will attempt to change institutional arrangements that serve them and as it will affect their success. Cottrell reviews the major powers in the areas of income maintenance, health, and housing for the aged. He concludes that the elderly can tip the political balance in policy-making, but are only a secondary force overall.

239   CRITTENDEN, JOHN. 1962. "Aging and Party Affiliation." *Public Opinion Quarterly*, 24(4):648–657.

Classic article that argues that the aging process has an effect on party affiliation independent of generational factors. Based on nation-wide surveys (1946–1958), the study performs age comparisons between cohorts. Results show a shift toward Republicanism for both high- and low-income groups. This shift is most prominent in middle-age groups. The author suggests that these tendencies can be explained by both generational differences in experiences and changes due to aging.

240   CUTLER, NEAL E. 1970. "Generation, Maturation, and Party Affiliation: A Cohort Analysis." *Public Opinion Quarterly*, 33:583–588.

Refutes John Crittenden's 1962 analysis that aging leads to increased Republican identification. Cutler uses cohort analysis of the data to demonstrate the need for cohort as well as maturational interpretations of observed age differences.

241   ———. 1974. "Aging and Generations in Politics: The Conflict of Explanations and Inference." In *Public Opinion and Political Attitudes*, edited by Allen R. Wilcox, 440–462. New York: Wiley.

Reviews the theoretical basis for using a cohort analysis rather than maturational analysis to explain age differences in political opinions. Using national public opinion data from 1946 to 1966, Cutler demonstrates that views on foreign policy issues are more consistent within cohorts over time than within fixed ages.

242   ———. 1976. "Resources for Senior Advocacy: Political Behavior and Partisan Flexibility." In *Advocacy and Age*, edited by Paul A. Kerschner, 23–40. Los Angeles: University of Southern California Press.

Suggests that political resources of the aged include their growing numbers, high political participation, the growth of stable age-based organizations, and the "partisan flexibility" of the aged. Cutler analyzes data that show little age change in the propensity to vote only along partisan lines.

243   ———. 1977. "Demographic, Social-Psychological, and Political Factors in the Politics of Aging: A Foundation for Research in 'Political Gerontology.'" *American Political Science Review*, 71(3):1011–1025.

Explores the argument that the American political system can expect increasing demands from older segments of the population. Cutler examines current and future demographics of the older population. He challenges the disengagement theory of political and social participation and considers alternatives to this theory. He discusses the concept of older Americans as a politically conservative group and concludes that the politics of aging will increase demands on the political system in the future.

244 ———. 1981. "Political Characteristics of Elderly Cohorts in the Twenty-First Century." In *Aging: Social Change*, edited by Sara Kiesler, James N. Morgan, and Valerie Kincade Oppenheimer, 127–157. New York: Academic Press.

Identifies and discusses political and nonpolitical aspects of aging in a historical-demographic context. Cutler considers demographic changes and secular trends (increases in educational level, declines of party preference, and age as a dimension of political organization) to determine the nature of politically relevant characteristics of elderly cohorts in the twenty-first century. He concludes that age consciousness will have important political implications in the future.

245 CUTLER, NEAL E., and BENGTSON, VERN L. 1974. "Age and Political Alienation: Maturation, Generation and Period Effects." *Annals of the American Academy of Political and Social Sciences*, 415(September):160–175.

Uses a cohort analysis to test possible maturation (age), cohort, and period effects as causes for changes in the feelings of political powerlessness among the aged. Using University of Michigan presidential opinion surveys from 1952, 1960, and 1968, the authors find that period effects are most important across age and education groups.

246 CUTLER, NEAL E.; PIERCE, ROBERT; and STECKENRIDER, JANIE. 1984. "How Golden Is the Future?" *Generations*, 9(1):38–43.

Examines the political interest and voting behavior as well as the political attitudes of older persons. The growing "age consciousness" among the elderly and the public perceptions of appropriate levels of the elderly's political influence are routinized. The authors forecast the potential for greater involvement of older people in development of aging policy as "age consciousness" is added to the other politically relevant aspects of their self-images.

247 CUTLER, NEAL E., and SCHMIDHAUSER, JOHN R. 1975. "Age and Political Behavior." In *Aging: Scientific Perspectives and Social Issues*, edited by Diana S. Woodruff and James E. Birren, 374–406. New York: Van Nostrand.

Reviews the literature on the effect of aging on political participation and behavior. The authors argue that a cohort analysis is more useful. Studies show the elderly are more attentive to and active in politics than younger adults, and the age of political leaders has increased. Cutler and Schmidhauser argue that age will become increasingly im-

portant in the future because of increased education, age consciousness, and acceptance of alternative forms of protest.

248   CUTLER, STEPHEN J. 1973. "Perceived Prestige Loss and Political Attitudes
among the Aged." *Gerontologist*, 13(1):69–75.
     Reports findings of a study of 170 noninstitutionalized respondents
age 65 and older. Cutler concludes that older persons who perceive the
aged as having low prestige in an age-stratified social system demonstrate attitudinal support for government intervention in behalf of the
elderly and for organized political activity. Socioeconomic status was
found to have an independent effect on each of the dependent variables. The author emphasizes the need for further examination of the
sources of variation in the political attitudes of the aged.

249   CUTLER, STEPHEN J., and KAUFMAN, ROBERT L. 1975. "Cohort Changes in
Political Attitudes: Tolerance of Ideological Nonconformity." *Public
Opinion Quarterly*, 39(1):69–81.
     Analyzes public opinion polls to show that all cohorts became more
tolerant of nonconformist beliefs between 1954 and 1973, contradicting
the claim that people become less tolerant with age. Younger cohorts
became tolerant faster, giving the false appearance of declining tolerance among the aged.

250   DAY, CHRISTINE L. 1990. *What Older Americans Think: Interest Groups
and Aging Policy*. Princeton, NJ: Princeton University Press. 164 pp.
     Comprehensively reviews the literature and provides data from in-
terviews of public officials and organizational representatives on the formation and current operation of old-age interest groups. The author
draws on exchange theory to explain the attraction to the elderly of
mass membership groups and predicts the continued influence of such
groups. An original analysis of opinion data shows that the elderly hold
diverse opinions about the role of the government in aging issues, with
economic status and party identification being more important than age
in predicting attitudes.

251   DIETRICH, T. STANTON. 1969. "Senior Citizens: A Political Minority
Group?" *Reports in Social Science*, 12(2):32–48.
     Defines "minorities" as groups that offer organized and aggressive re-
sistance to discrimination. Dietrich discusses several factors that indicate
that, using these criteria, senior citizens are becoming a minority group.
These are rapid growth of the elderly population, poverty among the elderly, and creation of advocacy groups. He evaluates the potential political
effect of senior citizens by analyzing voting behavior and demographics of
Florida elderly. This potential political power combined with the lack of
employment opportunities may identify the elderly as a minority group.

252   DOBSON, DOUGLAS. 1983. "The Elderly as Political Force." In *Aging and
Public Policy, the Politics of Growing Old in America*, edited by Wil-

liam P. Browne and Laura Katz Olson, 151–168. Westport, CT: Greenwood Press.

Questions whether the elderly constitute a distinctive political force in American politics. Dobson explores major areas of research relating to age and political behavior. He examines the political implications of aging as viewed by elected representatives and concludes that while the elderly appear to be more conservative, they are not a homogeneous political group. He suggests that the elderly of the twenty-first century will be better educated, in better health, and more politically experienced than their predecessors.

253 DOUGLASS, ELIZABETH B.; CLEVELAND, WILLIAM P.; and MADDOX, GEORGE L. 1974. "Political Attitudes, Age, and Aging: A Cohort Analysis of Archival Data." *Journal of Gerontology*, 29(6):666–675.

Examines the effect of age on political opinions as reported in Gallup surveys between 1940 and 1970. The authors present an overview of the methodological problems faced in using archival data. Their analysis shows that age is significant (and secondary to period) in political attitudes only for the issues that affect the immediate experience of the individual. Attitudes about broader community issues were sensitive to period, and national concerns were not influenced by period, age, or cohort.

254 FISHER, LLOYD H. 1962. "Research in the Politics of Aging." In *Politics of Age*, edited by Wilma Donahue and Clark Tibbitts, 36–47. Ann Arbor: University of Michigan Press.

Argues that age influences political beliefs and behaviors. Fisher suggests ways to study age-related beliefs and behavior, providing hypotheses concerning old-age movements.

255 FONER, ANNE. 1972. "The Polity." In *Aging and Society*, vol. 3. New York: Russell Sage Foundation. pp. 115–159.

Uses age stratification theory to explain the differential levels of political activity by age, the inconsistently conservative political attitudes of the aged, and the potential for intergenerational political conflict. Foner examines how cohort and period effects change political attitudes and analyzes the 1960s "youth rebellion" to show that membership in intergenerational groups and settings reduces the potential for intergenerational conflict.

256 ——. 1974. "Age Stratification and Age Conflict in Political Life." *American Sociological Review*, 39:187–196.

Explores the issue of age as a basis of political dissension. Foner utilizes the perspective of age stratification to examine the potential for age conflict in political life, the political struggles that erupt periodically between young and old, and the conditions that seem to foster these conflicts. She finds that in situations in which different strata have unequal power and opposing political views, conflict along age lines is likely.

257 GLENN, NORVAL D. 1969. "Aging, Disengagement, and Opinionation." *Public Opinion Quarterly*, 33:17–33.

Presents data that reject the disengagement theory hypothesis that individuals are less likely to hold or express opinions as they age. The observed increase in "no opinion" responses to opinion polls disappears when education is controlled for and is reversed when a cohort analysis is conducted. Cohort analysis also shows constant voter turnout until advanced age.

258 ———. 1974. "Aging and Conservatism." *Annals of the American Academy of Political and Social Sciences*, 415(September):176–186.

Reviews the evidence concerning the causes of the higher levels of political conservatism among the elderly. Research shows that the elderly are becoming less conservative than they were when they were young, but that the changes are slower than the decreasing conservatism among the young.

259 GLENN, NORVAL D., and GRIMES, MICHAEL. 1968. "Aging, Voting, and Political Interest." *American Sociological Review*, 33:563–575.

Utilizes data from 28 Gallup polls conducted from 1945 to 1965 to study age changes in voting and political interest among white persons. The analysis demonstrates a pronounced increase in participation from young adulthood to middle age. Voter turnout and political interest remained nearly constant from mid-life to advanced maturity. Flaws in interpretation of cross-sectional data are discussed. Disengagement theory and its relationship to the findings are analyzed.

260 GLENN, NORVAL D., and HEFNER, TED. 1972. "Further Evidence on Aging and Party Identification." *Public Opinion Quarterly*, 36:31–47.

Refutes the 1962 article by John Crittendon stating that individuals in the United States tend to become Republicans as they grow older. The authors utilize cohort analysis spanning 1945–1969 to conclude that there is no evidence that the process of aging leads to Republican party preference. They also cast doubt on the belief that the elderly tend to become more conservative in their political attitudes.

261 GUBRIUM, JABER F. 1972. "Continuity in Social Support, Political Interest, and Voting in Old Age." *Gerontologist*, 12(Winter):421–423.

Examines the consequences of widowhood and divorce on the political activity of 209 older persons in Detroit. Those with social losses reported less interest in politics and were less likely to vote.

262 HUDSON, ROBERT B., and BINSTOCK, ROBERT H. 1976. "Political Systems and Aging." In *Handbook of Aging and the Social Sciences*, edited by Robert H. Binstock and Ethel Shanas, 369–400. New York: Van Nostrand.

Reviews evidence on the political beliefs and behavior of the elderly, showing that beliefs remain relatively constant throughout one's life while participation increases. There is no evidence of an "aging vote," although patterned voting may occur around specific old-age interests. The authors review research to show that aging-advocacy organizations are not much different from other organizations and have limited power. They consider the forces that have made aging a concern of political systems.

263 HUDSON, ROBERT B., and STRATE, JOHN M. 1985. "Aging and Political Systems." In *Handbook of Aging and the Social Sciences*, (2nd ed.), edited by Robert H. Binstock and Ethel Shanas, 554–585. New York: Van Nostrand.

Examines the effects of aging on individuals' political orientations and behaviors and discusses why aging has become a concern of political systems. Cohort rather than age accounts for the party attachments of the aged, and issue priorities are similar to those of younger groups. The authors identify six different factors affecting aging policy that vary in importance by issue, period, and policy level. They predict that changing patterns of economic growth and the growing size of the elderly population could weaken the consensus support for programs for the elderly and make the role of the organized aged more important.

264 JENNINGS, M. KENT. 1979. "Another Look at the Life-Cycle and Political Participation." *American Journal of Political Science*, 23(4):755–771.

Examines the relationship between life stages and participation. Adequate understanding of this connection is hindered by ambiguous classifications of life stages and narrow conceptions of participation. Results indicate political participation varies in response to changing motivations and opportunity structures at different life stages rather than simply to chronological age. Jennings suggests that demographic changes could have a significant influence on political participation.

265 LIGHT, LARRY. 1981. "Democrats Hoping to Break Traditional GOP Loyalties of Voters Age 65 and Older." *Congressional Quarterly Weekly Report*, 39(48):2343–2344,2346.

Discusses Democratic party efforts to attract elderly voters away from the Republican party based primarily on reduction of Social Security benefits.

266 MILLER, ARTHUR H.; GURIN, PATRICIA; and GURIN, GERALD. 1980. "Age Consciousness and Political Mobilization of Older Americans." *Gerontologist*, 20(6):691–700.

Utilizes data from two national probability studies taken during the 1972 and 1976 national presidential elections. The authors examine age identification and political participation, noting human and economic factors that affect participation. Age denial is seen to have little to do with whether older people are politically engaged. A feeling of political powerlessness was observed in that individuals did not feel government was responsive to their needs. The authors conclude that the perception of organizational activity on the part of the elderly could act to stimulate political involvement.

267   MILLER, ARTHUR H.; GURIN, PATRICIA; GURIN, GERALD; and MALANCHUK, OKSANA. 1981. "Group Consciousness and Political Participation." *American Journal of Political Science*, 25(3):494–511.

Questions the use of group consciousness as an explanation for the higher political participation of some disadvantaged groups. The authors examine political participation according to race, class, age, and gender. The group consciousness model is refined to explore interactive, rather than strictly linear, relationships among both subordinated and dominant social groups. Factors affecting political participation for both groups are identified. Older people do not clearly fit pattern for subordinate or dominant groups. The authors conclude that interactive model of group participation is better than a linear, additive model.

268   NIE, NORMAN H.; VERBA, SIDNEY; and KIM, JAE-ON. 1974. "Political Participation and the Life-Cycle." *Comparative Politics*, 6(3):319–340.

Explores the relationship between age and political activity in Australia, India, Japan, Nigeria, and the United States. Survey data show similar participation rates among the young and the elderly, and higher participation rates for those in mid-life for all countries. Correcting for educational level reveals that the elderly participate at a rate similar to the average for all citizens. The apparent low participation rate of the elderly is attributed to their lower educational level, not decreasing participation in later life.

269   ODELL, CHARLES E. 1962. "Attitudes toward Political Activities among the Aging." In *Politics of Age*, edited by Wilma Donahue and Clark Tibbitts, 26–35. Ann Arbor: University of Michigan Press.

Argues that government concern with age follows election cycles and little is accomplished. Odell describes activities of retired auto workers in their union. He advocates increased involvement of seniors in social change.

270   PEIRCE, NEAL, and CHOHARIS, PETER. 1982. "The Elderly as a Political Force—26 Million Strong and Well Organized." *National Journal*, 14(37):1559–1562.

Asserts that the elderly are making a deep impression on American politics because of their voting participation, sheer numbers, political sophistication, and time to volunteer. The effective use of the media to increase public awareness of aging problems and the effectiveness of lobbying efforts in Congress are seen as key strengths in winning out in competition for government dollars.

271 PORTER, KIRK H., and JOHNSON, DONALD B. 1970. *National Party Platforms: 1840–1968*. Urbana: University of Illinois Press. 768 pp.

Provides the official party platforms of national parties, including clauses that indicate support for programs for the elderly. Health and/or retirement insurance for the aged were included in the planks of the 1908 Socialist party, 1912 Progressive party, 1916 Democratic and Prohibition parties, 1928 Republican party, and 1932 Democratic party. Starting in 1936, both major parties regularly included such planks in their platforms.

272 RIEMER, YOSEF, and BINSTOCK, ROBERT H. 1978. "Campaigning for 'The Senior Vote': Case Study of Carter's 1976 Campaign." *Gerontologist*, 18(6):517–524.

Analyzes politicians' perceptions of the aged as a potentially cohesive voting bloc and the importance of such a belief in shaping electoral campaign and public policy decisions. The authors utilize a case account of Jimmy Carter's 1976 campaign for the presidency. They outline Carter's positions on senior issues and the formation the Democratic Presidential Campaign Committee (DPCC) "Seniors Desk." They stipulate that further research is needed to understand what the politician's perception is regarding who has what kind of power over him or her. Such a study might provide greater insight into how older voters and aging-based organizations influence public policy.

273 RILEY, MATILDA WHITE, and FONER, ANNE. 1968. "Political Roles." In *Aging and Society*, vol. 1, 463–482. New York: Russell Sage Foundation.

Summary data of existing research on the continued political participation of the aged, partisan loyalties and affiliation, conservatism, and the impact of older people on the political system.

274 ROLLHAGEN, RICK E. 1984. "Age-Related Changing Levels of Voting Turnout across Time." *Gerontologist*, 24(2):205–207.

Analyzes two national panel studies from 1956–58–60 and 1972–74–76 to demonstrate that older persons do not differ substantially from members of other age groups in the "durability" of their voting turnout over time.

275 RULE, WILMA L. B. 1977. "Political Alienation and Voting Attitudes among the Elderly Generation." *Gerontologist*, 17(5):400–404.

Explores the elements of political alienation in a convenience sample of 51 elderly whites in a small midwestern town. The data showed that the elderly who felt inefficacious did not vote while those who felt cynical generally did vote. These reflect pre-Depression educational and historical attitudes, so later cohorts of the elderly are predicted to vote more and be more liberal.

276 SCHMIDHAUSER, JOHN R. 1958. "The Political Behavior of Older Persons: A Discussion of Some Frontiers in Research." *Western Political Quarterly*, 11(1):113–124.

Early application of political behavior and social psychological research to evaluate the political influence of the elderly. The author discusses the difficulties of defining "aged," the political importance of the elderly, and the demographic importance of the elderly in rural nonfarm areas. Schmidhauser explores the voting behavior of the elderly and identifies possible influences. Lack of data and ambiguous definitions of conservatism make it difficult for him to reach conclusions.

277 ———. 1968. "The Political Influence of the Aged." *Gerontologist*, 8(2):44–49.

Examines the gap that exists between the professionally recognized needs of the elderly and the public policy processes designed to meet those needs. Schmidhauser reviews demographics and voting behaviors and questions whether elders constitute a cohesive voting bloc. He asserts that the political role of the elderly is a complex phenomenon and recommends further research of the social environment in which political attitudes are developed and contemporary situations in which elderly find reinforcement for these attitudes.

278 SER, FRANCIS D. 1974. "The Importance of Age to Conservative Opinions: A Multivariate Analysis." *Journal of Gerontology*, 29(5):549–554.

Reports results of a study that postulates that the elderly are more conservative than young people with regard to controversial issues such as race, law enforcement, and patriotism. Age, size of childhood community, father's education and occupation, and respondent's occupation were among the variables explored. Results showed that age and conservative opinions were positively correlated even when social class, education, father's socioeconomic status, and the size of the respondent's childhood community were controlled.

279 STEPHENS, NANCY, and MERRILL, BRUCE D. 1984. "Targeting the Over Sixty-Five Vote in Political Campaigns." *Journal of Advertising*, 13(3):17–20.

Presents results of telephone interviews with 911 persons under age 65 and 198 aged 65 and over conducted one month before and one day after the 1982 general election. The subjects were registered voters in Arizona. The interviews demonstrated that the older group was more Republican, more interested in politics, and more likely to contribute than the under 65 group. Older people did not respond significantly differently from younger voters on most issues.

280 STRATE, JOHN M.; PARRISH, CHARLES J.; ELDER, CHARLES D.; and COIT, FORD, III. 1989. "Life Span Civic Development and Voting Participation." *American Political Science Review*, 83(2):443–464.

Examines the effects of aging and civic development on voting participation. The authors describe a model that uses cross-sectional data from nine presidential elections to represent civic development over the life span. Results are consistent with cross-sectional findings that show age and education are significant influences on voting behavior. The strength of the model lies in its ability to explain variations in voting participation usually attributed to the effects of aging. Most variations are explained by changes in level of community attachment, church attendance, strength of party attachment, government responsiveness, and civic competence.

281   TINGSTEN, HERBERT. 1963. "Age Groups in Politics." In *Political Behavior: Studies in Election Statistics*, edited by Vilgot Mannerling, 79–119. Totowa, NJ: Bedminster Press.

Extensively reviews the electoral participation rates by age in several European countries, with some U.S. data. Tingsten concludes that voting rates increase with age universally and that younger voters are more liberal.

282   TORRES-GIL, FERNANDO, and BECERRA, ROSINA M. 1977. "The Political Behavior of Mexican-American Elderly." *Gerontologist*, 17(5):392–399.

Examines the political activity of Mexican-American elderly in San Jose and Los Angeles, California. The authors posit a model that accounts for factors such as a sense of political efficacy and environmental and perceptive barriers that influence political behavior. They conclude that Mexican-Americans have low rates of political activity and suggest overcoming barriers such as low income and fear could serve to increase voter participation.

283   TURK, HERMAN; SMITH, JOEL; and MYERS, HOWARD P. 1966. "Understanding Local Political Behavior: The Role of the Older Citizen." In *Social Aspects of Aging*, edited by Ida Harper Simpson and John C. McKinney, 254–276. Durham, NC: Duke University Press.

Examines the political behavior of individuals on local community issues. The authors identify differences between local- and state-level political behavior and the importance of the aged in the political processes. They evaluate the self-interest and civic responsibility models of political participation, and the role of the aged voter. Using the civic responsibility model they analyze an urban community to examine the connection between community participation and political participation. The results show that persons with similar levels of community participation exhibit similar levels of political participation regardless of age, explaining varying rates of political activity.

284   WAGAR, LINDA. 1989. "Saying No to Grandma." *State Government News*, 32(3):10–14.

Depicts the political clout of seniors at the state level as a function of their voting rates and political organization. Wagar describes the benefits provided to all seniors in Alaska and Pennsylvania to demonstrate how undeserving elderly receive benefits and maintain them because of their political power.

285 WALKER, DAVID B. 1960. "The Age Factor in the 1958 Congressional Elections." *Midwest Journal of Political Science*, 4(1):1–26.

Analyzes the ages of winners and losers in the 1958 congressional elections in districts that were uncontested, fighting, marginal (close race), or switched. Walker finds that the age of Representatives does not vary by region of country and that Congress has become younger. The article provides a complex description of the conditions when younger or older candidates run for office.

Other Political Strategies

286 ACHENBAUM, W. ANDREW, and STEARNS, PETER N. 1978. "Essay: Old Age and Modernization." *Gerontologist*, 18(3):307–312.

Discusses conceptual problems and operational limitations of using modernization theory to analyze continuities and changes in the history of old age. The Western model of modernization cannot be applied globally because comparable phenomena—such as bureaucratization and urbanization—have affected Western and non-Western countries differently. Political modernization did not affect the elderly until the nineteenth century in the West, and most changes have not occurred until more recently.

287 ALWIN, DUANE F.; COHEN, RONALD L.; and NEWCOMB, THEODORE M. 1991. *Political Attitudes over the Life Span*. Madison: University of Wisconsin Press. 352 pp.

Examines the political attitudes among women who attended Bennington College in the 1930s and 1940s using a three-wave longitudinal panel and national election surveys from the 1950s to the 1980s. Findings support both persistence (direction of partisan support) and lifelong openness models of political attitudes. Political attitudes from the 1930s predicted 60 percent of attitudes in the 1980s.

288 BERKOWITZ, LOIS, and BENDERLY, BERYL L. 1989. *Building Bridges to Citizenship: How to Create Successful Intergenerational Citizenship Programs*. Arlington, VA: Close-Up Foundation. 91 pp.

Guide to creating citizenship programs based on an intergenerational model. The authors suggest ways to increase knowledge about the United States and provide suggestions for lobbying and media outreach.

289 BINSTOCK, ROBERT H. 1972. "Interest Group Liberalism and the Politics of Aging." *Gerontologist*, 12(3):265–280.

Classic article on the political power of senior citizens as a marginal interest group at the national level. It argues that the elderly's heterogeneity and lack of age consciousness are barriers to electoral power. It reviews the ten organizations for the aging that lobby for legislation and discusses their limited influence. Major senior organizations have been more successful in obtaining financial support from the government through "middleman programs" rather than by advocating income transfers to the poor aged. The author concludes that coalitions of the disadvantaged of all ages would be of more help to the aged poor than senior organizations.

290 BINSTOCK, ROBERT H., and LEVIN, MARTIN A. 1976. "The Political Dilemmas of Intervention Policies." In *Handbook of Aging and the Social Sciences*, edited by Robert H. Binstock and Ethel Shanas, 511–535. New York: Van Nostrand.

Examines the sources and instances of political limitations of effective policy interventions, describes the politics of policy adoption and of policy implementation, and suggests how adoption and implementation can be optimized despite politics. Electoral politics encourages legislators to favor policies that are immodest and tangible with quick results. Other problems include fragmented power, brokering of legislation, decentralization of programs, capture of programs by special interests, and bureaucratic self-interest.

291 BINSTOCK, ROBERT H.; LEVIN, MARTIN A.; and WEATHERLY, RICHARD. 1985. "Political Dilemmas of Social Intervention." In *Handbook of Aging and the Social Sciences* (2nd ed.), edited by Robert H. Binstock and Ethel Shanas, 589–618. New York: Van Nostrand.

Discusses the ways in which politics shapes the efficacy of social policies for the elderly. The authors describe legislators' needs to appeal to constituents and contributors in designing policy and the limits imposed by bureaucracies and service providers on implementing programs. The fragmentation of power in the American political system leads to fragmentation, competition for resources, and typically requires broad coalition building that can dilute the effectiveness of proposals. The needs of politicians can lead to policies that are only symbolic and perpetuate programs that are popular regardless of their effectiveness.

292 BORGATTA, EDGAR F., and MONTGOMERY, RHONDA J.V. (Eds.). 1987. *Critical Issues in Aging Policy: Linking Research and Values*. Beverly Hills: Sage Publications. 308 pp.

Emphasizes that study of aging policy is limited by options within existing frameworks and prevailing values. The authors use a broad perspective of policy analysis to identify issues. Authors advocate viewing aging policy as an element of larger public policy that reflects fluctuating societal values. They note that many social programs such as senior centers, living environments and preretirement programs focus on elders' well-being, but the common conceptualization, definition, and measurement of "well-being" are problematic. Other chapters focus on social support and programs designed to augment or substitute for the informal support system, retirement policy, and the inappropriate use of gender difference, housing issues, senior center policy, health care policy, and crimes committed by the elderly.

293   BROWNE, WILLIAM P. 1985. "Variations in the Behavior and Style of State Lobbyists and Interest Groups." *Journal of Politics*, 47(2):450–468.

Challenges interest group theory proposition that lobbyists need to acquire and maintain access. The report is based on interviews from Florida, Iowa, Michigan, and New Jersey with groups such as the AARP, Association of Homes for the Aging, and Michigan Society of Gerontology. Three patterns of access emerged: traditional proactive lobbyists with good legislative access, adversarial policy opponents, and policy dependents who mainly respond to legislative initiatives. Analysis of legislation found access type did not matter as long as some type of statewide action occurs on behalf of the constituency.

294   BROWNING, ROBERT X. 1981. "Political and Economic Predictors of Policy Outcomes: U.S. Social Welfare Expenditures." Ph.D. dissertation, University of Wisconsin. 206 pp.

Examines the predictors of increases in social spending, including Social Security and veterans' benefits. The author finds Social Security changes related to price increases and electoral cycles, while Aid to Families with Dependent Children (AFDC) is related to prices and wage growth.

295   CURTIS, THOMAS B. 1962. "The Republican Party." In *Politics of Age*, edited by Wilma Donahue and Clark Tibbitts, 167–174. Ann Arbor: University of Michigan Press.

Republican congressman explains the Republican Party position on the needs of the aged. He argues against targeted approaches.

296   DAY, CHRISTINE L. 1988. "Older Americans, Interest Groups, and Aging Policy." Ph.D. dissertation, University of California, Berkeley. 265 pp.

Examines the origin and maintenance of interest groups of the elderly, the source of their influence, and how well they represent the aged. The author finds the elderly divided in their opinions on key issues.

297   DOBELSTEIN, ANDREW, and JOHNSON, ANN BILAS. 1985. "Showdown at the White House Conference on Aging." *Southern Exposure*, 13(2–3):135–137.

A brief description of some of the political battles over agenda setting between Reagan supporters and other delegates to the 1981 White House Conference on Aging.

298   DONNELLY, HARRISON. 1981. "White House Conference: Delegates to Aging Conclave Seek to Focus U.S. Attention on Demographic Revolution." *Congressional Quarterly Weekly Report*, 39(48):2329,2332.

Lists political, social, and economic consequences of having a growing older population. Donnelly briefly discusses loss of Social Security benefits, preconference organization, and controversies.

299 ELDER, CHARLES D., and COBB, ROGER W. 1984. "Agenda-Building and the Politics of Aging." *Policy Studies Journal*, 13:115–129.

Examines the "agenda-building" decisional process as the combination of four elements: people, problems, solutions, and choice opportunities. Elder and Cobb focus on major mass membership organizations such as the AARP and the NCSC, as well as on individuals who have had a significant impact on defining aging issues. They emphasize that policy opportunities are governed in part by institutional practices and tend to ebb and flow. They urge reformers to make the most of opportunities that arise and to be persistent and patient.

300 ESTES, CARROLL L. 1976. "Goal Displacement in Community Planning for the Elderly." In *Community Planning for an Aging Society*, edited by M. Powell Lawton, Robert J. Newcomer, and Thomas O. Byerts, 309–316. Stroudsburg, PA: Dowden, Hutchinson.

Analyzes the activities of three community planning agencies for the aged, finding that their activities are more goal displacement than attainment oriented. One key problem with such agencies is that they are assigned a coordination role but have no real authority. This also leads them away from identifying basic problems such as income and medical care.

301 ———. 1976. "The Politics of Community Planning for the Elderly." *Policy and Politics*, 4:51–70.

Analyzes data from a study of four planning agencies for the aged. While members of the planning bodies were from both aging and non-aging service organizations, all the members with power were from the aging organizations. The planning organizations were dominated by a social work perspective and accomplished more to further their organizations and professions than to further the cause of the aged.

302 ———. 1980. "Social Policy for Elders in the 1980's." *Generations*, 4(1):4–5,50.

Reviews the pressures that the author predicts will be applied for both the expansion and limitation of benefits for the aged in the 1980s. The growing effectiveness of aging constituency groups along with trade associations and corporations are among the expansionary pressures.

303 ———. 1980. "Constructions of Reality." *Journal of Social Issues*, 36(2):117–132.

Reports on a study of local policy-making and service delivery organizations for the aged. The data show that the organizations largely exclude the elderly from their activities, the organizations' leaders are mostly professionals with social work backgrounds who have a negative perception of the aging process, and the organizations foster a service orientation that accommodates the status quo.

304   ———. 1986. "The Aging Enterprise: In Whose Interests?" *International Journal of Health Services*, 16(2):243–251.

Reviews social developments since the author's seminal 1979 book. Estes discusses the new business ideology that has infused the service approach to problems of the elderly, focusing particularly on Medicare. This shift results in creating markets more than serving needs. Single-interest age-based policies are criticized as a form of selfish separatism that impairs needed intergenerational coalitions.

305   ESTES, CARROLL L., and EDMONDS, BEVERLY C. 1981. "Symbolic Interaction and Social Policy Analysis." *Symbolic Interaction*, 4(1):75–85.

Adopts a symbolic interactionist framework to examine social policy for the elderly. The authors argue that three contextual properties of policy-making are important to consider: societywide uncertainty that allows for multiple definitions of a problem, policy ambiguity that allows a wide range of policy implementation, and political pluralism. The high level of possible negotiation also requires attention to the structural context within which policy unfolds.

306   FISCHER, DAVID HACKETT. 1979. "The Politics of Aging in America: A Short History." *Journal for the Institute for Socioeconomic Studies*, 4(2):51–66.

Traces the history of public intervention in the lives of the elderly and the role of advocates in this intervention. Fischer begins with nineteenth-century recognition of old-age poverty and the early twentieth-century development of industrial pensions. He describes recent successes of the gray lobby in its challenge of the American Medical Association over Medicare, and of large corporations over mandatory retirement and threats to Social Security. He emphasizes the necessity for advocate groups' recognition of elder autonomy.

307   FISHER, LLOYD H. 1950. "The Politics of Age." In *The Aged and Society*, edited by Milton Derber, 157–167. Champaign, IL: Industrial Relations Research Association.

Early discussion of the relationship between politics and the characteristics generally attributed to the elderly. Fischer describes statistical methods and sources of data that can be used to study aging and politics. He provides a brief analysis of old-age movements, party platforms, and Social Security legislation.

308   FONER, ANNE. 1975. "Age in Society: Structure and Change." *American Behavioral Scientists*, 19(2):144–165.

Describes an analysis of age wherein age operates as a basis for social stratification in a similar way to class. Age stratification allocates roles and influences individual experiences, group life, and social institutions. Age-based solidarity is likely because of shared experiences, age segregation, and mass communications. Solidarity is weakened because age is a transient affiliation. Forces exist that both encourage and dampen intergenerational conflict. Demographic changes in the future will change the shape of the age-stratification system.

309   FOX, PATRICK. 1989. "From Senility to Alzheimer's Disease: The Rise of the Alzheimer's Disease Movement." *Milbank Quarterly*, 67(1):58–102.

Describes establishment of the Alzheimer's disease movement. Alzheimer's has become a focus of advocacy efforts and is perceived as a significant health problem because of the efforts of a small group of scientists, interested in their own research goals, and the National Institute on Aging, which wished to establish the legitimacy of the disease. This interest led to the formation of alliances between scientists, government agencies, and the media. The distinction between Alzheimer's and senile dementia has been central to the success of the Alzheimer's movement.

310   FOX, RICHARD G. 1981. "The Welfare State and the Political Mobilization of the Elderly." In *Aging: Social Change*, edited by Sara Kiesler, James N. Morgan, and Valerie Kincade Oppenheimer, 159–182. New York: Academic Press.

Argues that determining whether the elderly will become a political group requires evaluating the question from a cultural evolutionary standpoint. This requires an examination of economic power, communication, and political control, which make up the welfare state. Fox compares the elderly, as an emerging political group, to ethnic nationalist movements to show how elites attempt to gain political power based on ascriptive characteristics such as race, gender, and age.

311   GELB, BETSY D. 1977. "Gray Power: Next Challenge to Business?" *Business Horizons*, April: 38–45.

Reviews the arguments on both sides concerning the potential power of senior citizens in the future. Data from 403 Houston, Texas, members of senior groups show that seniors are generally not likely to engage in disruptive activism that would affect business.

312   GURIN, PATRICIA; MILLER, ARTHUR H.; and GURIN, GERALD. 1980. "Stratum Identification and Consciousness." *Social Psychology Quarterly*, 43(1):30–47.

Analyzes national opinion data on the class, race, sex, and age consciousness of persons. Age identification was found to be stronger than sex identification and equal in strength to class identification. The elderly were as discontented with their social power as blacks were, and felt that their power had increased less than blacks perceived black power to have grown. Only one-third of the aged felt their group could increase its power.

313   HAMILTON, SANDY. 1979. "Florida's 'Silver-Haired Legislature.'" *Aging*,
      (297–298):22–25.
      Describes Florida's Silver-Haired Legislature, a program designed
      to help seniors understand the legislative process. The mock legislature
      nominates candidates, and identifies and votes on bills aimed at alleviat-
      ing the problems of the elderly. This session identified a number of spe-
      cific issues.

314   HAROOTYAN, ROBERT A. 1981. "Interest Groups and the Development of
      Federal Legislation Affecting Older Americans." In *The Aging in Politics*,
      edited by Robert B. Hudson, 74–85. Springfield, IL: Charles C Thomas.
      Argues that the effectiveness of the elderly as an interest group is
      fragmented because programs for the elderly are based on chronologi-
      cal age rather than functional ability. This heterogeneity works to de-
      crease group consciousness. The author claims that the elderly were
      most important for their symbolic legitimation role in Medicare, senior
      housing, and nutrition programs.

315   HESS, BETH B. 1978. "The Politics of Aging." *Society*, 15(5):22–23.
      Brief review of recent literature on the potential for political mobi-
      lization of the elderly. Hess considers the effect of government polity on
      the elderly.

316   HOLTZMAN, ABRAHAM. 1954. "Analysis of Old Age Politics in the United
      States." *Journal of Gerontology*, 9: 56–66.
      Discusses why the elderly have taken independent political ac-
      tion in the United States but not in European countries. The author
      attributes the problems of the aged to industrialization and eco-
      nomic inequality, compounded in the United States by a youth cul-
      ture. Strong unions in Europe incorporated the elderly and their con-
      cerns. The Depression combined with the structure of the American
      political system to encourage the development of special interest
      groups by the elderly. The author predicts that labor unions and po-
      litical parties will incorporate pension and other concerns of the el-
      derly so that there will be only limited independent political action
      by the elderly in the future.

317   HOWARD, EDWARD F. 1982. "Anatomy of a Victory for Older Americans."
      Perspective on Aging, 11(5):8–10.
      Analyzes the activities by aging advocates in achieving the congres-
      sional action that successfully overrode a presidential veto. President
      Reagan had vetoed a bill to continue funding for the Senior Community
      Services Employment Program under Title V of the Older Americans
      Act. Successful lobbying for the override constituted the biggest legisla-
      tive victory for elder advocates since a public outcry in 1981 scuttled the
      proposed cuts in Social Security benefits.

318 HUBBARD, LINDA. 1982. "Confrontation on the Future of America's Elderly." *Modern Maturity*, 25(1):72–73.

Highlights some of the discussion and politics involved in the 1981 White House Conference on Aging. The use of general revenue funds for Social Security was a key issue of discussion. In spite of turmoil, important resolutions dealing with older women, Medicaid and Medicare coverage and expansion, and development of home health care services were passed.

319 HUDSON, ROBERT B. 1978. "The 'Graying' of the Federal Budget and Its Consequences for Old-Age Policy." *Gerontologist*, 18(5):428–440.

Proposes that increasing financial demands of an aging population and competition for resources by a variety of social welfare groups will have an impact on old-age policy. There will be greater resistance to new appropriations and greater accountability will be demanded of agencies serving the elderly. Aging interest groups will face great challenges to exert political pressure and build a stronger constituency.

320 ———. 1980. "Old Age Politics in a Period of Change." In *Aging and Society: Current Research and Policy Perspectives*, edited by E. Borgatta and N. McClusky, 147–189. Beverly Hills: Sage Publications.

Reviews research on older persons' voting behavior, political cohesion, and variations produced by investigations confined to age-salient issues. Hudson summarizes findings on interest groups and the adequacy of the rising government effort on behalf of the aged. He analyzes factors that have helped the elderly attain their current standing.

321 HUDSON, ROBERT B., and GONYEA, JUDITH G. 1990. "Political Mobilization and Older Women." *Generations*, 14(3):67–71.

Asserts that neither the women's movement nor the old-age movement have appropriately addressed the concerns of older women. Cohort socialization and experience, socioeconomic status, race, and ethnicity are factors impeding political cohesion among women. The author notes that mass-based organizations for the aging have not separated out the unique need or interests of older women. Changing cohort characteristics, shifts in the political environment in which age-related policies are developed, and the manner in which older women identify and organize themselves will have a significant impact on their future political standing.

322 JACOBS, BRUCE. 1990. "Aging and Politics." In *Handbook of Aging and the Social Sciences* (3rd ed.), edited by Robert H. Binstock and Linda K. George, 349–366. San Diego: Academic Press.

Literature review covering the political attitudes and behavior of the aged, the politics of old-age programs as a function of political and economic conditions and interest groups, the place of old-age programs in American politics, and the types of debates that occur over old-age programs.

323 JOHNSON, HAROLD R.; MADDOX, GEORGE L.; and KAPLAN, JEROME. 1982. "Three Perspectives on the 1981 White House Conference on Aging." *Gerontologist*, 22(2):125–128.

Each author presents a short personal account of the conference by focusing on the issues of education, research, and services, respectively. A strong education platform was adopted over White House resistance as a result of the activation of a coalition of organizations in aging. All observed the democratic nature of the conference, although one noted that it was poorly organized in comparison to the 1971 conference.

324 KASSCHAU, PATRICIA L. 1978. *Aging and Social Planning: Leadership Planning.* New York: Praeger. 419 pp.

Analyzes interviews with 316 key public and private decision makers in Los Angeles to determine how their perspectives on aging and social policy are influenced. The author found the decision makers misinformed on the elderly and on aging policy. Their planning orientation was strongly influenced by their position in the policy process. The advocacy groups perceived the aged as sharing sufficient objective interests to provide the basis for organizing the elderly as an interest group. Business persons and income maintenance administrators were least likely to believe that the elderly were currently aware of those common interests. Respondents saw economic issues as the most central for the aged, but generally did not see the advocacy organizations of the aged as effective as labor, education, veterans, or minority organizations.

325 KENT, DONALD P. 1962. "Progress for Older People—How Far in the Coming Decade?" *Gerontologist*, 2:196–200.

Predicts that future issues for the elderly will include income, defining a valued role for the elderly, increasing the emphasis on rehabilitation versus curative medicine, developing senior housing, lifelong education, and improved planning and coordination of services.

326 KERIN, PAMELA B. 1986. "The Comparative Strength of Aging-Based Groups in Four States." Ph.D. dissertation, Emory University. 184 pp.

Examines the effectiveness of aging based interest groups in influencing policy on health care cost containment, mandatory retirement, and long-term care. The author finds groups are most powerful with amateur legislatures, active aging policy subsystems, and interpersonal lobbying.

327 KLEMMACK, DAVID L., and ROFF, LUCINDA L. 1980. "Public Support for Age as an Eligibility Criterion for Programs for Older Persons." *Gerontologist*, 20(2):148–153.

Evaluates the public opinion of a convenience sample of 332 adults in Alabama to determine the legitimacy of the use of age as a criterion for receipt of public benefits. Respondents did not support age as a sole criterion in general, but did support the use of age for specific senior services. The authors suggest that support is for a group that has a positive image but is viewed as having problems caused by forces beyond their control.

328 KLEYMAN, PAUL. 1991. "Aging Groups Criticize Thomas but Split on Opposing Him." *Aging Today*, 12(4):1–2.

Summarizes the positions of the National Council of Senior Citizens, National Caucus/Center of Black Aging, the American Association of Retired Persons (AARP), and the Leadership Council of Aging Organization on the nomination of Clarence Thomas to the U.S. Supreme Court. A few organizations opposed him because of his lack of vigorous enforcement of the Age Discrimination in Employment Act while he chaired the U.S. Equal Employment Opportunity Commission. Most took no position.

329 LAMMERS, WILLIAM W., and NYOMARKAY, JOSEPH I. 1980. "The Disappearing Senior Leaders." *Research on Aging*, 2(3):329–349.

Analyzes data on age patterns of cabinet members in Canada, France, Germany, the United Kingdom, and the United States. Findings show a decline in proportion of cabinet members over 65 in the post-industrial period for all countries. This decline is most pronounced in the 1970s, resulting in a greater concentration of middle-aged cabinet members. This pattern is due to bureaucratic emphasis on uniform career patterns in post-industrial societies and results in increasing underrepresentation for the elderly.

330 LEWIS, MYRNA I., and BUTLER, ROBERT N. 1972. "Why Is Women's Lib Ignoring Old Women?" *Aging and Human Development*, 3:223–231.

Argues that ageism has marginalized older women even in the women's movement. The authors review the stigmatized stereotypes of older women and their financial, employment, family, and health status. They argue that older women could be potent political allies.

331 LIGHT, LARRY. 1981. "The Organized Elderly: A Powerful Lobby." *Congressional Quarterly Weekly Report*, 39(48):2345.

Very brief description of the lobbying power and activities of the elderly. Light lists some major organizations in the aging lobby and briefly discusses increasing governmental paternalism toward the elderly as a result of lobbying activities.

332 LIGHT, PAUL C. 1985. *Artful Work: The Politics of Social Security Reform*. New York: Random House. 255 pp.

Analyzes the congressional politics leading to the 1983 Social Security Amendments. Basing his conclusions on interviews and observation, Light describes the difficulty in achieving congressional consensus on bills and the inherent stalemates between branches of government. Raising taxes and cutting benefits was not politically popular, even though it was to prevent Social Security from going bankrupt. He notes the limited public knowledge about the operation of the system, even though most adults pay into or receive Social Security. The National Council of Senior Citizens (NCSC) is credited with more effective lobbying than the American Association of Retired Persons (AARP) because the NCSC is more grass roots in nature, presented clear and firm positions, and had an overtly political orientation. Light discusses why advocacy coalitions are most effective at blocking versus advancing legislation and concludes that the Democratic Speaker of the House and the Republican president compromised behind the scenes on the final bill out of mutual fear versus public interest.

333 LOCKETT, BETTY A. 1983. *Aging, Politics, and Research: Setting the Federal Agendas for Research on Aging.* New York: Springer. 208 pp.

Employs the agenda-setting model to examine the founding of the National Institute on Aging (NIA) using original historical data. The author argues that a fragile coalition of a small group of researchers and leaders of age-based interest groups prevailed after 40 years of trying to foster federal support for research on aging. The large memberships of the American Association of Retired Persons and the National Council of Senior Citizens provided NIA advocates with grass-roots legitimacy during the push in Congress to establish the NIA during the early 1970s. Friction between NIA advocates who wanted only biomedical research and those who wanted social issues complicated the alliance. President Nixon vetoed a bill to establish the NIA in 1972 just before his landslide reelection, but signed a similar bill in 1974 while fending off calls for his impeachment. It took two years of further advocacy to obtain full implementation.

334 MARTIN, CAROL A. 1978. "Lavender Rose or Gray Panther?" *Aging,* (285–286):28–30.

Focuses on the largely female future of the elderly population. Martin evaluates the socialization processes experienced by today's older women and contrasts it with the independence and less traditional experience of today's younger women. She recommends greater political activism to meet the needs of older women.

335 MATTHEWS, SARAH H. 1982. "Participation of the Elderly in a Transportation System." *Gerontologist,* 22(1):26–31.

A case study of a transportation service that documents the erosion of an elderly constituent's effective participation. Organized as a small self-funded cooperative service, it grew in size and became a bureaucratic organization dependent on state funds to serve the needy. This shift in funding eroded elderly people's participation in the program and stigmatized the service.

336 MAYO, SELZ C. 1951. "Social Participation among the Older Population in Rural Areas of Wake County, North Carolina." *Social Forces,* 30(1).53–59.

Analyzes the organizational involvement of 144 rural persons age

60 and over in two North Carolina areas. The author found that participation in formal organizations drops off at age 60, with most activity of the aged being church related.

337 MCMURRY, DONALD L. 1922. "The Political Significance of the Pension Question, 1885–1897." *Mississippi Valley Historical Review*, 9(1):19–36.

Discusses the political power of Civil War veterans in influencing political parties to advocate war pensions. The Grand Army of the Republic was a key organization in lobbying and mobilizing the veteran's vote, influencing several close elections. In turn, Republicans exerted much influence over voters by their control of the pension bureaus. Claims agents were also politically active in promoting veteran pensions as a way to increase their business. Pensions were popular with northern manufacturers because they reduced the federal budget surplus created by protectionist tariffs.

338 MINKLER, MEREDITH, and ESTES, CARROLL L. (Eds.). 1984. *Readings in the Political Economy of Aging*. Farmingdale, NY: Baywood. 278 pp.

Depicts society's aging problem as a structural one, rooted in society's differential treatment of the aged as a group. The authors conclude that failure to address root causes of aging related problems can be linked to separatist thinking about the elderly. Contributing authors deal with such issues as health, older women, retirement, economic security in old age, and future social policy.

339 MOBLEY, G. MELTON. 1984. "Electronic Evangelists and Political Change in America: A Susceptible Population as a Bellwether." *Journal of Religion and Aging*, 1(1):31–47.

Analyzes the political impact of televangelists on their elderly audiences. Mobley describes overt attempts by Jerry Falwell, founder of the Moral Majority, and Pat Robertson of the 700 Club to affect the American political system directly. Data from seven Savannah, Georgia, Southern Baptist and United Methodist churches were utilized. Mobley concludes that televangelists have great financial success but little potential for influencing presidential politics among the elderly. The cultural tradition of the separation of religion and politics is viewed as an important factor.

340 MORGAN, EDWARD E., and SMITH, JEAN. 1988. "Tax Levies as a Source of Local Support for Funding Programs and Services for the Aging." *Journal of Applied Gerontology*, 7(2):242–247.

Finds that funding for senior centers under the Older Americans Act is not keeping pace with the increasing numbers of elderly using the facilities. A case study of the Wood County (Ohio) Committee on Aging is presented to describe local funding activities through a tax levy. The grass-roots activities by senior volunteers are described. The planning and organizing of the successful campaign is detailed.

341 NEUGARTEN, BERNICE L. 1974. "Age Groups in American Society and the Rise of the Young-Old." *Annals of the American Academy of Political and Social Sciences*, 415(September):187–198.

Argues that the changing demography of industrial societies is changing intergenerational relations. Because those age 55 to 75 are generally healthy, well educated, and possessed of free time, they are possible agents of social change such that society might become age irrelevant.

342 NEUGARTEN, BERNICE L.; MOORE, JOAN W.; and LOWE, JOHN C. 1968. "Age Norms, Age Constraints, and Adult Socialization." In *Middle Age and Aging*, edited by Bernice L. Neugarten, 22–28. Chicago: University of Chicago Press.

Analyzes opinions of 400 respondents to examine the constraints imposed by societal age norms and the adult socialization to those norms. The authors find most people report more restrictive age norms being held by other people than themselves. Adult socialization theory is supported.

343 O'GORMAN, HUBERT J. 1980. "False Consciousness of Kind." *Research on Aging*, 2(1):105–128.

Analyzes national survey data to explore patterns of perceived similarities and dissimilarities among the aged. The elderly overestimate the severity of problems experienced by most elderly persons; the more severe a problem is personally for an individual, the greater the tendency to falsely attribute it to the majority of other aged; and many elderly without serious problems believe themselves different from the rest of the aged. Findings are consistent regardless of social status. The author concludes that this false consciousness of kind is not peculiar to the elderly but is a form of pluralistic ignorance, or people's misconceptions about similarity and dissimilarity between themselves and others.

344 ORY, MARCIA G., and BOND, KATHLEEN (Eds.). 1989. *Aging and Health Care: Social Science and Policy Perspectives*. New York: Routledge. 265 pp.

Outlines the formal and informal health care for the elderly as a shifting spectrum of services with no clear boundaries between acute versus long-term care and community versus institutional care. The authors analyze patient movements between types and settings of care and assess factors associated with different utilization patterns. They also discuss technical policy issues.

345 PAMPEL, FRED C., and WILLIAMSON, JOHN B. 1989. *Age, Class, Politics and the Welfare State*. New York: Cambridge University Press. 199 pp.

Analyzes the impact of class factors and age structure on public spending on pensions and other welfare state programs. The authors use cross-national aggregate data with special attention given to the aged and their impact on spending policy. They find that age structure is more important than political power.

346 PEDERSON, JOHANNES T. 1976. "Age and Change in Public Opinion: The Case of California 1960–1970." *Public Opinion Quarterly*, 40(2):143–153.

Analyzes the relationship between age and changes in public opinion for various political questions based on survey data. Pedersen argues that the political conservatism usually attributed to the elderly is an exception rather than the rule. The elderly exhibit consistently stable attitudes only in the areas of party choice and political ideology. They remain flexible in candidate selection and opinion on political issues.

347 PETERS, GEORGE R. 1971. "Self-Conceptions of the Aged, Age Identification, and Aging." *Gerontologist*, 11(2):69–73.

Reviews and summarizes research on self-conception and age identification. Correlates of age identification, the consequences of age identification, age stereotyping, and the relationship between chronological age and age identification are presented as areas of research need. The volume has an extensive bibliography.

348 PHILLIPSON, CHRIS. 1982. *Capitalism and the Construction of Old Age*. London: Macmillan. 188 pp.

Argues that capitalism as a productive force and social system is incapable of meeting the needs of the elderly. Phillipson draws primarily on British history but also refers to U.S. data. The costs of social change have historically been forced on specific groups, with the aged bearing the brunt of recent change. While political activity around aging issues will increase, the aged are most likely to organize along broad class or single-issue lines.

349 POLLAK, OTTO. 1943. "Conservatism in Later Maturity and Old Age." *American Sociological Review*, 8(2):175–179.

Early discussion, which discounts the notion that the elderly are more conservative than the young; therefore, an intergenerational conflict exists. Pollack compares attitudes of people above and below age 40 based on questionnaire responses and performs statistical analyses to determine whether a higher percentage of elderly are conservative, and whether a conservative majority exists in either group. The findings indicate that a higher number of conservative people are in the older age group, in most cases a conservative majority exists in the older group, and most important, where a majority of the younger group favor progressivism, a majority of the older group do as well.

350 PRATT, HENRY J. 1978. "Symbolic Politics and White House Conferences on Aging." *Society* (July-August):67–72.

Reviews the White House Conferences on Aging from 1950 through 1971 to show how they have moved from primarily symbolic meetings to forums producing concrete results. This shift has been fostered by the development of advocacy groups and government bureaucracies. Delegates to the 1950 and 1960 meetings attended as unaffiliated individuals, allowing the deliberations to be managed by the White House to avoid strong policy resolutions. Leaders of senior organizations fought for a role in the planning and course of the 1971 Conference, which ended with more concrete resolutions.

351 PYNOOS, JON. 1984. "Setting the Elderly Housing Agenda." *Policy Studies Journal*, 13(1):173–184.

Proposes a redefinition of the nature of housing problems faced by the elderly. The author considers the political and economic situation affecting housing policy decisions and the importance of housing to the elderly. He identifies lobby groups and major actors that form an iron triangle and discusses the past, present, and future agenda of housing for the elderly.

352 RAGAN, PAULINE K., and DAVIS, WILLIAM J. 1978. "The Diversity of Older Voters." *Society*, 15(5):50–53.

Critiques attributions of homogeneity in characteristics usually attributed to the elderly. Income distribution among the aged reveals substantial differences. Most older persons do not have severe health problems. Race and nationality distinguish some groups of elderly. The elderly exhibit diverse political styles as evidenced by numerous advocacy groups. The authors conclude that recognizing the heterogeneity of the elderly is essential to understanding their political concerns.

353 RAGAN, PAULINE K., and DOWD, JAMES J. 1974. "The Emerging Political Consciousness of the Aged: A Generational Interpretation." *Journal of Social Issues*, 30(3):137–158.

Examines whether age-group political consciousness among the elderly will supersede established voting patterns based on social class, party affiliation, ethnicity, religion, and area of residence. The authors explore the connection between participation in social movements and group consciousness by analyzing different theories of social movements. They question the dominance of maturational, period effect, and cohort analyses of the politicizing of old age and suggest a model for politics of old age based on participation in social movements. This model would make it possible to identify the generational aspects of the potential political consciousness among the elderly.

354 RILEY, MATILDA WHITE. 1971. "Social Gerontology and the Age Stratification of Society." *Gerontologist*, 11(Spring):79–87.

Presents an overview of Riley's theory of age as an element of stratification in society that is interdependent with other types of stratification. The article discusses how the age structure of society affects attitudes and behaviors, the relationships between and within different age groups, the dynamics of cohort flow, and the relationship between social change and age.

355 ———. 1979. "Aging, Social Change and Social Policy." In *Aging from Birth to Death: Interdisciplinary Perspectives*, edited by Matilda White Riley, 109–121. Washington, DC: American Association for the Advancement of Science.

The heterogeneity of the varying cohorts along with the "plasticity" of the aging process are seen as forces for social change. Policy implications are discussed.

356 ———. 1985. "Age Strata in Social Systems." In *Handbook of Aging and the Social Sciences* (2nd ed.), edited by Robert H. Binstock and Ethel Shanas, 369–411. New York: Van Nostrand.

Argues that age is a central dimension of stratification in society. Aging and social change are interdependent, although poorly synchronized. Social roles are differentiated and allocated by age depending on the historical period. Changes in the stratification system can result from the conflict between the demands of individuals who are growing older and the demands of the changing society.

357 RODERICK, SUE S. 1984. "The White House Conferences on Aging: Their Implications for Social Change." D.P.A. dissertation, University of Southern California.

Examines the functioning of the White House Conferences on Aging (WHCoA) between 1950 and 1981 using documents, interviews, and participant observation. Roderick concludes that the gray lobby, including the elderly themselves, control the senior movement's political influence, which has increased greatly. The WHCoAs have contributed to that increase.

358 ROSE, ARNOLD M. 1965. "Group Consciousness among the Aging." In *Older People and Their Social World*, edited by Arnold M. Rose and Warren A. Peterson, 19–36. Philadelphia: F.A. Davis.

Classic article that analyzes the degree to which older people are developing a group identity and mobilization in response to the role losses of aging. Rose analyzes data from 200 seniors, half of whom were selected from aging related local voluntary organizations. Findings of high and continued social involvement contradict disengagement theory. The age-group conscious are more likely to associate primarily with other aged than the nonconscious. Rose concludes that no single type of personality or social type becomes age-group conscious.

359 ———. 1965. "The Subculture of the Aging: A Framework for Research in Social Gerontology." In *Older People and Their Social World*, edited by Arnold M. Rose and Warren A. Peterson, 3–16. Philadelphia: F.A. Davis.

Widely cited article that develops a theory of a subculture of the aged. Subcultures arise when a group is drawn together through positive affinity or social exclusion. Both forces affect the aged. Socially integrating forces include family, the mass media, employment, and resistance to accepting an aged identity. The author suggests that group consciousness is increasing and can act as a political force.

360 ———. 1966. "Class Differences among the Elderly: A Research Report." *Sociology and Social Research*, 50(3):356–360.

Surveyed 210 noninstitutionalized middle- and lower-class elderly to identify their attitudes toward aging and the problems of aging. Middle-class elderly were more likely to have fewer problems associated with increased free time and interpersonal relationships, think of religion as a comfort, participate more in voluntary organizations, and vote more often than lower-class elderly.

361 ROSENBAUM, WALTER A., and BUTTON, JAMES W. 1989. "Is There a Gray Peril? Retirement Policies in Florida." *Gerontologist*, 29(3):300–306.

Analyzes the political impact of retirees migrating to Florida. Based on survey data, three hypotheses are considered. The growing elderly population will (1) increase political activism, (2) stimulate political mobilization of the elderly, or (3) motivate the elderly to resist political expenditures which do not benefit them. Results show that even where political activity is high, organization is lacking. Advocacy organizations vary in effectiveness and intensity of efforts. There is little direct evidence that the elderly have had significant political impact.

362 ROSOW, IRVING. 1962. "Old Age: One Moral Dilemma of an Affluent Society." *Gerontologist*, 2(4):182–191.

Views old age as a social problem that should be seen as part of the larger social order. Rosow asserts that the elderly are stripped of roles and statuses that are frequently found in less-advanced societies. He suggests establishment of programs to provide for material welfare and security.

363 ———. 1970. "Old People: Their Friends and Neighbors." In *Aging in Contemporary Society*, edited by Ethel Shanas, 57–67. Beverly Hills: Sage Publications.

Identifies the positive and negative consequences of age segregation that is the result of public programs or social trends. Rosow asserts that elders are more comfortable among peers as friendships and interaction with neighbors increase dramatically when elders reside among other elders.

364 SHAPIRO, ROBERT Y., and SMITH, TOM W. 1985. "The Polls: Social Security." *Public Opinion Quarterly*, 49(4):561–572.

Summarizes the results of several public opinion polls about Social Security for the period 1935–1985. Findings show that many social welfare programs are now perceived as rights of citizenship, support for Social Security is consistent, public opinion is stable, and existing or higher levels of government spending for Social Security are consistently approved by the public.

365 SHEPPARD, HAROLD L. 1962. "Implications of an Aging Population for Political Sociology." In *Politics of Age*, edited by Wilma Donahue and Clark Tibbitts, 48–59. Ann Arbor: University of Michigan Press.

Argues that the demographics of aging will increase the salience of aging in politics. Sheppard presents polling data from 1960 showing the relationship between the percentage of elderly in a state and the percentage in the state identifying "old age problems" as an important issue in the 1960 presidential election. The author notes the importance of family and local community in advocating a politics of aging.

366 SKIDMORE, MAX J. 1970. *Medicare and the American Rhetoric of Reconciliation*. University, AL: University of Alabama Press. 198 pp.

Focuses on the popular ideology of the nation and the rhetoric surrounding the debates over Social Security and Medicare. The analysis of the passage of Medicare includes an extensive discussion of the American Medical Association's efforts to delegitimize the program. The programs required that conflicting rhetoric be reconciled, such as that of individual achievement versus universal benefits.

367 SMITH, JOHN PATRICK, and MARTINSON, OSCAR B. 1984. "Socio-Political Bases of Senior Citizen Mobilization: Salient Issues beyond Health Policy." *Research on Aging*, 6(2):213–224.

Examines the potential for issues to act as a catalyst to mobilize the elderly, in the light of the financial problems of health care issues and the shift in Administration on Aging (AoA) discretionary power from federal to state levels. Data from a mock North Dakota Silver-Haired Legislative election were examined to identify salient issues. Issues identified were services within the home, concern for legal issues, health services and funding, and community services and facilities. The authors summarize surveys among North Dakota senior citizens to determine agreement or disagreement with salience of these issues. They conclude that political mobilization of the elderly is occurring because of government efforts to avoid the financial burden of social programs for the elderly.

368 SOMERS, ANNE R. 1985. "Toward a Female Gerontocracy? Current Social Trends." In *The Physical and Mental Health of Aged Women*, edited by Marie R. Haug, Amasa B. Ford, and Marian Sheafor, 16–26. New York: Springer.

Three major demographic trends are described: the aging of the population, the growing proportion of women in the population, and the shrinking family size. The potential societal consequences of these changes are discussed. These include rising total health care costs, increasing reliance on Social Security, and a different political climate. Somers concludes that a number of changes are called for: a redefinition of "old age"; strengthening of Social Security, Medicare, and state and local governments; and development of shared housing.

369   SPENGLER, JOSEPH J. 1969. "The Aged and Public Policy." In *Behavior and Adaptation in Late Life*, edited by Ewald W. Busse and Eric Pfeiffer, 367–383. London: Little, Brown.

Examines ideological and historical forces behind increasing public provision for the aged since 1930. The combined effects of the Depression, increasing elderly population coupled with decreasing employment opportunities, growth in disposable income, and larger awareness of inflation created a trend toward an expansion of assistance for the elderly. This was accompanied by expanding capacity of governments to provide assistance and a move toward collectivism and a growth in public spending. Spengler concludes that the future of the elderly will be bleak as the need for all types of public assistance comes in conflict with a loss of national productivity and continuing inflation.

370   STONE, ROBYN I., and KEMPER, PETER. 1990. "Spouses and Children of Disabled Elders: How Large a Constituency for Long-Term Care Reform?" *Milbank Quarterly*, 67(3–4):485–504.

Reviews data on the number of primary and secondary caregivers who also have paid employment to show that they comprise a small constituency and will not overwhelm employee leave programs. For elderly who help with activities of daily living, a relatively small number of children and spouses both provide assistance and are in the labor force. Including those not employed, 7 percent of U.S. adults are spouses or children of disabled elders.

371   STREIB, GORDON F. 1968. "Are the Aged a Minority Group?" In *Middle Age and Aging*, edited by Bernice L. Neugarten, 35–46. Chicago: University of Chicago Press.

Argues that the elderly do not meet any of the criteria for being considered a minority group. The economic and health problems of the elderly are a function of biologically determined status rather than of society.

372   ———. 1976. "Social Stratification and Aging." In *Handbook of Aging and the Social Sciences*, edited by Robert H. Binstock and Ethel Shanas, 160–185. New York: Van Nostrand.

Examines the role of age in the stratification system of society. Streib argues that the aged are not group conscious and the diversity of the aged leads to different stratification places for them. He reviews the socioeconomic status of black and Spanish-speaking aged.

373   ———. 1985. "Social Stratification and Aging." In *Handbook of Aging and the Social Sciences* (2nd ed.), edited by Robert H. Binstock and Ethel Shanas, 339–368. New York: Van Nostrand.

Reviews the various bases for stratification between and among age groups, examining the consequences for the class position, status, and power of the elderly. The author considers how occupation, income, property, education, and the dual economy affect the class position of the aged. Status reflects membership groups, style of life, and subjective status. Power comes from holding political offices and voting. The author argues that the aged do not function as a minority group and provides comparative material from England and the Soviet Union.

374 STREIB, GORDON F.; FOLTS, W. EDWARD; and LA GRECA, ANTHONY J. 1985. "Autonomy, Power, and Decision-Making in Thirty-Six Retirement Communities." *Gerontologist*, 25(4):403–409.

Examines community autonomy in 36 retirement communities of varied sizes in four states. The authors find that most residents are satisfied letting the community operate at the status quo, as long as they can continue to enjoy the life-style, services, and amenities at what they consider a reasonable price. Residents were able to mobilize quickly when the community or a large number of its residents were threatened. Findings contradict the authors' expectation that healthy retired persons would be active in the politics of their retirement communities.

375 SUNDERLAND, GEORGE. 1978. "National Organizations Launch Crime Prevention Programs." *Aging*, 281-282:32–34.

Outlines training seminars developed in 1973 by the American Association of Retired Persons under a grant from the Law Enforcement Assistance Administration to assist law enforcement agencies and older persons understand the problems of crimes against the elderly. Joint efforts of the police and elderly residents in Arizona, Florida, and California are discussed.

376 TRELA, JAMES E. 1976. "Status Inconsistency and Political Action in Old Age." In *Time, Roles, and Self in Old Age*, edited by Jaber F. Gubrium, 126–147. New York: Human Sciences Press.

Examines the consequences of status inconsistency on the level of collective action by the aged. Trela shows how earlier social movements were made up of aged persons whose status had rapidly declined. He argues that in the future, status will decline with age and voluntary associations of the aged will increase age consciousness, enhancing the potential for political activism.

377 TROPMAN, JOHN E. 1987. *Public Policy Opinion and the Elderly, 1952–1978*. New York: Greenwood Press. 247 pp.

Analysis of public opinion polls shows that the views of the elderly are not substantially different from those of other age groups. Largest differences are in the areas of trust in government, rights of accused criminals, women's rights, and ideal family size. Support for health programs that directly benefit the aged is no higher among the elderly than among other age groups, contrary to rational self-interest theory.

378 U.S. SENATE, SPECIAL COMMITTEE ON AGING. 1973. *Post–White House Conference on Aging Reports, 1973*. Washington, DC: U.S. Government Printing Office. 859 pp.

Summary of conference recommendations and administration response. Topics include assuring an adequate income, appropriate living arrangements, independence and dignity, institutional responsiveness and a new attitude toward aging. The reports include full study panel recommendations and administration responses. Advocacy suggestions and legislation needed are discussed.

379 VELEZ-I., CARLOS G.; VERDUGO, RICHARD; and NUÑEZ, FRANCISCO. 1980. "Politics and Mental Health among Elderly Mexicanos." In *Chicano Aging and Mental Health*, edited by Manuel Miranda and René A. Ruiz, 118–155. Rockville, MD: National Institute of Mental Health.

Reviews the literature that shows participation and attitudes in politics remaining constant through the life cycle. Research shows Mexican-American elderly political participation is low while structural and ethnic barriers to their participation are high. Historic discrimination and a consequent emphasis on family and community led to low levels of political participation earlier in life.

380 VINYARD, DALE. 1978. "The Rediscovery of the Elderly." *Society*, 15(5):24–29.

Traces the social and public involvement in problems of the elderly. The elderly played a limited role in local poor laws in the 1920s and the development of state pension laws in the 1930s. The Townsend movement and subsequent passage of Social Security saw age-based groups playing a peripheral role in policy formation. Even in the 1960s with the creation of the National Council of Senior Citizens, the elderly played a supporting rather than a leading role in political action. Today's mass-membership groups are having an impact, such as with Medicare and the Older Americans Act. The elderly today are represented by many stable permanent organizations and will demand a greater role in the future.

381 WARD, RUSSELL A. 1977. "Aging Group Consciousness: Implications in an Older Sample." *Sociology and Social Research*, 61(4):496–519.

Analyzes data from 323 older persons from Madison, Wisconsin, to determine whether they belonged to a subculture of aging. Few elders were age-group conscious. Belonging to age-segregated organizations fostered group consciousness. Those with group consciousness of aging have higher self-esteem than those who see themselves as elderly. This was a result of reference-group comparisons rather than normative changes from a subculture. Ward sees limited potential for age-related political action.

382 WEAVER, JERRY L. 1976. "The Elderly as a Political Community: The Case of National Health Policy." *Western Political Quarterly*, 29(4):610–619.

Proposes that the isolation and separation that characterize many elderly citizens are the beginnings of a political community. Political issues that are important to the elderly will unite seniors as a political group. Using health care as an example, national survey data concerning attitudes toward low-cost health care are analyzed. National opinion data from 1968–1972 show that the elderly are homogeneous and progressive in most preferences and attitudes, while other age groups vary according to socioeconomic status.

383 WILLIAMSON, JOHN B.; EVANS, LINDA; and MUNLEY, ANNE. 1980. "Status, Power, and Politics." In *Aging and Society*, edited by J.B. Williamson, L. Evans, and A. Munley, 120–146. New York: Holt, Rinehart.

An analysis of the aged in American society using Wirth's conception of a minority group. The authors compare stereotypes used in describing the aged as opposed to those used to describe women and blacks. They discuss sources of political influence of the elderly such as resource control.

384 WILLIAMSON, JOHN B.; EVANS, LINDA, and POWELL, LAWRENCE A. 1982. "Senior Power." In *The Politics of Aging: Power and Policy*, 75–101. Springfield, IL: Charles C Thomas.

Traces the history of the senior movement using Mauss's model of social movements combined with pluralist theory. The incipiency stage is 1920–1950 when the aged developed multiple ad hoc organizations to push for social insurance. A coalescence phase (1950–1965) founded more permanent organizations and worked for programs such as Medicare. The post–1965 period has been an institutionalization phase as federal programs have become established and movement priorities bureaucratized. In each phase coalitions with nonaging groups have been key ingredients for success. The authors argue that the fragmentation and demise phases are unlikely to occur in the near future. (See also entry 30.)

385 WILLIAMSON, JOHN B.; EVANS, LINDA; POWELL, LAWRENCE A.; and HESSE-BIBER, SHARLENE. 1981. "The Political Influence of Older Americans." *Journal of Sociology and Social Welfare*, 8:771–795.

Explores the future prospects for political influence by the elderly in the United States. The authors evaluate arguments that the next 50 years will see an increase in the political influence of the elderly, and arguments that the elderly are not a significant force today nor will be. They claim that there will be a sharp increase in the political resources of the elderly, which may or may not translate into a substantial political influence.

386 YELAJA, SHANKAR A. 1989. "Gray Power: Agenda for Future Research." *Canadian Journal on Aging*, 8(2):118–127.

Provides a historical review of the concept of gray power. The term became popular in the 1970s with the advent of advocacy organizations and political lobbying on behalf of the elderly. The elderly are taking direct action more often and relying less on advocacy groups. Current research is contradictory: despite growth in advocacy organizations, the elderly remain marginal as a politically influential group.

387 YOUMANS, E. GRANT. 1973. "Age Stratification and Value Orientations."
     International Journal of Aging and Human Development, 4(1):53–65.
          Analyzes the value orientations of samples of men and women aged
     20–29 and 60 and over in a rural county and urban center in the South-
     ern Appalachian region. Values differed between generations in both
     the rural and urban areas on issues including authoritarianism, depen-
     dency, achievement, religiosity, and anomia. A likely cause of the differ-
     ences is the social change that has occurred between the two cohorts.
     The findings suggest that the values of younger persons will lead them
     to develop a sense of group identity when they become elderly.

3

The Issues

Public Policies and Government, General

388 • 1989. *Annual Report to the President 1988*. Washington, DC: U.S. Federal Council on the Aging.

  Describes the functions and organization of the U.S. Federal Council on the Aging. Activities of the Council during 1988 include developing a plan for the 1991 White House Conference on Aging, reviewing the practice of targeting federal funds to designated groups, developing guidelines for guardianship laws, producing a demographic report, and calling on the insurance industry to encourage individuals to provide for long-term health care through savings plans. The report outlines proposed activities of the council and summarizes policy recommendations.

389 ACHENBAUM, W. ANDREW. 1983. *Shades of Gray: Old Age, American Values, and Federal Policies since 1920*. Boston: Little, Brown. 216 pp.

  Utilizes a historical perspective to assert that the elderly are among the last to be affected by the long-term process of modernization. The social values underlying the formation of Social Security and those involved in the Great Society policy dilemmas are discussed. The economic issues of inflation, energy, and growth in the "Shocking, Sobering Seventies" induced doubts about policy directions. The author suggests a "double-decker social welfare program"—the first layer including income maintenance, health-care and social-service programs using objective eligibility standards, and the second layer to include aged-based standards. Achenbaum considers the early years of Reaganomics inconclusive, but they could prove a milestone in forging a coherent policy for the aging

390 AFFELDT, DAVID A. 1975. "Legislation on Aging: A View from Capitol Hill." In *Legal Problems of Older Americans*, edited by Dorothy Heyman, 29–

36. Durham, NC: Center for the Study of Aging and Human Development, Duke University.

Reviews legislation passed during 1973–74, noting that significant activity occurred in 1972. The author provides a point-by-point critique of a *Washington Post* column by David Broder that claimed the elderly are receiving too large a share of the federal budget.

391 ARMOUR, PHILIP K.; ESTES, CARROLL L.; and NOBLE, MAUREEN L. 1980. "Implementing the Older Americans Act." In *Aging in Politics, Process and Policy*, edited by Robert Hudson, 199–219. Springfield, IL: Charles C Thomas.

Identifies the issues and problems in developing and implementing national aging policy through such legislation as the Older Americans Act. The authors focus particularly on the Title III individual service model and the needs for institutional change. Community participation is required but poorly defined. Contradictory elements of the act include decentralization versus bureaucratic control, rational planning versus political process, and a mandate for targeting those in greatest economic need versus prohibiting means testing. More than incremental changes in the act are called for.

392 AUSTIN, CAROL D., and LOEB, MARTIN P. 1982. "Why Age Is Relevant in Social Policy and Practice." In *Age or Need? Public Policies for Older People,* edited by Bernice L. Neugarten, 263–288. Beverly Hills: Sage Publications.

Forecasts that chronological age will remain the determining criterion in "a continuum of allocative principles" for the present time. Occasional inclusion of need-based or other factors may produce incremental changes but age remains "familiar, easy to understand, simple to determine and politically useful for constituencies."

393 BEATTIE, WALTER M., JR. 1976. "Aging and the Social Services." In *Handbook of Aging and the Social Sciences*, edited by Robert H. Binstock and Ethel Shanas, 619–642. New York: Van Nostrand.

Reviews the historical development of numerous social services for the aged. Attributes the late development of services for the elderly to the curative, individualistic, and child development-oriented theories held by medicine and the helping professions. The author discusses contemporary models of social services that address the needs of the aged.

394 BENJAMIN, A. E.; ESTES, CARROLL L.; SWAN, JAMES H.; and NEWCOMER, ROBERT J. 1980. "Elders and Children: Patterns of Public Policy in the Fifty States." *Journal of Gerontology*, 35(6):928–934.

Analyzes data from 50 states on spending and eligibility for Supplemental Security Income, Medicaid, Aid to Families with Dependent Children, education, and juvenile justice to determine the relationship between public policy patterns for the elderly and youth. The study shows that general state policy orientations and contexts are important. States that are most generous to children show the greatest variability in programs for the aging. Least generous states are meager with both age groups. This finding suggests that aging politics is most important in more generous states.

395 BINSTOCK, ROBERT H. 1967. "What Sets the Goals of Community Planning for the Aging?" *Gerontologist*, 7(1):44–46.

Describes how seven demonstration projects in social planning for the elderly evolved their goals sporadically, with little technical knowledge, and often based on political needs. Professional staff and "national experts" had the primary input, with the elderly having almost none.

396 BROWNE, WILLIAM P. 1989. "The Aged Agenda in State Legislatures: A Comparative Perspective." *Policy Studies Journal*, 17(3):497–513.

Analyzes over 2,000 bills and resolutions affecting the aged in four states between 1956 and 1978 to determine how state legislatures respond to the needs of the elderly. Tax breaks for seniors were common issues, while nutrition, education, and age discrimination were rarely addressed. About one-third of proposed legislation in each state was unique to that state, suggesting that states have an independent role in policy-making. Bills affecting service providers and administrators had a higher passage rate than bills directly benefiting the aged in three of the four states. No dominant legislator advocates were identified in any state, indicating decentralized policy-making.

397 BROWNE, WILLIAM P., and RINGQUIST, DELBERT J. 1985. "Sponsorship and Enactment: State Lawmakers and Aging Legislation 1956–1978." *American Politics Quarterly*, 13(4):447–466.

Analyzes legislative patterns and outcomes of age-related issues for the period 1956–1978 in Florida, Iowa, Michigan, and New Jersey. Results show large numbers of legislators sponsor age-related bills, yet few could be considered specialists in aging legislation. Legislative committees play an important role in screening sponsored legislation. Gubernatorial vetoes increase when unusually high percentages of bills are reported.

398 CALIFANO, JOSEPH A., JR. 1978. "U.S. Policy for the Aging—A Commitment to Ourselves." *National Journal*, November 30:1575–1581.

Edited testimony of the then-Secretary of Health, Education and Welfare before the Senate Special Committee on Aging in July 1978. Discusses the demographic and financial trends of the aged that will affect government policy. Califano reviews the current status and policy needs regarding retirement income and health care. He calls for a rational, comprehensive, and efficient system to deliver health services, including long-term care.

399 CHUNN, JAY. 1978. "The Black Aged and Social Policy." *Aging*, 287–288: 10–14.

Summarizes the needs of older blacks and the political barriers to meeting those needs. The author sees income as the primary need.

400 CLARK, ROBERT L., and MENEFEE, JOHN A. 1981. "Federal Expenditures for the Elderly: Past and Future." *Gerontologist*, 21(2):132–137.

Seeks to identify factors that affect federal outlays for the elderly, especially public policy decisions. Using data for 1960–1978, the authors analyze price level and age structure changes. They find the growth of public spending for the elderly has been caused by the federal government's response to the perceived needs of the elderly and/or their growing political power. Projections of outlays through 2025 are offered.

401 COHEN, ELIAS S. 1962. "An Aging Population and State Government." *State Government*, 35(3):168–175.

Reviews the potential impact on state government health and income maintenance programs of the growing number of elderly. Cohen describes the functions and administrative structures of state units on aging that existed in about half of U.S. states.

402 ———. 1962. "The State Unit on Aging: A Point of View on Structure." *Gerontologist*, 2(1):14–17.

Reviews and summarizes several state initiatives made before the Older Americans Act of 1965 necessitated formation of state units. The form most frequently employed was independent governors' commissions. Cohen argues for placing state units within the regular framework of state government.

403 ———. 1970. "Research and Public Policy: Relevance for Decisionmaking." *Gerontologist*, 10(3):198–201.

Urges development of new relationships by universities and operating agencies in order to increase utilization of research findings in public policy decisions.

404 ———. 1970. "Toward a Social Policy on Aging." *Gerontologist*, 10(4), Pt.II: 13–21.

Cautions that social policy development must take into account the relationship of the value system and attitudes of the general population, and these must be counterbalanced against the characteristics of the elderly population. Cohen recommends a systematic approach to expand knowledge and to link research to appropriate social policy and action.

405 COOMBS, SUSAN R. (Ed.). 1985. *An Orientation to the Older Americans Act*. Washington, DC: National Association of State Units on Aging. 122 pp.

Thorough explanation and history of the Older Americans Act.

Coombs describes the role of organizations of the aging in the development of public policy. Legislative changes, the Discretionary Grant Program, and the role of state and area agencies on aging are presented. The book incorporates an alphabetical listing of Leadership Council on Aging members.

406 CORKER, BRUCE D. 1973. "Nutrition Program for the Elderly: Amendments to the Older American Act of 1965." *Harvard Journal on Legislation*, 10(2):198–216.

Reviews the legislation and philosophy of the 1972 amendments to the Older Americans Act establishing the nutrition program for the elderly. The author suggests that electoral year politics, senior lobbying, and targeting amendments led President Nixon to reverse his opposition to the bill.

407 COUNCIL OF STATE GOVERNMENTS. 1955. *The States and Their Older Citizens*. Chicago: Council of State Governments." 176 pp.

An early policy document that provides an overview of the problems of aging, including employment, income, living arrangements, health, use of health care institutions, and leisure time. The document provides action recommendations oriented to state governments in each area and describes existing efforts by states toward the aged.

408 CUTLER, NEAL E. 1984. "Federal and State Responsibilities and the Targeting of Resources within the Older Americans Act: The Dynamics of Multiple Agenda Setting." *Policy Studies Journal*, 13(1):185–196.

Analyzes targeting strategy in the Older Americans Act (OAA) and the agenda-setting dynamics that led to the development of targeting. Targeting is defined as a means of allocating limited funds to those subpopulations in greatest need; this requirement was mandated by 1978 Amendments to OAA, which also required states to develop a quantitative formula to identify the elderly in greatest need. Cutler suggests that targeting was implemented to give more latitude to state and local planning agencies. He concludes that targeting was developed in response to the demands of special interests.

409 ESTES, CARROLL L. 1974. "Community Planning for the Elderly: A Study of Goal Displacement." *Journal of Gerontology*, 29(6):684–691.

Reviews the work of three planning organizations for the aging to assess the implementation of their mandates. The study shows that most outcomes were more symbolic than instrumental, oriented more to legitimating the work and expert status of the organizations' members. This result is caused in part by the organizations' being relatively weak and facing a hostile environment.

410 ———. 1975. "New Federalism and Aging." In *Developments in Aging: 1974 and January–April 1975*, 150–157. A Report of the U.S. Senate

Special Committee on Aging. Washington, DC: U.S. Government Printing Office.

Reviews the arguments made in favor of general revenue sharing (GRS) and assesses the results after three years of the program. The author notes that little GRS money has gone to programs for the aged or other social services, despite the claim that local officials who administer GRS funds are more sensitive than federal officials to public concerns.

411   ———. 1979. *The Aging Enterprise*. San Francisco: Jossey-Bass. 283 pp.

Influential critique of social policy and services for the elderly. Estes shows how the Older Americans Act and other policies work to isolate, stigmatize, and create dependency among the aged. She argues that professionals working in the aging enterprise benefit more from public policies than do the aged.

412   ———. 1982. "Austerity and Aging in the United States: 1980 and Beyond." *International Journal of Health Services*, 12(4):573–584.

Discusses how perceptions that a fiscal crisis exists, that national policies should be decentralized, and that old age is an individual problem affect policies for the aged. The author also argues that policies concerning the aging reflect a two-class system with different types of benefits based on legitimacy rather than need.

413   ———. 1986. "The Politics of Ageing in America." *Ageing and Society*, 6(2):121–134.

Discusses the policy trends of austerity, federalism, deregulation, and the growing medicalization of aging. These trends are shown within the context of the capitalist needs for new sources of investment and profits.

414   ———. 1991. "The Reagan Legacy: Privatization, the Welfare State, and Aging in the 1990s." In *States, Labor Markets, and the Future of Old-Age Policy*, edited by John Myles and Jill Quadagno, 59–83. Philadelphia: Temple University Press.

Examines the consequences of the privization of health and social services initiated by the Reagan administration. Estes argues that federal policies and the rhetoric used to justify those policies contributed to hightened intergenerational conflict and reduced access of the aged to public services.

415   ETHEREDGE, LYNN. 1984. "Aging Society and the Federal Deficit." *Milbank Memorial Fund Quarterly*, 62(4):521–543.

Recommends reconsideration of federal policy on aging, which is viewed as "highly successful and expensive" in light of the federal deficit and improved living standards of many elderly. Etheredge suggests that control of rising health costs and improvement of retirement security will be key factors in the success of national policy for the elderly.

416 ETZIONI, AMITAI. 1976. "Old People and Public Policy." *Society*, November–December:21–29.

Reviews some of the major policy areas that affect the elderly, including health care, income maintenance, and family policy. Etzioni argues that the most effective public policies are those based on universal achievement rather than on ascribed policies targeted on specific groups, such as the aged. He critiques policies that hinder multigenerational families and those that set complete independence as an unquestioned goal.

417 FRANKE, JAMES L. 1985. "Citizen Input and Aging Policy, the Case of Florida." *Research on Aging*, 7(4):517–533.

Interviews elderly and county and city officials in 10 counties in Florida to determine what effect citizen input had on development of policy positions of public officials. Franke concludes that citizen input is not critical to the policy positions expressed by local officials. He suggests that officials must be reacting to other factors such as constituency demographics, role orientation, personal attitudes, or professional advocates.

418 GOLD, BYRON D. 1974. "The Role of the Federal Government in the Provision of Social Services to Old People." *Annals of the American Academy of Political and Social Sciences*, 415(September):55–69.

Reviews the fragmentation of federal social services for the elderly between the social welfare system, one title of the Older Americans Act (OAA) that mandates meeting locally defined needs, and one title of the OAA that mandates federally defined services. Gold suggests that the Supplemental Security Income program will make unmet needs more visible, but sees the continuation of multiple approaches to meet those needs.

419 HARBERT, ANITA S. 1976. *Federal Grants in Aid: Maximizing Benefits to the States*. New York: Praeger. 173 pp.

Analyzes the impact of federal strategies on the implementation of programs by the 50 states by studying the Older Americans Act (OAA), OAA nutrition programs, and vocational rehabilitation programs. Despite federal intent, there is a wide variation among the states in their spending on those programs. Determinants of state policy include state demographics, and especially economic and political factors.

420 HUDSON, ROBERT B. 1974. "Rational Planning and Organizational Imperatives: Prospects for Area Planning Agencies." *Annals of the American Academy of Political and Social Sciences*, 415(September):41–54.

Analyzes the 1973 Older Americans Act amendments that established local Area Agencies on Aging (AAAs). The act established the contradictory goals of developing linkage services using federal funds and mobilizing local resources. This action occurred because the legislation assumed a rational goal model while ignoring typical organizational be-

havior models. Hudson predicts that AAAs will follow organizational imperatives and develop following the vertically designed federal program
rather than responding to local needs.

421   ———. 1987. "Tomorrow's Able Elders: Implications for the State." *Ger-*
ontologist, 27(4):405–409.
     Reviews the policy issues that result from the demands the able
elderly make on government and the demands that society and government may make on these elders. The formalized identity of "able elderly" as a socially and self-defined group could result in making the frail
elderly a socially residual category. Advocates for the aging would have
to provide additional rationale for rights-based benefits that are not con-
tingent on demonstrable economic or functional need.

422   ———. 1988. "Renewing the Federal Role." *Generations*, 12(2):23–26.
     Critiques the conservative attack on government spending for the
aged. Hudson argues that rather than cutting benefits for the aged, the
government should extend benefits to all ages as a right of citizenship.
He shows that neither local government nor families can increase their
responsibility.

423   KENT, DONALD P. 1966. "Social Services and Social Policy." In *Aging and*
Social Policy, edited by John C. McKinney and Frank T. de Vyver, 198–
220. New York: Appleton-Century-Crofts.
     Considers the social context of the social problems of the aged.
Kent notes that problems reflect social circumstances, values, and economic conditions. Income programs are used most for the aged, while
service programs are more common for children. He claims that no social policy is enacted until it reaches a national consensus. He sees social
values as moving social policy toward the elimination of the material
need of the aged.

424   KLEMMACK, DAVID L., and ROFF, LUCINDA L. 1981. "Predicting General and
Comparative Support for Government's Providing Benefits to Older Persons." *Gerontologist*, 21(6):592–599.
     Evaluates the public opinion of 1,015 adults in Alabama to deter-
mine the comparative support for using taxes to support old-age versus
other programs. Overall support for government programs for the aged
is very high, ranking only after defense as a use for federal dollars. General programs that assist the elderly, such as Medicaid, had less support.
The authors discuss potential problems in mobilizing supporters of benefits for the aged.

425   LAKOFF, SANFORD A. 1976. "The Future of Social Intervention." In *Hand-*
book of Aging and the Social Sciences, edited by Robert H. Binstock and
Ethel Shanas, 643–663. New York: Van Nostrand.
     Discusses variations in the basis of the concept of justice for the
elderly. Lakoff applies the concepts of justice to the role of government

in post–industrial societies, suggesting that rational planning should supplant interest groups in deciding aging policy.

426 LAMMERS, WILLIAM W. 1981. "Congress and the Aging." In *Aging: Prospects and Issues* (3rd ed.), edited by Richard H. Davis, 274–296. Los Angeles: University of Southern California Press.

Provides a historical review of legislation, decade by decade, from the early 1960s through the early 1980s. Lammers illustrates the changing focus in congressional priorities through the years and discusses the impact of state experiments on federal policy.

427 LAMMERS, WILLIAM W., and KLINGMAN, DAVID. 1984. *State Policies and the Aging.* Lexington, MA: Lexington Books. 252 pp.

Analyzes changes in state level policies that affected the aged from 1955 to 1975 in eight states: California, Florida, Iowa, Maine, Minnesota, North Carolina, Ohio, and Washington. The policy areas examined are income maintenance, health and long-term care, regulatory protection, and social services. The analysis showed that the efforts and successes of advocacy groups for the aged was highest in states with a tradition of political liberalism and high fiscal capacity. The authors found that elderly interest groups were able to raise issues but had little role in the development of policy.

428 LEINBACH, RAYMOND M. 1977. "The Aging Participants in an Area Planning Effort." *Gerontologist,* 17(5):453–458.

Explores differences in attitudes between 58 elderly and 63 nonelderly members of Area Agency on Aging advisory committees. Data showed no significant difference by age on attitudes toward the planning effort, but higher income and education were found to determine improved understanding of the planning purpose and process. Leinbach suggests ways to improve the planning input provided by low-income elderly.

429 MCCLOMB, GEORGE E. 1984. "Public Policy and the Aging: A Comparative Analysis of the Implementation of Title III of the Older Americans Act of 1965." Ph.D. dissertation, University of Pittsburgh. 258 pp.

Examines the role of implementation strategies in the performance of public policy. McClomb finds that strategies affect the direction of performance but not the level, that expressive goals of policies conflict with the instrumental capacity of implementation, and that prior strategic decisions shape implementation.

430 MERRILL, GREG. 1989. "State Agenda for the Aged." *State Government News,* 32(3):15–16.

A staff member of the American Association of Retired Persons discusses the broadening set of issues in which the elderly are involved in at the state level, including health topics, long-term care, finances, and consumer interests.

431   MYLES, JOHN F. 1983. "Conflict, Crisis, and the Future of Old Age Secu-
      rity." *Milbank Memorial Fund Quarterly*, 61(4):462–472.
          Argues that the aging of the population is a potential crisis only
      because of the role of our democratic state in our market economy. The
      author contends that old-age security programs have been attacked be-
      cause they operate outside of the market economy. The future will re-
      quire either a reassertion of the market or a further introduction of
      democratic principles into the market.

432   NELSON, GARY. 1980. "Social Services to the Urban and Rural Aged: The
      Experience of the Area Agencies on Aging." *Gerontologist*, 20(2):200–
      207.
          Critiques funding and staffing policies for rural agencies on aging.
      Nelson finds care and services for frail, at-risk elderly to be inadequate.
      He recommends establishment of minimum funding levels and suggests
      that allocation formulas consider rural factors.

433   ———. 1982. "Social Class and Public Policy for the Elderly." *Social Ser-
      vice Review*, 56(1):85–107.
          Argues that public policy for the elderly is split into means-tested
      welfare programs for the poor, compulsory earnings-related Social Se-
      curity programs for the middle- and lower-middle income elderly, and
      publicly supported private programs like private pensions for the
      upper-middle class and wealthy. Nelson shows how medical and social
      service programs fit this classification. Policy changes in the early 1980s
      have hurt programs for the poor and benefited the wealthy.

434   ———. 1982. "Support for the Aged: Public and Private Responsibility."
      Social Work, 27(2):137–143.
          Examines the interrelationship between government and family aid
      to the elderly. The author discusses how some government programs
      replace existing family support, complement it, or fill in for absent fam-
      ily support. He suggests how policy should be modified to support ex-
      isting family aid to the elderly while serving as a fallback for those with-
      out family aid.

435   NEUGARTEN, BERNICE L. (Ed.). 1983. *Age or Need? Public Policies for
      Older People*. Beverly Hills: Sage Publications. 288 pp.
          Examines methods for enhancing the welfare of the older popula-
      tion that are constructive to the whole society. Central to the public de-
      bate are the age-targeted federal programs. Contributing authors rec-
      ommend reexamination of existing programs with recommendations
      for improvements.

436   ORIOL, WILLIAM E. 1981. "'Modern' Old Age and Public Policy." *Gerontol-
      ogist*, 21(1):35–45.
          Reviews the changes in public policy from 1960 to 1980 during
      which time aging disappeared as a national "problem." Oriol primarily

reviews congressional action addressing issues of the aged, concluding that progress has been made although problems continue to exist.

437 ———. 1983. "New Direction of Old Themes Revisited? The Present Federal Role in Service Entitlements." *Gerontologist*, 23(4):399–401.

Presents, as part of the First Annual Ollie Randall Symposium, a review of federal legislation that seems to favor upper-income groups at the expense of lower-income individuals. Oriol focuses on the problems of the 1981 Social Service Block Grant in decreasing federal funding while increasing state responsibility. He cautions against the focus on today's elderly as the "wealthiest and healthiest" in our history.

438 ———. 1984. "A Quarter Century of Focus by the Senate Aging Committee." *Perspective on Aging*, 13(4):7–9.

Outlines the 25-year history of the Senate Special Committee on Aging. Created in 1959 as a subcommittee to review problems of the aged and aging, it studies aging issues and makes recommendations to standing committees with legislative jurisdiction. The committee was instrumental in the passage in 1965 of Medicare legislation and the Older Americans Act, and in the 1972 Social Security legislation.

439 ———. 1985. "Medicaid Essential—Provides Critical Protection for 23 million." *Perspective on Aging*, 14(4):4–8.

Highlights 20 years of Medicaid accomplishments and failings. Oriol discusses concerns over spiraling expenditures and offers alternative structures. The article contains a study guide and extensive references.

440 ORLOFF, ANN S. 1988. "The Political Origins of America's Belated Welfare State." In *The Politics of Social Policy in the United States*, edited by M. Weir, A. S. Orloff, and T. Skocpol, 37–80. Princeton, NJ: Princeton University Press.

Discusses the reasons for the late development in the United States of social insurance and pensions. Orloff argues that neither popular demand nor social problems led to the programs. Instead, political and bureaucratic elites are shown to use those programs to incorporate the working class into the established political system. This process was delayed in the United States because the patronage system delayed the development of a bureaucracy capable of implementing national pension programs. Civil War pensions are discussed as evidence of the problems inherent with patronage versus bureaucratic control. Social Security legislation marked a shift toward professional administration.

441 PIFER, ALAN. 1986. "The Public Policy Response." In *Our Aging Society: Paradox and Promise,* edited by Alan Pifer and Lydia Bronte, 391–413. New York: Norton.

Outlines the principal policy issues that will face the nation. Pifer analyzes how these issues will affect policy formation and considers the ways public values will inform the policy process. He identifies four major policy areas: to make the wisest use of resources, to use the senior population productively, to determine responsibility for meeting the social needs of the aged, and finally, to achieve intergenerational equity. The nature and extent of the government role in addressing these problems is examined.

442   POWELL, LAWRENCE A., and WILLIAMSON, JOHN B. 1985. "The Reagan-Era Shift toward Restrictiveness in Old Age Policy in Historical Perspective." *International Journal of Aging and Human Development*, 21:81–86.

A historical analysis of the ebb in the liberalization trend in Social Security during the 1970s and the clear reversal of the liberalization trend during the 1980s. The authors view this reversal as an example of the recurrent pattern of welfare policy reform and reaction. Analysis of a similar trend during the early 1800s is presented. During the 1820s, as during the 1980s, the objective of welfare reform was to reduce public expenditures. In both periods the aged poor were caught in a political cross-fire between irate taxpayers and a presumably sizable number of able-bodied poor.

443   SAINER, JANET S. 1982. "Human Services Constraints at State and Local Levels." *Gerontologist*, 23(4):402–405.

Traces the growth of human services from the poorhouses through Social Security, Medicare, and the Older Americans Act. Sainer outlines the political and societal cross-currents that constrain services at the state and local levels. She cautions against a shift from federal responsibility to the state and local levels. She stresses that more than ever it is necessary for professionals to act as advocates for the elderly, not only in human service areas but across all sectors of society.

444   SARASIN, RONALD A. 1977. "Over the Hill?" *Connecticut Law Review*, 9(3):427–434.

A congressman reviews the problems faced by the aged and the legislation introduced in Congress during 1975–76 that addressed some of those problems.

445   SCHRAM, SANFORD F. 1979. "Elderly Policy Particularism and the New Social Services." *Social Service Review*, 53(1):75–91.

Examines state eligibility and spending patterns of Title XX social services to show that the elderly are not benefiting from the increased discretion being given the states. Services offered on a universal basis are rarely those for the aged. The author warns of the divisiveness of advocating special treatment for the aged.

446   SCHULDER, DANIEL J. 1985. "Older Americans Act: A Vast Network of Public, Private Agencies." *Perspective on Aging*, 14(5):4–7.

Describes the evolution of the Older Americans Act from its modest beginnings to date. On the twentieth anniversary of the enactment of this legislation, the author reviews the wide range of programs offered under this act by state and area agencies as well as private agencies.

447 SHEPPARD, HAROLD L. 1982. "Aging Services a Right, Most Say." *Gerontologist*, 11(1):6–32.

Polls of persons both below and above age 65 indicate general support for government to assume greater responsibility for social programs for the elderly. Some skepticism was expressed about the capability of business and private sources to fill in the gaps left by reductions in government funding.

448 SHINDUL-ROTHSCHILD, JUDITH, and WILLIAMSON, JOHN B. 1991. "Future Prospects for Aging Policy Reform." In *Critical Perspectives on Aging*, edited by Meredith Minkler and Carroll L. Estes, 325–340. Amityville, NY: Baywood.

Discusses the pros and cons of policies that are universal versus those targeted on subgroups of the aged. The authors describe the implications of these two approaches in health care, income maintenance, and Social Security. They see the aged and their organizations as continuing to be important forces in moving aging policy.

449 SKINNER, JOHN H. 1990. "Targeting Benefits for the Black Elderly: The Older Americans Act." In *Black Aged*, edited by Zev Harel, Edward A. McKinney, and Michael Williams, 165–182. Newbury Park, CA: Sage Publications.

Describes the problem of the Older Americans Act (OAA), which is underfunded given its mission to serve the entire aged population. Skinner explains that allocation of funds is targeted to those in greatest social and economic need, with race often being part of the allocation formula. This places minority elderly in competition with other elders. He suggests using functional status and other need criteria rather than race in allocation formulas.

450 STANLEY, MARY B. 1987. "Elders, Objects and Agents: Citizenship, Political Culture and Aging Policy." Ph.D. dissertation, Syracuse University. 924 pp.

Argues that notions of citizenship shape the way policy is made. Stanley draws from the history of social work and human services, publications of the Gerontological Society, and interviews with federal policymakers. She concludes that experts and policymakers hold limited notions of the aged that reflect a limited concept of them as citizens.

451 TABER, MERLIN, and FLYNN, MARILYN. 1971. "Social Policy and Social Provision for the Elderly in the 1970s." *Gerontologist*, 2(4):51–54.

Analyzes 400 agencies, programs, and institutions in three Illinois counties. The study shows that services are negligible and depersonalized in medical and social services, income maintenance, education,

public housing, recreation and employment. Modest direct money payments predominate and policy for the aged seem to be one of disengagement.

452   TAVANI, CHARLES. 1979. "Meeting the Needs of the Oldest of the Old."
      Aging, 291–292:2–7.
          Offers a rationale for federal programs that focus on the special
      needs of those aged 85 and over. The author suggests provision of in-
      creased income and other help to the oldest poor to ensure standards
      of essential personal care assistance.

453   TIBBITTS, CLARK. 1951. "Summary of Activities of Federal Agencies." In
      Conference on Problems of Aging. Transactions of the Thirteenth Con-
      ference, edited by Nathan W. Shock, 96–105. New York: Josiah Macy Jr.
      Foundation.
          Briefly reviews the work of the Federal Security Agency and the
      1950 National Conference on Aging. The author reviews the number of
      conferences and committees on aging at state and local levels.

454   TOWNSEND, PETER. 1981. "The Structured Dependency of the Elderly: A
      Creation of Social Policy in the Twentieth Century." *Ageing and Society*,
      1(1):5–28.
          Argues that dependency of the elderly on society is created socially
      and is more severe than necessary. Townsend examines the effects of
      retirement, pensions, and institutional care in creating social depen-
      dence. He concludes that this structural dependency results from twen-
      tieth-century political, social, and economic factors.

455   VINYARD, DALE. 1972. "The Senate Special Committee on Aging." *Geron-
      tologist*, 12(3):298–303.
          Describes the historical development, functions, and accomplish-
      ments of the United States Senate Special Committee on Aging estab-
      lished in 1961. The author views the committee as more influential than
      just as a study group even though it lacks the authority to receive and
      act on legislation. While it takes an active role in formation of aging pol-
      icy, its activities are limited.

456   ———. 1973. "The Senate Committee on the Aging and the Develop-
      ment of a Policy System." *Michigan Academician*, 5(3):281–294.
          Examines the role of the Senate Committee on Aging in the federal
      policy system. Policy creation often takes place within a closed system.
      Aging policy is unique because of the nature of aging issues, the role of
      interest groups, and the committee's lack of legislative authority. The
      history and functions of the committee are described. Its role as a sym-
      bol, personal vehicle, legislation catalyst, monitoring agency, and forum
      are explored.

457   ———. 1980. "Public Policies and the Aged: Some Additional Ques-
      tions." *Social Thought* (Spring):31–40.
          Addresses two issues: whether current programs assist those aged

most in need and whether the aged are receiving privileged treatment over other disadvantaged groups. Vinyard suggests that the most advantaged are best equipped to press their claims so that policy becomes skewed against the most disadvantaged. Increases in Social Security payments, which resulted in reductions of state assistance programs, had a negative impact on the most needy. Programs that finance medical care have had little impact on quality and distribution of care. It does appear the aged have been among the major beneficiaries of the welfare state.

458 ————. 1983. "Public Policy and Institutional Politics." In *Aging and Public Policy: The Politics of Growing Old in America,* edited by William Brown and Laura Katz Olson, 181–199. Westport, CT: Greenwood Press.

Examines the legislative and executive branch components of the aging-policy system. Fragmentation and a decentralized policy structure in both the Congress and the executive branch are the result of the rapid growth and the diversity of programs. Founded to overcome fragmentation in social services, the Administration on Aging is largely symbolic because of inadequate resources and no political power. While providing public forums and serving as catalysts for aging programs, the Senate Special Committee on Aging and the House Select Committee on Aging are unable to report bills directly to the floor. The author concludes that the vital function of policy implementation is with the executive branch.

459 WALLACE, STEVEN P., and ESTES, CARROLL L. 1989. "Health Policy for the Elderly: Federal Policy and Institutional Change." In *Policy Issues for the 1990s,* edited by Ray Rist, 591–613. Policy Studies Review Annual, 9. New Brunswick, NJ: Transaction.

Analyzes present and future trends in health policy as they affect the elderly. Reliance on the biomedical model, the changing shape of federalism, the fiscal crisis of the states, and deregulation are discussed, as political and economic conditions that frame changes in health policy. The authors suggest that those influences will bring additional medicalization, growth in the medical-industrial complex, and increased codification of health care for the aged. They advocate coalition building between the aged and other groups to restructure the medical care system around human needs.

460 WERSHOW, HAROLD J. 1981. "Issues of Public Policy: How Do We Best Serve Public Policy?" In *Controversial Issues in Gerontology,* edited by Harold J. Wershow, 147–173. New York: Springer.

Comments on the contributions of the guest authors on a variety of topics. Wershow identifies inadequacies of federal policies, factors affecting health care delivery, and proposals for broadening the tax base for social programs. He utilizes the nutrition program to demonstrate how incremental single-purpose programs can take on a life of their own.

461   WILLIAMS, HARRISON A. 1962. "Implications of an Aging Population for Political Sociology." In *Politics of Age*, edited by Wilma Donahue and Clark Tibbitts, 158–167. Ann Arbor: University of Michigan Press.

Democratic congressman explains the Democratic party position on the needs of the aged.

462   WILLIAMSON, JOHN B.; SHINDUL, JUDITH A.; and EVANS, LINDA. 1985. *Aging and Public Policy: Social Control or Social Justice?* Springfield, IL: Charles C Thomas. 332 pp.

Historical perspective on policy origins that examines the shift in public policy from concerns with equity and social justice to concerns about cost containment. Theoretical perspectives of political economics, functionalism, and labeling theory are used to examine social control aspects of public policy. Health policy is criticized in three chapters and another chapter deals with revisions in long-term care. The impact of advances in medical technology and the influence of mass media on public perception of the elderly are presented. Recommendations for future public policy are given.

463   ZONES, JANE SPRAGUE; ESTES, CARROLL L.; and BINNEY, ELIZABETH A. 1987. "Gender, Public Policy and the Oldest Old." *Ageing and Society*, 7:275–302.

Examines the consequences of the expanding number of very elderly women combined with a political climate that opposes helping to fulfill family functions. The authors show how the historical events in older women's lives, especially those involving family and employment, have shaped their experiences and current condition. They then review different approaches to public policies for income maintenance, health care financing, and long-term care as they would affect older women.

Social Security

464   • 1937. Helvering v. Davis, 301 United States 619, 57 Supreme Court 904, 81 L. Ed 1307 (1937).

Key Supreme Court decision upholding the constitutionality of the Social Security Act of 1935 by invoking the public welfare clause of the Constitution.

465   • 1969. "Reports to Congress on OASDHI Studies." *Social Security Bulletin*, 32(3):10–14.

Summarizes the results of several studies required by the Social Security Amendments of 1967. Studies deal mainly with the extension of Medicare benefits.

466 • 1969. "Social Security in Review." *Social Security Bulletin*, 32(3):1–3.
Lists issues considered by the Secretary of Health, Education and Welfare in determining the Medicare Part B premium rate. The program operations of Social Security are described.

467 AARON, HENRY J.; BOSWORTH, BARRY P.; and BURTLESS, GARY. 1989. *Can America Afford to Grow Old? Paying for Social Security*. Washington DC: Brookings Institution. 144 pp.
Addresses the long-run stability of the Social Security system. The authors analyze the impact on workers of providing pension and health benefits for the retiring baby-boom generation. They assert that including the Social Security trust fund in the overall federal budget conceals the true size of the federal budget deficit and conclude that future workers will be required to pay greatly increased taxes to support the costs of promised benefits.

468 ACHENBAUM, W. ANDREW. 1986. "The Elderly's Social Security Entitlements as a Measure of Modern American Life." In *Old Age in a Bureaucratic Society: The Elderly, the Experts, and the State in American History,* edited by Donald Van Tassel and Peter Stearns, 156–192. New York: Greenwood Press.
Traces the political and historical evolution of Social Security. The need to question common, often-mistaken assumptions about the fundamental principles behind Social Security is emphasized, along with recommendations to explore "a persistent failure to recognize the incongruency between entitlements and expectations."

469 ———. 1986. *Social Security: Visions and Revisions*. New York: Cambridge University Press. 300 pp.
Traces the convoluted history of Social Security from the New Deal to the Reagan Era. The author describes a number of contemporary crises, and illustrates how the legislation has served in promoting congressional self-interest and political power brokering. In outlining the 1972 amendments, he asserts that in an election year, ill-considered programs were approved for the wrong reasons. He recommends that future policy changes be historically informed. He advocates removing Medicare and Medicaid from income security programs because the Social Security model does not suit health care needs. Recommendations for the future include homemaker "credits" to address the problems of aging women. The book provides detailed, well-documented material on the complex history of Social Security.

470 ALTMEYER, ARTHUR J. 1968. *The Formative Years of Social Security*. Madison: University of Wisconsin Press. 314 pp.
Often-cited insider history of the debates around Social Security. Altmeyer explains why nonpension programs are administered by states, why Social Security pensions are contributory, why disability benefits were not added until 1956, and why health benefits were not in-

cluded. Administrative decisions determined whether old age pensions would become the primary type of old age security, whether public assistance would be equitable and consistent within each state, and whether states would develop civil services. The author participated in many of these developments and details his ongoing fight to keep Social Security dependent on employment taxes with benefits tied to contributions.

471   BALL, ROBERT M. 1978. *Social Security Today and Tomorrow*. New York: Columbia University Press. 528 pp.

Detailed overview of the operation of and controversies about Social Security by a former Social Security commissioner. Ball uses a question and answer format to discuss eligibility, benefits, financing, and adequacy and equity in the system. He argues that the current contributory pension system is the best type of social insurance against poverty.

472   BEATTIE, WALTER M. 1983. "Economic Security for the Elderly: National and International Perspectives." *Gerontologist*, 23(4):406–410.

Contends that issues of Social Security must be assessed from a "life-span/intergenerational framework" that recognizes the economic problems of older women and minorities related to their limited employability and earnings. The author argues that traditional incremental public policy will fail and recommends movement to an integrated public-private income security system in old age.

473   BORGER, GLORIA. 1986. "Thinking the Unthinkable: A Cut in Social Security?" *Newsweek*, 107(5):20.

Explores the possibility of reducing Social Security benefits as a solution to the federal budget deficit. Borger suggests that what was once considered untouchable may now be used to deal with the mounting budget crisis.

474   BRENTS, BARBARA G. 1986. "Policy Intellectuals, Class Struggle and the Construction of Old Age: The Creation of the Social Security Act of 1935." *Social Science and Medicine*, 23(12):1251–1260.

Historical review of the Social Security Act. Brents argues that age-based inequities in legislation and the institutionalization of retirement resulted from workplace class conflicts. Those conflicts centered on changes in worker productivity, new methods of production, and an ageist view of aging as decline. Capitalists used a biological concept of aging as a weapon against workers.

475   ———. 1987. "The Class Politics of Age Politics: The Development of the 1935 Social Security Act." Ph.D. dissertation, University of Missouri, Columbia. 342 pp.

Examines the class struggle present in the formation of Social Security policy. Brents finds that the state mediated between factions of the capitalist class and worker insurgency. She argues that focusing the debate on age served to silence potential discussion based on class inequalities.

476   BROWN, JAMES DOUGLAS. 1972. *An American Philosophy of Social Security: Evolution and Issues*. Princeton, NJ: Princeton University Press. 244 pp.

Describes Social Security as a "three-layer approach" with social insurance supported by needs-tested public assistance and private pensions. Brown, one of the leaders in the design and development of the Social Security system, provides a clear account of its philosophical evolution. The book gives a nontechnical picture of "why the system is in its present form and why further evolution is necessary."

477   BURKHAUSER, RICHARD V. 1979. "Are Women Treated Fairly in Today's Social Security System?" *Gerontologist*, 19(3):242–249.

Analyzes data from Old Age Survivors Insurance (OASI) to question the model of the family on which tax and transfer policy is based. The conflict between OASI goals of providing a safe financial instrument for retirement and providing a means of redistribution of income in the name of social adequacy is addressed. The author concludes that with the increase of two-earner households and the lifetime commitment of women to the labor force, the redistributive features of the legislation need revamping.

478   BUTLER, STUART, and GERMANIS, PETER. 1983. "Achieving a 'Leninist' Strategy." *Cato Journal*, 3(2):547–556.

Discusses a strategy for building political support for privatizing Social Security into an Individual Retirement Account-type system. The authors note that existing beneficiaries need to be reassured because of the political power of the aged, the public needs to be educated about the problems of Social Security, and successful alternatives must be publicized. Financial institutions and young workers are two groups most likely to form the core of a coalition for privatization.

479   CLARK, TIMOTHY B. 1983. "Congress Avoiding Political Abyss by Approving Social Security Changes." *National Journal*, March 19:611–615.

Analyzes the political activities surrounding Social Security reforms. Clark discusses activities by federal employees, the American Association of Retired Persons, the Chamber of Commerce of the United States, and the National Federation of Independent Business. He provides charts on the trust funds and figures on potential long- and short-term deficits.

480   COHEN, RICHARD E. 1983. "Democrats in a Pickle." *National Journal*, March 19:621.

Provides an account of the congressional politics behind raising the retirement age for Social Security. Cohen discusses the role of partisan politics, labor unions, and the American Association of Retired Persons in the debate.

481   COHEN, WILBUR J. 1957. *Retirement Policies under Social Security*. Berkeley: University of California Press. 105 pp.

Reviews the legislative history of proposals concerning the age for retirement under Social Security and the design of the retirement test. Age 65 was the only eligibility age considered by those drafting Social Security for reasons of economic and political feasibility, given the Depression. Cohen describes the legislative decisions in proposals to add early retirement at age 62, disability pensions, and changes in the retirement test.

482   CONGLETON, ROGER D., and SHYGHART, WILLIAM F. 1990. "Growth of Social Security: Electoral Push or Political Pull?" *Economic Inquiry*, 28(1):109–132.

Examines the growth of benefit levels in Social Security programs from 1946 to 1980. The authors describe three different models representing the political process that influences retirement benefit levels. They analyze growth in Social Security expenditures to determine whether special interest groups or public demands are responsible for the increase in benefit levels. Results show that the best explanation is provided by the median voter model, which states that voters are motivated by both altruism toward the elderly and concern for their own retirement income. This conclusion suggests that the Social Security focus on personal pensions and redistribution of income reflects public interest in both activities.

483   DEMOTT, JOHN S. 1985. "New Look at the Elderly." *Time*, 125(7):81.

Reviews the annual report of the President's Council of Economic Advisers, which describes the elderly as no longer economically disadvantaged. Advocates for the elderly claim the report supports efforts to cut Social Security benefits.

484   DERTHICK, MARTHA. 1979. "How Easy Votes on Social Security Came to an End." *The Public Interest*, 54(Winter):94–105.

Examines the context of the Social Security crises of the late 1970s and how Congress was forced to take unpopular measures. The author finds that the growth of the program and favorable economic conditions allowed Social Security benefits and eligibility to be expansive at a low cost until the 1970s. Social Security has become a more difficult political issue because the system is maturing, there are few new groups to cover that will increase revenues, and flexibility in benefit levels was eliminated with indexing.

485   ———. 1979. *Policymaking for Social Security*. Washington, DC: Brookings Institution. 446 pp.

Widely cited book that examines how Social Security was successfully institutionalized and why it faced a crisis beginning in the 1970s. The author describes the different groups that influence Social Security policy, both inside and outside government. She finds organized labor one of the most important external supporters and notes how program officials tried to maximize general public support. She explains the system and its expansion into disability, health care, and larger cash benefits, and she analyzes the causes and politics around the system's deficit of the 1970s. Derthick finds that the program faced little conflict and discussion in the past because its policy-making was dominated by a few experts whose predictions were uncritically accepted and because it promised a fair return on the taxes levied.

486   DOMHOFF, G. WILLIAM. 1970. *The Higher Circles: The Governing Class in America*. New York: Random House. 367 pp.
      Essays on the ways in which the upper class in the United States predominates in the policy process as a result of common material interests and resources, social position, and background. Domhoff emphasizes the importance of policy organizations of both reformers and business. He explains the influence of the American Association for Labor Legislation and elite reformers in shaping Social Security and shows that big business was generally favorable to the plan.

487   ———. 1986–87. "Corporate-Liberal Theory and the Social Security Act: A Chapter in the Sociology of Knowledge." *Politics and Society*, 15(3):297–330.
      Analyzes three rival class theories that explain the passage of the Social Security Act of 1935: structuralist, state-oriented, and corporate-liberal. Domhoff argues that the power of big business was central in shaping Social Security, reaffirming a corporate-liberal position. He shows how differences between the theories have been exaggerated by factors external to the theories themselves.

488   ESTES, CARROLL L. 1983. "Social Security: The Social Construction of a Crisis." *Milbank Memorial Fund Quarterly*, 61(3):445–461.
      Describes how the Social Security crisis of the 1980s was "socially constructed" so that it delegitimized the elderly and reduced expectations of the program. It also diverted attention from the consequences of federal fiscal policy.

489   EVANS, LINDA, and WILLIAMSON, JOHN B. 1981. "Social Security and Social Control." *Generations*, 6(Winter):18–20.
      Argues that despite its many benefits, the Social Security Act of 1935 functioned as a form of social control of the elderly. The authors claim that it provided a strong inducement for the elderly to leave the labor force and contributed to the institutionalization of mandatory retirement age rules. They criticize efforts by corporate America to undercut the public pension approach in favor of privatized alternatives.

490 EVANS, LINDA, and WILLIAMSON, JOHN B. 1984. "Social Control of the Elderly." In *The Political Economy of Aging*, edited by Carroll L. Estes and Meredith Minkler, 47–72. Farmingdale, NY: Baywood.

An analysis of the rise of the pension movement at the turn of the century. The authors review the reasons that pensions were considered un-American historically. The authors argue that current gerontologists are agents of social control in that their studies and services underscore the separateness of older Americans and perpetuate the elderly's definition as a problem group. The article highlights the social control aspects of a variety of welfare programs for the aged.

491 FERRARA, PETER J. 1983. "The Prospect of Real Reform." *Cato Journal*, 3(2):609–620.

Takes issue with the 1983 Social Security legislation for providing insufficient reforms. Ferrara describes the program as a burden on the young, who will never reap the benefits, and a burden on the economy because it affects employment and has a negative impact on personal savings. Noting that Social Security provides both welfare and insurance functions, he suggests expansion of Individual Retirement Accounts (IRAs) as one plausible replacement.

492 ———. 1988. "Social Security: Look at Your Pay Stub." In *Assessing the Reagan Years*, edited by David Boaz, 201–209. Washington, DC: Cato Institute.

Reviews the early proposals of the Reagan administration on Social Security. Ferrara argues that Reagan failed to reform the program according to his vision, which would have required the privatization of the program.

493 FLOWERS, MARILYN R. 1983. "The Political Feasibility of Privatizing Social Security." *Cato Journal*, 3(2):557–561.

Discusses some of the political problems of privatizing Social Security, especially the resistance of current workers who may perceive a loss of benefits.

494 FREEMAN, GARY, and ADAMS, PAUL. 1982. "The Politics of Social Security: Expansion, Retrenchment, and Rationalization." In *The Political Economy of Public Policy*, edited by Alan Stone and Edward J. Harpham, 241–261. Beverly Hills: Sage Publications.

Reviews the development of Social Security to show how pay as you go financing and interest groups led to incremental expansion until 1972. The first expression of "crisis" began then because of bad economic conditions, a maturing pension population, and the baby-boom generation. These circumstances led to a struggle between those who would make economic policy primary and those who would make social insurance policy primary. The authors predict that the Reagan years will move past the impasse of the previous 10 years to subordinate Social Security to larger economic policy.

495 GOODWIN, LEONARD, and TU, JOSEPH. 1975. "The Social Psychological Basis for Public Acceptance of the Social Security System." *American Psychologist*, 30:875–883.

Analyzes survey data from 615 residents of three large cities to determine the basis for public support of Social Security. The authors find that linking contributions to benefits increases the high acceptance of a mandatory system. Most respondents did not believe they were getting a good return on their contributions and thought they would make more if the money were invested elsewhere. The insurance metaphor used by the system increases its acceptance.

496 GORDON, MARGARET S. 1970. "Aging and Income Security in the United States Thirty-Five Years After the Social Security Act." *Gerontologist*, 10(4):23–31.

Recommends adoption of a guaranteed minimum income with negative income tax features for the entire population as a substitute for the Supplemental Security Income program (SSI). A thorough and useful analysis of the act and discussion of adequate social insurance programs are presented.

497 GRAEBNER, WILLIAM. 1982. "From Pensions to Social Security: Social Insurance and the Rise of Dependency." In *The Quest For Security,* edited by John N. Schacht, 19–33. Iowa City, IA: Center for the Study of Recent History of the United States.

Examines the relationship between social insurance and social dependency. Graebner gives a brief account of the history of private and public pension plans, and the labor force participation rate as a measure of the rise of old-age insurance. The author argues that the social insurance system creates dependency by institutionalizing the elderly. He discusses three cases that illustrate the relationship between dependency and social insurance and explains how the Social Security Act of 1935 works as retirement legislation. He concludes that social insurance has been consciously used to create dependency of the elderly during times of severe unemployment.

498 HOLLISTER, ROBINSON. 1974. "Social Mythology and Reform: Income Maintenance for the Aged." *Annals of the American Academy of Political and Social Sciences*, 415(September):19–40.

Provides a summary and critiques of how Social Security works, before and after the 1972 amendments. The author reviews the debate over reforming Social Security, arguing that the legitimacy of Social Security rests on a myth that could be easily shattered by proposed changes. The myth is that Social Security is contributory social insurance when it is really an intergenerational transfer with features that redistribute income from wealthy elderly to poorer elders.

499 JENKINS, J. CRAIG, and BRENTS, BARBARA G. 1989. "Social Protest, Hegemonic Competition, and Social Reform: A Political Struggle Interpreta-

tion of the Origins of the American Welfare State." *American Sociological Review*, 54:891–909.

Examines the forces leading to the establishment of Social Security. The authors argue that economic uncertainty and waves of protest created a feeling of crisis among policymakers and divided capitalists. Liberal capitalists were central in placing Social Security policies on the political agenda in that context.

500   KAHNE, HILDA. 1981. "Women and Social Security." *International Journal of Aging and Human Development*, 13(3):195–208.

Suggests immediate and long-term reforms for the inadequacies in the Social Security provisions for women. Kahne cites "unfortunate disjunction between the assumptions upon which present social security provisions are based and the contemporary roles and lifetime living patterns of women" as a partial explanation of the system's inadequate treatment of women.

501   KAPLAN, BARBARA. 1985. "Social Security 50 Years Later." *Perspective on Aging*, 14(2):4–7+.

Emphasizes simplistic aspects of the 1980s political environment with its focus on the "graying of the budget." The long-range action taken in the 1983 Social Security amendments has led to growth in the Social Security trust fund, a positive development that is ignored in this focus.

502   KINGSON, ERIC R. 1984. "Financing Social Security: Agenda Setting and the Enactment of the 1983 Amendments to the Social Security Act." *Policy Studies Journal*, 13(1):131–155.

Provides a detailed account of the legislative actions taken between 1972 and 1983 to keep Social Security solvent. In the early 1970s financing issues replaced system expansion as the major issue because the 1972 indexing of Social Security to inflation occurred just before the economy experienced a long period of high inflation and high unemployment. Amendments in 1977 were to have adjusted the program for those economic conditions, but the economy worsened further and created a new deficit. The Reagan administration heightened public and political attention by proposing drastic cuts in the program in 1981, requiring creation of a bipartisan commission to develop a politically feasible plan for keeping the system solvent.

503   ———. 1989. "Don't Panic; It's Working: What Baby Boomers Need to Know about Social Security." *Generations*, 13(2):15–20.

Reviews the Social Security programs to show how the baby-boom generation will be able to count on Social Security for a substantial portion of its retirement income. Kingson describes how projections are made to ensure that the program is financially sound and argues that the program is fair to both workers and retirees.

504 KINGSON, ERIC R., and WILLIAMSON, JOHN B. 1991. "Is the Goal Generational Equity or the Privatization of Social Security?" *Society*, 28(3).

Discusses why the debate over intergenerational equity has emerged and how those who favor privatizing Social Security benefit from this debate. The authors suggest that the debate is fostered by those who want to shrink the role of the welfare state.

505 LIGHT, PAUL C. 1985. *Artful Work: The Politics of Social Security Reform.* New York: Random House. 255 pp.

See entry 332.

506 ———. 1985. "Social Security and the Politics of Assumptions." *Public Administration Review*, 45(3):363–371.

Discusses the importance of economic and social assumptions in Social Security budgeting from 1972 to 1984. Indexing has made the process more important since program expenditures grow automatically. Light demonstrates that almost all Social Security Administration (SSA) projections have been overly optimistic. He attributes the errors in part to politics, with predictions being tailored to support the political agenda of the White House.

507 LUBOMUDROV, SLAVA. 1987. "Congressional Perceptions of the Elderly: The Use of Stereotypes in the Legislative Process." *Gerontologist*, 27(1):77–81.

See entry 766.

508 LUBOVE, ROY. 1968. *The Struggle for Social Security, 1900–1935.* Cambridge, MA: Harvard University Press. 276 pp.

Often-cited book analyzing how the value of voluntarism dominated debates over public pensions and describing the movement of policy toward a national system. Lubove describes the efforts of the American Association for Labor Legislation and its leaders in informing the public and policymakers about the benefits of social insurance. The experience with workers' compensation, mothers' pensions, and the attempts to secure health insurance framed the debate over old-age pensions.

509 MUNNELL, ALICIA. 1977. *The Future of Social Security.* Washington, DC: Brookings Institution. 190 pp.

Examines old-age and survivors insurance rather than the entire Social Security system. The author identifies an "ambivalence of goals" in this system, which seeks to combine social insurance and welfare goals. She raises questions of sufficient funding. A legislative history is included in the appendix.

510 MYLES, JOHN F. 1985. "The Trillion-dollar Misunderstanding." In *Growing Old in America: New Perspectives in Old Age,* edited by Beth Hess and Elizabeth Markson, 507–523. New Brunswick, NJ: Transaction.

Urges new debate on social security. Myles suggests that proposed cuts of Social Security in 1981 were directly related to "conservative as-saults . . . spanning a decade." He emphasizes the importance of fresh approaches to the problems instead of continued criticism.

511 ———. 1988. "Postwar Capitalism and the Extension of Social Security onto a Retirement Wage." In *The Politics of Social Policy in the United States,* edited by M. Weir, A. S. Orloff, and T. Skocpol, 265–292. Princeton, NJ: Princeton University Press.

    Old-age policy is the only part of the American welfare state that is well developed. Myles argues that this development did not occur until the passage of reforms under President Nixon. He explains the subse-quent business backlash that attempted to reduce the "retirement wages" provided by Social Security. The alliance of the middle classes and the poor prevented significant cuts.

512 ORLOFF, ANN S. 1988. "The Political Origins of America's Belated Welfare State." In *The Politics of Social Policy in the United States,* edited by M. Weir, A. S. Orloff, and T. Skocpol, 37–80. Princeton, NJ: Princeton Uni-versity Press.

    See entry 440.

513 OZAWA, MARTHA N. 1982. "Who Receives Subsidies through Social Secu-rity and How Much?" *Social Work,* 27(2):129–134.

    Considers current retiree benefits from the standpoint of past con-tributions. Ozawa calculates the amount of these benefits that are paid by past contributions plus interest. She presents suggestions for changes to provide greater equity for low-income persons.

514 QUADAGNO, JILL S. 1984. "Welfare Capitalism and the Social Security Act of 1935." *American Sociological Review,* 49(October):632–647.

    Examines the original Social Security Act as the result of mediation by the state between the conflicting interests of monopoly and non-monopoly business. Labor unions were relatively uninvolved and Townsend movement pressures were politically conservative.

515 ———. 1987. "The Social Security Program and the Private Sector Alter-native: Lessons from History." *International Journal of Aging and Human Development,* 25(3):239–246.

    Analyzes the 1970s debate about the capacity of Social Security to survive into the twenty-first century. The author addresses the relation-ship of the Social Security fund to the federal deficit. Conservatives view the fund as a drain on the economy and recommend greater reliance on private sector benefits. Historical evidence shows that private sector programs fail to provide adequately for older citizens, with benefits in-equitably distributed on the basis of social class and gender. She con-cludes that increased reliance on the private sector would only add to existing inequities.

516 ———. 1988. *The Transformation of Old Age Security*. Chicago: University of Chicago Press. 266 pp.

> See entry 604.

517 ———. 1991. "Interest Group Politics and the Future of U.S. Social Security." In *States, Labor Markets and the Future of Old Age Policy*, edited by John Myles and Jill Quadagno, 36–58. Philadelphia: Temple University Press.

> Argues that the key to the political invulnerability of Social Security is its incorporation of the middle-class elderly, giving them a stake in the program. The middle class was not fully incorporated until the program expanded to cover most workers and the benefits increased significantly in the late 1960s and early 1970s. The repeal of the Medicare Catastrophic Coverage Act shows that the middle-class elderly will fight for their own interests.

518 ROSE, NANCY E. 1985. "The Political Economy of Welfare: Social Reproduction and the Constraints on Work Relief in the 1930s." Ph.D. dissertation, University of Massachusetts. 365 pp.

> Explains why work relief was not included in the 1935 Social Security Act. Rose argues that the Federal Emergency Relief Administration violated three principles of welfare in a capitalist society, leading capitalists to block the inclusion of those programs in Social Security.

519 SANDERS, DANIEL S. 1973. *The Impact of Reform Movements on Social Policy Change*. Fairlawn, NJ: R. E. Burdick. 205 pp.

> See entry 138.

520 SCHERSCHEL, PATRICIA M. 1985. "Social Security Freeze? Facts behind the Furor." *U.S. News and World Report*. 98(3):81–82.

> Analyzes the financial status of Social Security and presents conflicting arguments behind the move to freeze Social Security benefits.

521 SCHULZ, JAMES H. 1978. "Liberalizing the Social Security Retirement Test: Who Would Receive the Increased Pension Benefits?" *Journal of Gerontology*, 33(2):262–268.

> Discusses the controversial retirement test that makes payment of benefits dependent on partial or total cessation of specified employment. Schulz suggests that considerable liberalization of the requirements could occur without benefiting the higher-income aged disproportionately.

522 ———. 1985. "To Old Folks with Love: Aged Income Maintenance in America." *Gerontologist*, 25(5):464–471.

> Reviews Social Security as an income source designed to provide stability of benefits and dignity for its recipients. Schulz asserts that because it relies on payroll taxes, the system will soon prove inadequate. He explains why private pensions and SSI could not compensate for reduced Social Security.

523   SKOCPOL, THEDA, and AMENTA, EDWIN. 1985. "Did Capitalists Shape Social
      Security?" *American Sociological Review,* 50(4):572–575.
         Challenges a previous article by Jill Quadagno, "Welfare Capitalism
      and the Social Security Act of 1935." The authors claim that Quadagno
      exaggerates the influence of big business, underestimates long-term
      labor influences, misportrays Congress as a vehicle for translating capi-
      talist interests into conservative policy, and does not provide adequate
      explanation of the establishment of old-age Social Security.

524   TYNES, SHERYL R. 1988. "Turning Points in Social Security: Explaining
      Legislative Change, 1935–1985." Ph.D. dissertation, University of Ari-
      zona. 361 pp.
         Analyzes factors that have contributed to the political success of
      Social Security. Tynes distinguishes between unique factors and histori-
      cal trends.

525   U.S. HOUSE SELECT COMMITTEE ON AGING. 1982. Cost of living adjust-
      ments under the Old Age, Survivors and Disability (Social Security) pro-
      gram. Washington, DC: U.S. Government Printing Office. 28 pp.
         Informative and concise history and summary of the effects and
      proposed changes in the social security cost-of-living adjustments
      (COLA). The report discusses the impact of price-indexing on Old Age,
      Survivors, and Disability Insurance (OASDI) beneficiaries.

526   U.S. SENATE, SPECIAL COMMITTEE ON AGING. 1985. Fifty Years of Social Se-
      curity: Past Achievements and Future Challenges. Washington, DC: U.S.
      Government Printing Office. 87 pp.
         Analyzes both the ambiguities and achievements of the social secu-
      rity system. The contributing authors present a historical perspective
      and discuss intergenerational and disability issues, labor market policy,
      and the evolving roles of women. Some international comparisons are
      included.

527   WALSH, KENNETH T. 1985. "Graying Armies March to Defend Social Secu-
      rity." *U. S. News and World Report*, 101(3):25–26.
         See entry 153.

528   WITTE, EDWIN E. 1962. *The Development of the Social Security Act*. Mad-
      ison: University of Wisconsin Press. 220 pp.
         An account by the executive director of the Committee on Eco-
      nomic Security (CES) of the committee's development of the proposal
      for Social Security and its movement through Congress. Witte reviews
      the activities of the CES, its technical board, its staff, the National Con-
      ference on Economic Security, the Advisory Council on Economic Secu-
      rity, and the congressional debates. He repeatedly notes the impact of
      the Townsend movement on congressional attitudes.

Pensions, Poverty, and Other Economic Issues

529   • 1926. "Public Pensions for Aged Dependents." *Monthly Labor Review*, 22(6):1–9.

Summarizes numerous state reports on old-age pensions. Most identify increasing life span and unemployment among the elderly, resulting from industrialization, as being responsible for a growing number of elderly on pensions. The article outlines progress of the movement for aging legislation and existing pension laws and compares pensions in various states and other countries.

530   • 1948. Inland Steel Co. v. NLRB, 170F 2d 247, 22 LRRM 2505 (CA 7, 1948).

Key federal court decision upholding a National Labor Relations Board ruling that found pensions were subject to collective bargaining.

531   ABEL, BRUCE J., and HAYSLIP, BERT, JR. 1987. "Locus of Control and Retirement Preparation." *Journal of Gerontology*, 42(2):165–167.

Small study of a retirement preparation program on the locus of control and adjustment to retirement. The interventions included a corporate program and an American Association of Retired Persons program. The authors find that retirees with retirement preparation showed higher externality of control than those without.

532   ANDREWS, JOHN B. 1923. "Progress in Old Age Pension Legislation." *American Labor Legislation Review*, 13(1):47–48.

Reviews the progress in states introducing and adopting compulsory old age pensions. Andrews mentions the advantages of pensions over poor houses, and lists types of organizations that favor pensions.

533   ANGLIM, CHRISTOPHER, and GRATTON, BRIAN. 1987. "Organized Labor and Old Age Pensions." *International Journal of Aging and Human Development*, 25(2):91–107.

Examines 1910–1920 convention proceedings of 18 state labor federations to determine whether organized labor opposed public welfare programs. Focusing on Massachusetts, the authors' analysis indicates that organized labor consistently supported state welfare programs and was instrumental in campaign efforts to establish old-age pensions. These findings demand reexamination of the traditional views of the working class and the role of organized labor in the creation of the welfare state.

534   BARFIELD, RICHARD E., and MORGAN, JAMES N. 1978. "Trends in Planned Early Retirement." *Gerontologist*, 18(1):13–18.

Repeats a Survey Research Center study by the University of Michigan to compare age patterns of contemporary plans for early retirement with those of 10 years ago. Findings seem to demonstrate that historic events have altered the position of different cohorts. Economic factors still were very important in retirement decisions but the economic history of each generation can influence choices of early retirement.

535 BERKOWITZ, EDWARD D. 1988. "Social Insurance for the Disabled and Elderly in Historical Perspective." *Educational Gerontology*, 14(5):411–418.

Presents a historical perspective on social welfare insurance for the disabled and the elderly. Berkowitz notes that the first social insurance, workmen's compensation, was to assist the disabled. Civil War veterans' pensions began as disability pensions but later became old-age pensions. Benefits for the elderly were largely state and local responsibilities until the early twentieth century. The author contends that old age benefits continue to be more secure than disability entitlements.

536 BORZILLERI, THOMAS C. 1978. "The Need for a Separate Consumer Price Index for Older Persons: A Review and New Evidence." *Gerontologist*, 18(3):230–236.

Questions the adequacy of the consumer price index (CPI) in reflecting accurately the purchasing power of the elderly. The author notes that the CPI is not a cost-of-living index. Using data from the Bureau of Labor Statistics from 1960–1973, he finds prices increased 4 percent faster for the elderly than is reflected in the CPI. Medical care expenses showed the most significant increase for this group.

537 BRIDGES, BENJAMIN, JR., and PACKARD, MICHAEL D. 1981. "Price and Income Changes for the Elderly." *Social Security Bulletin*, 44(1):3–15.

Assesses the impact of inflation on the resources of the elderly. The market basket of goods and services used by the elderly rose at a rate higher than the economywide index during the 1970s, largely because of medical inflation. The income of the elderly rose between 1970 and 1974, then fell from 1974 to 1977, probably because of increases in early retirement.

538 BUREAU OF NATIONAL AFFAIRS, INC. 1978. *1978 Age Discrimination Act Amendments*. Washington, DC: Bureau of National Affairs. 130 pp.

Explains the 1978 Age Discrimination Act Amendments that prohibited mandatory retirement before age 70. Includes the conference report, text of the act, and House and Senate committee reports.

539 BURKE, VINCENT J., and BURKE, VEE. 1974. *Nixon's Good Deed: Welfare Reform*. New York: Columbia University Press. 243 pp.

Focuses on President Nixon's attempts to change the welfare system. During the debate, most attention centered on a guaranteed annual family income, a proposal contested by unions, social workers, Congress, and business. The authors claim that Supplemental Security Income passed with little notice among major players because of controversy over the other aspects of Nixon's proposals.

540 BURKHAUSER, RICHARD V., and TOLLEY, GORDON S. 1978. "Older Americans and Market Work." *Gerontologist*, 18(5):449–453.

Suggests that the ending of mandatory retirement will have little impact on employment levels of older Americans. The authors recommend a policy format that will provide greater options for work in later years. They take a dim view of the Social Security retirement test.

541 CALIFANO, JOSEPH A., JR. 1978. "The Aging of America: Questions for the Four-Generation Society." *Annals of the American Academy of Political and Social Science*, 438:96–107.

The then-Secretary of Health, Education and Welfare calls for new policies and ideas to address issues arising from the "graying" of the federal budget. He examines trends toward early retirement and its economic impact. Califano questions whether Medicare and Medicaid have the potential to keep up with spiraling health care costs and explores methods for greater federal support to family caregiving.

542 CAMPBELL, SHIRLEY. 1979. "Delayed Mandatory Retirement and the Working Woman." *Gerontologist*, 19(3):257–263.

Focuses on the long-range effects on women workers of the 1978 legislation raising the mandatory retirement age from 65 to 70. While most of the discussion emphasizes the impact on male workers, equally profound consequences apply to women employees. One such consequence might be more flexibility for those women whose careers began in middle life.

543 CANTRELL, STEPHEN R., and CLARK, ROBERT L. 1980. "Retirement Policy and Promotional Aspects." *Gerontologist*, 20(5):515–580.

Reviews the Age Discrimination Act amendments of 1978 that prohibited job discrimination because of age until age 70. Using an age-structure model, the authors demonstrate that raising the mandatory retirement age will slow the pace of promotion only slightly.

544 CARP, FRANCES M. 1972. "The Mobility of Older Slum-Dwellers." *Gerontologist*, 12(1):57–65.

Surveys older persons who live in slums and those who live elsewhere to determine the causes of different transportation patterns. The elderly poor tend to stay within their own neighborhood and have greatest contact with family members. The neighborhood focus is attributed more to the lack of inexpensive and convenient transportation than to cultural preferences.

545 CLAGUE, EWAN. 1940. "The Aging Population and Programs of Security." *Milbank Memorial Fund Quarterly*, 18(4):345–358.

Describes dependency and unemployment among the elderly and the implications of this for public welfare programs. Clague discusses three types of old-age support: public assistance based on need, public pensions, and private pensions. He concludes that private pensions are the best means of providing support. He considers unemployment of older workers to be largely a result of industrialization. To counter this, older workers should be retrained in joint public and private programs.

546   CLARK, ROBERT L., and BAUMER, DAVID L. 1985. "Income Maintenance Policies." In *Handbook of Aging and the Social Sciences* (2nd ed.), edited by Robert H. Binstock and Ethel Shanas, 666–695. New York: Van Nostrand.

Describes public and private income maintenance policies and their effect on the income and retirement decisions of the elderly and on the national economy. The authors show that the real income of the elderly has risen in the past 20 years, primarily because of government programs.

547   CLARK, ROBERT L., and SUMNER, DANIEL A. 1985. "Inflation and the Real Income of the Elderly: Recent Evidence and Expectations for the Future." *Gerontologist*, 25(2):146–152.

Examines the impact of the inflationary period of the 1970s on the real income of the elderly. The authors report the findings of the Retirement History Study conducted for the Social Security Administration in 1969. The results show that general inflation will have only minor impact on the well-being of the elderly compared with persons in other demographic groups, and that most sources of income of the elderly rise in response to increasing prices.

548   CLEMENT, PRISCILLA FERGUSON. 1985. "History of United States Aged's Poverty Shows Welfare Program Changes." *Perspectives on Aging*, 14(2):20–23.

Traces the history, from the colonial era to the present, of programs to aid the indigent aged, highlighting the disruptions in that aid. Clement presents Social Security as the most efficient anti-poverty program and asserts that it is subject to fewer flaws than welfare programs designed only to assist the poor.

549   CONYNGTON, MARY. 1926. "Industrial Pensions for Old Age and Disability." *Monthly Labor Review,* 22(1):21–56.

Describes the growth and extent of private pension systems. Conyngton discusses types, purposes, and features of private pension plans. The article provides the date the pension plan was established, the number of employees included, the source of funds, and benefit amounts for over 100 private companies. There is an extensive discussion of various features of pension plans, employer and employee attitudes toward pensions, and the value of private pensions.

550   COOK, FAY LOMAX, and KRAMEK, LORRAINE M. 1986. "Measuring Economic Hardship among Older Americans." *Gerontologist,* 26(1):38–47.

Reports a telephone survey of 1,422 elderly Chicago residents to examine the status of food, housing, and access to medical care. Focusing on the use of the poverty level to measure hardship, the authors found that elderly respondents were no more likely to suffer hardship than adults of other ages, perhaps because of the success of existing federal social programs.

551 CUMMINGS, FRANK. 1974. "Reforming Private Pensions." *Annals of the American Academy of Political and Social Sciences*, 415(September):80–94.

Reviews the structure of private pensions and the ways the 1974 pension reform bill would eliminate some of the problems with them. Cummings identifies the major problems as underfunding, lack of vesting rights, no portability, and overfunding.

552 CUTLER, NEAL E. 1981. "The Aging Population and Social Policy." In *Aging: Prospects and Issues* (3rd ed.), edited by Richard Davis, 236–259. Los Angeles: University of Southern California Press.

Examines the dynamics of changing demographics and how they influence sociopolitical trends. The interconnectedness of these two is often overlooked or misunderstood. Cutler uses the issue of changing retirement patterns to illustrate the link between demographics and sociopolitical trends. Dependency ratios are examined.

553 DENTZER, SUSAN. 1989. "The People Tax Reform Left Behind." *U.S. News and World Report*, 106(15):24–25.

Describes the inequity in the 1986 federal income tax simplification that taxes high-paid professionals at a higher rate than the group with the greatest income. Dentzer argues that the elderly with large incomes are affected most adversely by the reform.

554 DONNELLY, HARRISON. 1981. "Employment Past Age 65: Hard to Sell." *Congressional Quarterly Weekly Report*, 39(48):2335.

Discusses possible effects of eliminating mandatory retirement on the basis of age.

555 EPSTEIN, ABRAHAM. 1928. *The Challenge of the Aged.* New York: Vanguard. 435 pp.

Examines the problems of old-age dependency caused by increasing longevity and employment discrimination in industry. Epstein discusses the inadequate provision for the aged of charity and pensions. He reviews congressional bills to establish national pensions and state laws that have instituted state-level pensions. He also briefly describes pension systems in other countries.

556 ———. 1938. *Insecurity, a Challenge to America, a Study of Social Insurance in the United States and Abroad* (2nd ed., rev.). New York: Random House. 939 pp.

Comprehensive overview of the need for federal social insurance for unemployment, illness, old age, disability, and widowhood by a leader in the movement for U.S. social insurance. Epstein argues that the absence of strong unions in the United States has contributed to the lack of worker protections. First published in 1933, the 1938 edition includes a critique of the limitations of the 1935 Social Security Act. The author reviews data on the economic insecurity and dependency of the aged and the limited public and private provisions for them. He discusses the variations in state-level pension programs and contributory pension programs in other nations. He provides an extensive summary of the deliberations of the Committee on Economic Security concerning development of the proposal for Social Security. Epstein critiques elements of the way Social Security programs were implemented, especially the lack of general revenues in the pension program.

557 FESSLER, PAMELA. 1981. "Tax Incentives for Savings." *Congressional Quarterly Weekly Report*, 39(48):2336.

Very brief discussion of tax incentives for retirement savings.

558 FESSLER, PAMELA, and DONNELLY, HARRISON. 1981. "Congress Seeking to Assure Retirement Income Security." *Congressional Quarterly Weekly Report*, 39(48):2333–2334,2336.

Discusses the failure of Social Security, private pensions, and retirement savings plans to provide retirement income. The authors consider congressional attempts to deal with these shortcomings.

559 FILLENBAUM, GERDA C.; GEORGE, LINDA K.; and PALMORE, ERDMAN B. 1985. "Determinants and Consequences of Retirement among Men of Different Races and Economic Levels." *Journal of Gerontology,* 40(1):85–94.

Criticizes current retirement policies, "which support those at the ends of the economic spectrum" but provide little aid to the "marginal man" who must rely on enforced saving and limited pension income. Alternative pension formats are discussed.

560 FOLSOM, JOSEPH K. 1940. "Old Age as a Sociological Problem." *American Journal of Orthopsychiatry,* 10(1):30–39.

Reviews the existing data on the increasing numbers of elderly, their decreasing employment, and their sources of economic support, political activity, and attitudes. Folsom describes the ways American values affect the aged, suggests directions for social action, and outlines needed research.

561 FREEMAN, RICHARD B. 1985. "Unions, Pensions, and Union Pension Funds." In *Pensions, Labor, and Individual Choice,* edited by D. A. Wise, 89–121. Chicago: University of Chicago Press.

An economic analysis of the effect of unions on pensions, using models of unions as a collective voice and as a monopoly power. Freeman finds that unions give greater weight to the preferences (voice) of older, relatively permanent employees as shown by the structure and benefits of union pensions compared to private nonunion pensions.

562   GILLIN, JOHN LEWIS. 1926. *Poverty and Dependency: Their Relief and Prevention*. New York: Century. 836 pp.

  Written as a college text, the book provides a historical perspective on the social problems of poverty and dependency. Chapters deal with the economic, social, and political aspects of problems. Part IV addresses the special needs of the dependent aged. Savings for old age, almshouses, care by relatives, boarding homes, insurance, and industrial and public service pensions are among the topics considered. The author concludes by advocating a national noncontributory old-age pension plan and humane care for the elderly poor.

563   GLASSON, WILLIAM H. 1900. *History of Military Pension Legislation in the United States*. New York: Columbia University Press. 135 pp.

  Provides a detailed history and statistics of national military pensions from 1776 to 1899. The political context of each pension bill is discussed. The first national pensions were for Revolutionary War officers and all service disabled veterans. Coverage was later added for indigent veterans, widows, and survivors. Subsequent wars led to other pensions. The author details the lobbying of veterans for more and increased pensions, claiming that budget surpluses and the legitimacy of veterans made pensions popular. He details many abuses and administrative problems.

564   ———. 1904. "A Costly Pension Law—Act of June 27, 1890." *South Atlantic Quarterly*, 3(4):361–369.

  Historic article that describes legislation granting Civil War pensions on the basis of disability not directly related to military service. Glasson criticizes the extravagance and generosity of the pension system, which did not discriminate on the basis of length of service and ability or inability to perform manual labor. He lists yearly pension expenditures for 1891–1904 and concludes that the pension law is an unnecessary public expense for the privileged class.

565   ———. 1918. *Federal Military Pensions in the United States*. New York: Oxford University Press. 305 pp.

  Examines the political, economic, and moral consequences of federal military pensions, with additional information on their administration. Glasson reviews pension laws chronologically from 1776 to 1917. He notes that interests supporting military pensions include veterans and the politicians courting their votes, pension attorneys and claims agents, employees of the pension bureaucracy, and industries that benefited from the high tariffs that generated surplus revenues to pay the pensions. He discusses the activities of the Grand Army of the Republic and the unrelated, privately published *National Tribune* in lobbying for increased pensions. The book is well indexed.

566   GORDON, MARGARET S. 1960. "The Older Worker and Retirement Policies." *Monthly Labor Review*, 83(6):577–585.

  Analyzes the attitudes and practices of large and small firms in the

San Francisco Bay Area toward employment of older workers. Most large firms have involuntary retirement policies, which were influenced by the presence or absence of pension plans and union policy. Gordon lists the rationales given by large firms in favor of involuntary retirement. Most small firms have voluntary retirement practices and exhibited greater flexibility toward loss of productivity among older workers. The author concludes that structural and economic factors, as well as employer attitudes, are important determinants of retirement policy.

567   GRAEBNER, WILLIAM. 1980. *The History of Retirement. The Meaning and Function of an American Institution, 1885–1978.* New Haven, CT: Yale University Press. 293 pp.

Traces the course of American capitalism to describe major events in the history of retirement. The work reflects the important interplay between public policy, private employment, and individual worker expectations. It includes an extensive review of the legislative changes in the 1970s at which time every level of government began to review various retirement institutions. The author cautions about the costs of eliminating mandatory retirement.

568   GRATTON, BRIAN. 1987. "The Labor Force Participation of Older Men: 1890–1950." *Journal of Social History,* 20(4):689–710.

An analysis of census data on labor force participation rates (LFPR) of U.S. males age 65+ for the years 1890, 1930, and 1950 and changes in LFPR for 1890–1930 and 1930–1950. Challenging the common historical explanation that structural change was the result of the shift from an agricultural to an industrial economy, the findings suggest that racial and ethnic factors played a role in LFPR and that the Social Security Act provided an incentive for retirement by older workers.

569   GRIMALDI, PAUL L. 1982. "Measured Inflation and the Elderly: 1973–1981." *Gerontologist,* 22(4):347–353.

Challenges the belief that the national consumer price index (CPI) understates the impact of inflation on the elderly. The results of Grimaldi's study showed no difference in the inflation experienced by the elderly and the general population. The author states that growth in home ownership costs after 1977 may have resulted in the aged being overcompensated by Social Security's indexing benefits.

570   HENDERSON, CHARLES R. 1908. *Industrial Insurance in the United States.* Chicago: University of Chicago Press. 429 pp.

Analyzes the development of industrial insurance. Henderson identifies the nature of the demand for industrial insurance and analyzes the benefits offered by the trade unions and fraternal societies such as the National Fraternal Congress and the Associated Fraternities of America. He examines the role of private insurance companies in providing burial and casualty insurance for employees and shows that railroad companies promote industrial insurance by assuming the entire cost of old-age pensions. The author reports mechanisms for providing insurance for municipal workers and teachers and details the paucity of coverage for police, firemen, and educators. He concludes that an American "social policy" is lacking and that our social philosophy of individualism has limited progress on this front. Henderson proposes expansion of federal constitutional powers to provide a national insurance law.

571 KAHNE, HILDA. 1985. "Not Yet Equal: Employment Experience of Older Women and Older Men." *International Journal of Aging and Human Development,* 22(1):1–13.

Identifies the many disadvantages experienced by the older woman worker. Kahne notes that women aged 45 and over make up nearly 30 percent of the female labor force and 40 percent of the older labor force. She urges affirmative action at the federal level and better employment counseling.

572 KAPLAN, KENNETH M., and LONGINO, CHARLES F., JR. 1991. "Gray in Gold: A Public-Private Conundrum." In *Growing Old in America* (4th ed.), edited by Beth B. Hess and Elizabeth W. Markson, 389–398. New Brunswick, NJ: Transaction.

Argues that the discovery of the elderly as a market by business is mostly positive. The authors critique Minkler's (1989) essay that warned of the problems of this discovery. They emphasize the diversity in wealth and needs of the aged.

573 KING, FRANCIS P. 1982. "Indexing Retirement Benefits." *Gerontologist,* 22(6):488–492.

Overview of the primary ways that postretirement pension adjustments are made in response to inflation and the financial implications of those methods. King notes that most public but few private pensions have automatic index-related pension increases. Only federal pensions typically provide open-ended adjustments tied to the consumer price index.

574 KIRCHNER, WAYNE K., and DUNNETTE, MARVIN D. 1954. "Survey of Union Policy toward Older Workers." *Journal of Personnel Administration and Industrial Relations,* 1(3):156–158.

Results of a Minneapolis-St. Paul study to determine union attitudes toward issues raised by the increasing proportion of older workers. There is significant disagreement among unions concerning the desirability of mandatory retirement. Most unions focus on pension plans, seniority clauses, and death benefits as the primary means of supporting the older worker. The authors conclude that the unions' lack of flexibility and failure to consider psychological problems of older workers facing retirement limit their effectiveness in aiding the older worker.

575 KOSTERLITZ, JULIE. 1986. "Getting Out Early." *National Journal,*
     18(40):2374–2378.
         Reviews the causes and consequences of early retirement. Causes
     include available pensions, employer incentives related to work force
     reductions, and age discrimination. Consequences include possibly
     lower income for the individual and the loss of skills, workers, and taxes
     for society during a period when there are fewer young people entering
     the work force. The article reviews congressional proposals.

576 LASLETT, PETER. 1985. "Societal Development and Aging." In *Handbook
     of Aging and the Social Sciences* (2nd ed.), edited by Robert H. Binstock
     and Ethel Shanas, 199–230. New York: Van Nostrand.
         Presents historical data from England, the United States, and else-
     where to argue that the position of the elderly in the family has changed
     little from its status in preindustrial Western societies. The author
     claims that if the elderly are a policy problem, it is because of their in-
     crease in numbers rather than a change in their situation.

577 LAZER, WILLIAM. 1985. "Inside the Mature Market." *American Demo-
     graphics,* 7(3):22–27.
         Challenges the perception that older Americans are a poor market.
     Lazer divides the mature market into four different market segments
     and explores the demographics of each segment, identifying products
     appropriate to each. He reports that mature consumers currently head
     one-third of all households with discretionary incomes and concludes
     with possible changes in purchasing patterns resulting from increasing
     proportions of older people who are college educated.

578 LEBRUN, HARVEY. 1936. "Evolution of the American Pension System,
     1883–1936." *Sociology and Social Research,* 20(5):453–462.
         Describes early pension plans provided by states and local govern-
     ments from 1883 to 1936. Most pensions during this period were for the
     institutionalized or needy elderly. Lebrun shows that early pension ef-
     forts were plagued by inadequate financing and ambiguous legislation.
     More effective pension programs resulted from state supervision and
     mandatory financing requirements for pension programs. The author
     identifies trends in early pension legislation.

579 LICHTIG, ALLISON. 1982. "Older Unemployed Suffer Most." *Perspective
     on Aging,* 11(6):11–12,18.
         Summarizes findings of a study by the House Select Committee on
     Aging, which reveals that unemployment for workers 55+ rose by 24
     percent in 1982, compared with 16 percent for all age groups. Issues of
     age discrimination and a 76 percent increase in age discrimination suits
     are discussed. The author offers recommendations for new legislation
     in areas such as pension portability and job retraining.

580 LINDSEY, FRED D. 1957. "Expanding Markets: The Oldsters." *Nation's Business,* 45(11):38–39,87.

Early examination of the economic implications of the growing number of elderly in the population. Although the elderly lack the earning potential of younger people, their financial resources still provide substantial purchasing power. Lindsey discusses geographic location, family status, and financial resources of the elderly.

581 LINFORD, ALTON. 1949. *Old Age Assistance in Massachusetts.* Chicago: University of Chicago Press. 418 pp.

Reports a study that examines the origin, growth, and development of the old-age assistance (OAA) program in Massachusetts, the first state to study and research an old-age assistance law. Full documentary materials are cited from the law's initial inception in 1903 to enactment of the law in 1930. The organization for administration, criteria for eligibility, and other standards are presented. Mechanisms for standards of assistance and for financing the program are defined. The author notes that the OAA in Massachusetts was ultimately over five times more expensive than had been expected at its inception. The book contains many charts and graphs comparing Massachusetts's programs to those of other states.

582 McCONNEL, CHARLES E., and DELJAVAN, FIROOZ. 1983. "Consumption Patterns of the Retired Household." *Journal of Gerontology,* 38(4):480–490.

Examines consumption patterns of retired and employed elderly using the 1972–73 Bureau of Labor Statistics Consumer Expenditure Survey. The study shows that marginal health care expenditures, transportation costs, and gifts and donations are as high or higher for the retired, while costs for clothing and food away from home decline. Overall, marginal spending on necessities remains constant.

583 McEADDY, BEVERLY J. 1975. "Women in the Labor Force: The Later Years." *Monthly Labor Review.* 98:17–24.

Examines the decline in labor force participation by women 55 and over during the first half of the 1970s. From 1950 to 1974, these women accounted for only one-third of the growth in the total number of women 55 and over, but they represented four-fifths of the women's labor force growth. Data on marital and household status, unemployment, types of occupations, educational attainment, income, and retirement benefits are presented. The author notes that in 1973 the proportion of families headed by women 55 and over living below the poverty line was twice as high as the proportion headed by men.

584 McMURRY, DONALD L. 1922. "The Political Significance of the Pension Question, 1885–1897." *Mississippi Valley Historical Review,* 9(1):19–36.

See entry 337.

585   McWILLIAMS, CAREY. 1949. "Pension Politics in California." *Nation,*
      169(14):320–322.
      See entry 112.

586   MINKLER, MEREDITH. 1989. "Gold in Gray: Reflections on Business' Dis-
      covery of the Elderly Market." *Gerontologist,* 29(1):17–23.
      Explores the pros and cons of the sudden interest of the business
      community in the elderly market. The privatization of care and services
      for the elderly has helped fuel the growth in products in the aging mar-
      ket. Minkler discusses concepts of mainstreaming, consumerism, and
      the geriatric "social industrial complex." She shows that mainstreaming
      can give visibility and legitimacy to the elderly and potentially change
      societal attitudes toward elderly people; however, targeting the elderly
      as consumers may lead to distorted perceptions of their financial status
      and negatively impact support for needed public services for this group.

587   MINKLER, MEREDITH, and STONE, ROBYN I. 1985. "The Feminization of
      Poverty and Older Women." *Gerontologist,* 25(4):351–357.
      Discusses the triple jeopardy of being old, poor, and female. The
      authors find women overrepresented in secondary sector industries. El-
      derly women's poverty rate is the highest of all age groups and in 1980
      half of all older women had annual incomes below $5,000. Federal and
      state budget cuts and changes in work-force trends could worsen the
      older women's plight.

588   MOON, MARILYN. 1986. "Impact of the Reagan Years on the Distribution
      of Income of the Elderly." *Gerontologist,* 26(1):32–37.
      Examines the economic status of the elderly during 1980–1984. Ris-
      ing asset income and Social Security increased the inflation-adjusted
      disposable income of older individuals 9.8 percent: 11.5 percent for the
      highest income quintile and 7.4 percent for the lowest income quintile.
      This shift increased income inequality among the aged. Social Security
      indexing and tax cuts helped the elderly feel federal budget cuts less
      than other age groups.

589   MORGAN, JAMES N. 1977. "The Ethical Basis of the Economic Claims of
      the Elderly." In *Social Policy, Social Ethics, and the Aging Society,* ed-
      ited by Bernice L. Neugarten and Robert J. Havighurst, 67–68. Washing-
      ton, DC: U.S. Government Printing Office.
      Argues that there is no basic economic impossibility in providing
      adequately for the aged in industrial societies. The demands on the
      economy by the aged should be seen as deferred earnings that were
      diverted into economic growth (business investments and profits) dur-
      ing the working years of the elderly.

590   MORRIS, ROBERT, and BASS, SCOTT A. 1988. "A New Class in America: A
      Revisionist View of Retirement." *Social Policy,* 18:38–43.
      Describes the increasing number of retired but healthy elderly who

can continue to contribute to society. The authors explain that many retired people want to continue to engage in productive activities, and they suggest ways to utilize this new group.

591 MORRISON, MALCOLM H. 1976. "Planning for Income Adequacy in Retirement: The Expectations of Current Workers." *Gerontologist,* 16(6):538–543.

Surveys 588 employees (male hourly wage earners) to ascertain retirement income needs. The study shows that employees are not saving and that they hold unrealistic expectations about supplementary pension benefits. Morrison recommends adoption of preretirement programs to help workers begin planning 10 to 15 years before retirement.

592 ———. 1986. "Work and Retirement in an Older Society." In *Our Aging Society: Paradox or Promise?,* edited by Alan Pifer and Lydia Bronte, 341–365. New York: Norton.

Asserts that a new concept of retirement that acknowledges "a productive life stage between middle and older age" is tomorrow's social imperative. The author urges a reexamination of current attitudes and practices to achieve a social consensus.

593 MYLES, JOHN F. 1989. *Old Age in the Welfare State: The Political Economy of Public Pensions* (Rev. ed.). Lawrence: University of Kansas Press. 162 pp.

Argues that the economic well-being of the aged is the result of a political process in which the relative power of the working class is the most important factor. The book is a study of international differences in the "retirement wage," that is, the income provided to the elderly that corresponds to their preretirement wage. Myles tests various theories of welfare state development with cross-national data on pension quality (level, distribution, and accessibility). The revised 1989 edition of the book has a new chapter reviewing scholarship of the 1980s on the topic and reaffirming the author's class analysis.

594 NICHOLSON, TOM. 1985. "Early-Retirement Binge." *Newsweek,* 105(18):55.

Suggests that early-retirement inducements being offered by many major corporations such as DuPont, Caterpillar Tractor, and certain California aerospace companies do not allow employees adequate time for preretirement planning.

595 OLIVER, JOHN WILLIAM. 1917. *History of the Civil War Military Pensions, 1861–1885.* Bulletin No. 844, History Series, vol. 4, no. 1. Madison: University of Wisconsin Press. 120 pp.

Details the development of Civil War military pensions. Oliver explains the importance of pensions as an incentive for enlistment during the war. Subsequent benefits were shaped by the political power of pension agents and pensioners after the war. The author describes the political efforts of the Grand Army of the Republic and its newspaper to influence pension legislation and elections. He discusses the politicization of the Pension Bureau in the successful efforts of a Republican administration to increase its share of the veteran vote.

596 ORLOFF, ANN S. 1985. "The Politics of Pensions: A Comparative Analysis of the Origins of Pensions and Old Age Insurance in Canada, Great Britain and the United States, 1880s–1930s." Ph.D. dissertation, Princeton University. 339 pp.

Examines the contribution of changes in social demand and political structures to explain policy outcomes. The author argues that the move from poor laws to modern pensions was a result of elite sponsorship and state administrative capacity rather than popular pressure or other forces.

597 OSSOFSKY, JACK. 1985. "Trade Deficit, Loss of Jobs in US: An Older Worker Problem." *Perspective on Aging,* 14(5):17–18.

Reviews congressional testimony indicating that over five million workers who had lost jobs since 1980 were 55 or over. The large number of plant closings and moves and the attendant loss of pensions is attributed to the U.S. trade deficit. The author presents a legislative agenda for displaced workers proposed by the National Council on Aging.

598 PALMORE, ERDMAN B. 1972. "Compulsory versus Flexible Retirement: Issues and Facts." *Gerontologist,* 12(4):343–348.

Notes that current compulsory retirement policies affect about one-half the male wage and salary workers retiring at age 65. The pros and cons of forced retirement are discussed and various proposals for flexible retirement are suggested.

599 PARKER, FLORENCE E. 1934. "Experience under State Old-Age Pension Acts in 1933." *Monthly Labor Review,* 39(2):255–272.

Describes state pension systems in 1933. Tendencies show increased legislation and reduction of actual pension operations because of limited funds. Parker identifies increases and decreases in the number of pensioners and number of counties participating in state pension programs. She describes existing pension systems in various states and compares their development, cost, and average benefits.

600 POLNER, WALTER. 1962. "The Aged in Politics: A Successful Example of the NPA and the Passage of the Railroad Retirement Act of 1934." *Gerontologist,* 2:207–215.

See entry 126.

601 PUTNAM, JACKSON K. 1970. *Old-Age Politics in California.* Stanford, CA: Stanford University Press. 211 pp.

See entry 130.

602 QUADAGNO, JILL S. 1984. "From Poor Laws to Pensions: The Evolution of Economic Support for the Aged in England and America." *Milbank Memorial Fund Quarterly,* 62(3):417–446.

Historical account of the economic support for the elderly in England and the United States. The author describes England's Poor Laws and early colonial law that recognized state responsibility to care for the indigent. Wars and social changes in the eighteenth century created increasing numbers of poor and the need for additional public relief. Social movements in the nineteenth century differentiated among various categories of the poor and resulted in more specific legislation and relief programs. The author discusses the establishment and growth of the pension concept and development of Social Security. She concludes that there has been a gradual transformation from local, informal provisions for old-age security to extensive state- and federal-based provisions.

603 ———. 1986. "The Transformation of Old Age Security." In *Old Age in a Bureaucratic Society: The Elderly, the Experts and the State in American History,* edited by Donald Van Tassel and Phillip Stearns, 129–155. New York: Greenwood Press.

Traces the history of social relief from colonial times to the present. Social Security is described as a complex mixture of various types of welfare systems including the nineteenth-century poor laws.

604 ———. 1988. *The Transformation of Old Age Security.* Chicago: University of Chicago Press. 266 pp.

Detailed social history of U.S. pensions from the 1800s to the 1970s. The author shows how the poor laws were transformed into old-age pensions. Factors shaping the transition include the power held by private industry, differences between mass-production workers and craft workers, and conflict between the economic needs of the planter economy in the South and the industrial economy in the North. Local control of old-age relief benefited the South in keeping blacks bound to agriculture, while public pensions benefited the North by absorbing federal budget surpluses created by protectionist industrial tariffs. Although the primary actors were organized labor and big business, the Townsend movement catalyzed the adoption of Social Security. The author discusses the political context and battles between labor and business over the expansion of Social Security and private pensions after World War II.

605 QUADAGNO, JILL S., and MEYER, MADONNA HARRINGTON. 1989. "Organized Labor, State Structures, and Social Policy Development: A Case Study of Old Age Assistance in Ohio, 1916–1940." *Social Problems,* 36(2):181–196.

See entry 132.

606 ———. 1990. "Gender and Public Policy." *Generations,* 14(3):64–66.

Argues that benefit rules are political decisions and not the "inevitable consequence of inexorable forces." The authors evaluate public old-age pensions, noting that Social Security disregards household labor. Women's access to private pensions varies widely. When women are covered they receive less than men. When family status allows them income, many pension systems pay only half benefit to widows. The authors suggest that women be fully credited for their nonmarket labor and that private pensions be equalized between men and women.

607   QUINN, JOSEPH F. 1981. "The Extent and Correlates of Partial Retirement." *Gerontologist,* 21(6):634–643.

Analyzes the longitudinal Retirement History Study (1969–1979). Partial retirement for the self-employed was predominant while only 5 percent of wage and salary respondents considered themselves partially retired. The author suggests that part-time arrangements could reduce demands on social security.

608   RENO, VIRGINIA. 1971. "Why Men Stop Working at or before Age 65: Findings from the Survey of New Beneficiaries." *Social Security Bulletin,* 34:3–17.

Reports results of the survey of newly entitled beneficiaries conducted in 1968 by the Office of Research and Statistics. Declining health was found to be the major factor for claiming Social Security benefits prior to age 65. Compulsory retirement policies were the primary reason those over 65 claimed Social Security benefits. Only two in five of this latter group reported wanting to retire.

609   RICH, SPENCER. 1983. "Survey Shows Elderly Exceeded Average Income." *Washington Post,* August 19:A1ff.

From a census report that finds the elderly better off than previously believed and paying the lowest tax rate of any group. The article predicts that these findings will be used in the battles over Social Security and Medicare.

610   RONES, PHILIP L. 1978. "Older Men—The Choice between Work and Retirement." *Monthly Labor Review,* 101:3–10.

Focuses on older men who continue to work after retirement. Factors such as race, health, sources of retirement income, job satisfaction, number of dependents, and local unemployment conditions are considered. The author concludes that as fewer young persons enter the job market and the growing elderly population increases the burden on the nation's major retirement systems, incentives may have to be developed to encourage older persons to continue to work.

611   SCHIEBER, SYLVESTER. 1982. "Trends in Pension Coverage and Benefit Receipts." *Gerontologist,* 22(6):474–481.

Examines the historical growth of private pensions from 1950 to 1980. Using data from the Employee Benefit Research Institute (EBRI). The author claims that the 1981 Economic Recovery Tax Act with its expanded tax incentives for retirement savings will enhance the role of private provision for retirement. Further Social Security policy options will be affected by these components of the retirement system.

612 SCHILLER, BRADLEY R., and SNYDER, DONALD C. 1982. "Restrictive Pension Provisions and the Older Worker." *Gerontologist,* 22(6):482–487.

Examines requirements of private pensions that encouraged earlier retirement in medium and large firms in 1974. Almost half of private pensions had a mandatory retirement, half would not accrue pension credits after age 65, and one quarter barred pensioners from working for another company. Almost all pensions contained at least one type of restrictive provision.

613 SCHULZ, JAMES H. 1982. "Inflation's Challenge to Aged Income Security." *Gerontologist,* 22(2):115–116.

Highlights the impact of inflation on the near-poor aged. Schulz suggests that full indexing of Social Security plus Supplemental Security Income, federal pensions, and food stamps help provide protection. He recommends government policy shifts to greater dependence on private pensions to make these government programs more helpful.

614 SCHULZ, JAMES H., and MYLES, JOHN F. 1990. "Old Age Pensions: A Comparative Perspective." In *Handbook of Aging and the Social Sciences* (3rd ed.), edited by Robert H. Binstock and Linda K. George, 398–414. San Diego: Academic Press.

Examines the history of public and employer pensions as a response to the economic needs of the aged and the debates over social assistance versus social insurance approaches. The authors provide comparative international data.

615 SMEEDING, TIMOTHY M. 1986. "Nonmoney Income and the Elderly: The Case of the 'Tweeners.'" *Journal of Policy Analysis and Management,* 5(4):707–724.

Analyzes 1980 census data to show that the most economically vulnerable elderly have incomes between 100 and 200 percent of the federal poverty line. This group does not benefit from programs for the poor from tax breaks for the wealthier. The elderly overall are shown to be no less vulnerable to inflation than are those in other age groups.

616 SQUIER, LEE WELLING. 1912. *Old Age Dependency in the United States.* New York: Macmillan. 361 pp.

Details the causes of old-age dependency and the limitations of private pensions in providing economic security in old age. Squier reviews the provisions of most existing private and public pension programs and charity relief for the aged in the country. He concludes that the average worker is too poor to save or purchase an annuity and that service pensions should be provided.

617 TREAS, JUDITH. 1986. "The Historical Decline in Late Life Labor Force Par-
     ticipation in the United States." In *Age, Health, and Employment,* ed-
     ited by James E Birren, Pauline K. Robinson, and Judy E. Livingston,
     158–175. Englewood Cliffs, NJ: Prentice-Hall.

     Argues that 1890–1920 declines in labor force participation of the
     elderly were a result of industrialization of the economy and not Civil
     War military pensions. Treas discusses the evolution and scope of Civil
     War pensions. She analyzes labor-force trends for the elderly between
     1890 and 1920 and compares the level of industrialization in states to
     declines in employment of elderly men. She concludes that institution-
     alization of retirement is due to industrialization of the economy.

618 U.S. DEPARTMENT OF LABOR. 1929. *Care of Aged Persons in the United
     States.* Bulletin of the United States Bureau of Labor Statistics, No. 489.
     Washington, DC: U.S. Government Printing Office. 310 pp.

     Exhaustive review of retirement and pension plans in the United
     States, including public, labor, and private sponsors as well as alms-
     houses. The report includes extensive documentation of old-age homes
     sponsored by unions, religious organizations, fraternal organizations,
     nationality groups, and public agencies.

619 UEHARA, EDWINA S.; GERON, SCOTT; and BEEMAN, SANDRA K. 1986. "The
     Elderly Poor in the Reagan Era." *Gerontologist,* 26(1):48–55.

     Reports a study of Chicago public-aid recipients in 1983, examining
     cash and in-kind benefits, and describes the losses caused by policy
     changes in cash benefits, health care, and food programs. The authors
     find that Supplemental Security Income (SSI) frequently fails to provide
     a "safety net" when other programs experience cutbacks and show that
     the elderly are lacking in both formal and informal supports. They urge
     policymakers to consider ramifications of policy changes and to provide
     greater assistance to the vulnerable elderly.

620 WAITE, EDWARD F. 1893. "Pensions: The Law and Its Administration."
     Harper's New Monthly Magazine, 86(512):236–243.

     Describes the pension legislation of the 51st Congress showing
     that pensions constitute the chief item in the nation's budget. Waite ex-
     plains the qualifications and amounts of benefits offered and discusses
     problems of fraudulent claims and pension administration. He con-
     cludes, "In the unparalleled munificence of our pension system there
     lurk serious evils."

621 WALKER, ALAN. 1980. "The Social Creation of Poverty and Dependency in
     Old Age." *Journal of Social Policy,* 9(1):49–75.

     Examines the ways in which social policies contribute to poverty
     and dependency in old age. Walker claims that retirement is a primary
     cause and that government policies reinforce inequality in the labor
     force and devalue the retired. He argues that policies treat symptoms
     rather than causes.

622 ———. 1981. "Toward a Political Economy of Old Age." *Aging and Society,* 1(1):73–94.

Challenges the functionalist theory of aging that contributes to the perception of the elderly as a distinct and homogeneous group with special needs. Walker proposes an approach to aging based on political economy to explore the differential impact of social processes on the elderly. He explores dependent status as a social creation and examines the socioeconomic conditions leading to a depressed economic and social status among the elderly. The author concludes that most poverty among the aged results from two factors: low socioeconomic status prior to retirement and the increased reduction in social status that can be attributed to retirement.

623 WATSON, WILBUR H. 1986. "Crystal Ball Gazing: Notes on Today's Middle-Aged Blacks with Implications for Their Aging in the 21st Century." *Gerontologist,* 26(2):136–139.

Finds that in spite of civil rights efforts and affirmative action, blacks continue to function predominantly in peripheral occupations. This situation yields a steady decline in black family income. The author is pessimistic about changes in the future and calls for strenuous enforcement of antidiscrimination laws.

624 WEILER, N. SUE. 1986. "Family Security or Social Security? The Family and the Elderly in New York State during the 1920s." *Journal of Family History,* 11(1):77–95.

Examines the impact of industrialization and immigration on family responsibility for the aged and family security using census manuscripts of 1,815 persons. Weiler concludes that as long as work and pensions for the elderly were scarce, dependence on children in old age predominated. Industrialization theory predictions of urban-rural differences were not supported. Eastern and southern European immigrants emphasized children as insurance in old age. Western Europeans and Americans valued independence between generations.

625 WILLIAMSON, JOHN B. 1984. "Old Age Relief Policy Prior to 1900. The Trend toward Restrictiveness." *American Journal of Economics and Sociology,* 43:369–384.

Historical account of the evolution of old-age relief policy during the seventeenth, eighteenth, and nineteenth centuries that informs an analysis of recent shifts in public policy for the elderly. Williamson asks why old-age relief policy in the United States became increasingly restrictive between the eighteenth and the nineteenth centuries, and why relief policy became more restrictive in the United States than in England by the middle of the nineteenth century. One factor was the emerging market economy and the ideological concomitants. The influx of immigrants who did not share a common background with those who came earlier, and environmental factors such as the abundance of land, contributed to a more individualistic ethic in this country than in England.

626   WITTE, EDWIN E. 1950. "Social Provisions for the Aged." In *The Aged and Society,* edited by Milton Derber, 115–136. Champaign, IL: Industrial Relations Research Association.

Shows that the elderly need assistance with income. Witte discusses industrial pensions, old-age assistance, social security, and other government programs that provide some, but not enough, assistance. The essay is well documented.

Health Care

627   • 1989. *"Aging in America: The Federal Government's Role."* Washington, DC: Congressional Quarterly Press. 95 pp.

Describes the elderly population, aging issues, and the federal government's role in providing services to the aged. The book includes a discussion of the establishment, growth, and financing of the Social Security system and measures taken to address financial problems. Establishment of Medicaid and Medicare, cost problems encountered by both programs, and the impact of changes enacted to control costs are described. Activities preceding the passage of the Medicare Catastrophic Coverage Act, basic features of the bill, and the surrounding debate are outlined.

628   AMERICAN ASSOCIATION OF RETIRED PERSONS (AARP). 1989. Opinions of Americans Age 45 and Over on the Medicare Catastrophic Coverage Act: Report on a Survey. Washington, DC: AARP Research and Data Resources Department. 13 pp.

Results of a December 1988 survey of 1,750 persons that finds strong support for the Medicare Catastrophic Coverage Act, especially its benefits. Opinion was divided on the tax surcharge and whether respondents thought they would personally receive benefits. Most had some knowledge of the program.

629   ATKINS, G. LAWRENCE. 1990. "The Politics of Financing Long-Term Care." *Generations,* 14(2):19–22.

Reviews reasons for the failure of Medicare's catastrophic coverage, particularly the high costs for both the wealthy and poor elderly, combined with an unattractive package that provided benefits most affluent elderly already had. Groups favoring new government involvement in long-term care include organizations representing the elderly; businesses and insurance companies prefer private solutions. The author advocates broad-based taxation to fund long-term care benefits, noting that these would benefit primarily the middle class. He predicts little action until political leadership develops on the issue and effective public pressure is applied.

630 BALL, ROBERT E. 1978. "Health Care for the Elderly." *Social Security Today and Tomorrow.* New York: Columbia University Press. pp. 96–105.

Cites accomplishments of the Medicare program while highlighting the threats of rising health care costs to Medicare recipients. Ball urges revisions to include long-term care that incorporates both home-based and institutional care.

631 BALL, ROBERT M. 1969. "Medical Prices and Their Control." *Social Security Bulletin,* 32(3):4–9.

An address delivered by the Commissioner of Social Security to a conference dealing with rising health care costs. Ball relates problems with the provision and pricing of medical care and the importance of access to health care to the growing success of the health profession. The medical care cost problem includes the overuse of expensive resources. He argues that financial incentives for economical and quality health care need to be established.

632 BAUMGARTNER, LEONA. 1961. "Public Health and Aging." *Gerontologist,* 1(4):160–161.

Traces federal legislation that would lead to Medicare and Medicaid. The author discusses the problems of fragmented, uncoordinated medical care. She notes the responsibility of states to cut waste and improve their public assistance medical care programs for the aged.

633 BAYER, RONALD. 1985. "Coping with Cost Containment." *Generations,* 9(2):39–42.

Presents the structure of Medicare's prospective payment system as a possible threat to both the quality of and the access to care. Bayer suggests that recent increases in Medicare participants' "cost-sharing" serves as a measure to "reprivatize" the cost of the Medicare program. Models that would ease the treatment of "marginal" cases are offered.

634 BERG, DON L. 1985. "What They Really Want from You." *Medical Economics,* 62(9):44–49.

Opinions of a panel composed of a private physician, a geriatrics specialist, a staff member of the Senate Special Committee on Aging, a member of the legislative council of the American Association of Retired Persons, and a member of the National Council of Senior Citizens. Issues include the difficulties of medical management of elders with chronic and multiple problems, polypharmacy, home care, and accessibility of care. The complexities of Medicare, diagnosis-related groups, malpractice, and increasing health care costs are among the concerns discussed.

635   BERK, MARC L., and WILENSKY, GAIL R. 1985. "Health Care of the Poor Elderly: Supplementing Medicare." *Gerontologist,* 25(3):311–314.

Demonstrates how out-of-pocket health care costs for the poor and near-poor elderly increased markedly from 1977 to 1982. Such increases were especially significant for those ineligible for Medicaid. The impact of the cost of supplemental insurance is highlighted.

636   BINSTOCK, ROBERT H. 1990. "The 'Catastrophic' Catastrophe: Elitist Politics, Poor Strategy." *The Aging Connection,* 11(1):9.

Briefly reviews the reasons that the Medicare Catastrophic Coverage Act was repealed. Binstock notes that the program was designed by public officials with little input or support from the elderly.

637   BRADLEY, WILLIAM V. 1977. "The South Carolina Nursing Home Ombudsman Project." In *Handbook of American Aging Programs,* edited by Lorin A. Baumhover and Joan Dechow Jones, 132–139. Westport, CT: Greenwood Press.

Describes the first three years of South Carolina's demonstration ombudsman project. Bradley explains the administrative organization and goals of the program.

638   BRANDON, WILLIAM P. 1989. "Cut Off at the Impasse without Real Catastrophic Health Insurance: Three Approaches to Financing Long-Term Care." *Policy Studies Review,* 8(2):441–454.

Examines the problems in providing long-term health care. Brandon claims it is possible to restructure the health care system to provide long-range care before the twenty-first century. He outlines three methods of accomplishing this: maintain the current system and add additional programs, institute compulsory social insurance, and develop private insurance programs. The author discusses the advantages and disadvantages of each and suggests means of improving the present health care system. He suggests that the elderly may not obtain the political power necessary to accomplish this until after the baby-boom generation retires.

639   BREHM, HENRY P., and COE, RODNEY M. 1980. *Medical Care for the Aged.* New York: Praeger. 143 pp.

Provides a history of health policy for the elderly, focusing on the value of individualism as it affects social security and health care. The book presents data from 1969–1971 surveys of doctors and elderly in Kansas City, Missouri, concerning Medicare. The authors conclude that there is a mismatch among the problem, the policy as formulated, and the program as implemented. The problem of the elderly was defined as ability to pay for health care, which was addressed by Medicare. An implicit need was for chronic illness care and a continuum of services. Medicare decreased financial barriers and doctors knew about the services available, but neither the medical system nor practice styles were changed by Medicare. Slowly changing values are the primary problem.

640   BRODY, STANLEY J. 1971. "Prepayment of Medical Services for the Aged: An Analysis." *Gerontologist*, 11(2):152–157.

Analyzes health maintenance organization (HMO) utilization by seniors eligible for Medicare. Brody discusses a legislative proposal currently before Congress. He cautions against viewing prepaid health care programs as a panacea, especially as their experience with an aged population is limited.

641   BRODY, STANLEY J.; POULSHOCK, S. WALTER; and MASCIOCCHI, CARLA F. 1978. "The Family Caring Unit: A Major Consideration in the Long-Term Support System." *Gerontologist*, 18(6):556–561.

Reports the findings of a study to identify variables governing institutional versus community placement of functionally disabled elderly. Family support was the key to placement. The authors suggest that support of the family as a caring unit should be given critical policy consideration.

642   BUTLER, ROBERT N. 1986. "How to Create Effective Care Spectrum? 'Money Is There' for Needed Health System Reforms." *Perspective on Aging*, 15(3):4–6.

Argues that the American health care enterprise has failed to adapt to the demographic changes the country is experiencing. Because of its emphasis on acute care, the Medicare system is "antigeriatric." The author recommends a publicly funded community-based focus for the spectrum of care.

643   CALLAHAN, DANIEL. 1986. "Health Care in the Aging Society: A Moral Dilemma." In *Our Aging Society: Paradox and Promise*, edited by Alan Pifer and Lydia Bronte, 319–339. New York: Norton.

As population aging continues, social values and economic realities will conflict. Callahan predicts that the elderly will suffer a sharp disadvantage unless clear ethical issues are heeded. He recommends reassessment of moral, social, and cultural values that form the basis for current high health care costs for the elderly.

644   CANTOR, MARJORIE, and MAYER, MARY. 1976. "Health and the Inner City Elderly." *Gerontologist*, 16(1):17–24.

Utilizes a sample of 1,552 elderly persons age 60 and over residing in 26 of the poorest neighborhoods of New York City to report on concerns regarding health care. Most respondents report fair health and a low hospitalization rate with increasing functional incapacity. Barriers to health care were found to include a lack of money, fragmentation of services, and depersonalization of the system.

645   CARLSON, ELLIOT. 1986. "Join the Wellness Revolution." *Modern Maturity*, 29(3):36–39+.

Discusses the establishment of the Healthy Older People program in 1985 by the Department of Health and Human Services, Office of

Health, Disease Prevention, and Health Promotion. The author explores life-style changes for healthier aging.

646   CARLUCCI, TIMOTHY N. 1986/87. "The Asset Transfer Dilemma: Disposal of Resources and Qualification for Medicaid Assistance." *Drake Law Review*, 36(2):369–387.

Reviews the history of efforts beginning in 1980 to prevent the elderly and others from transferring their assets in order to qualify for Medicaid. The author explains Iowa's law and reviews case law nationally on transfer of assets.

647   CHAPMAN, CARLETON B., and TALMADGE, JOHN M. 1970. "Historical and Political Background of Federal Health Care Legislation." *Law and Contemporary Problems*, 35(2):334–347.

Provides a general history of federal health care measures, beginning postindependence when most efforts concerned quarantines. Until the beginning of the twentieth century most federal legislation generated much states' rights controversy. After the 1920s, most opposition came from the American Medical Association. The authors discuss the development of federal health care up to the passage of Medicare.

648   CIEPLIK, CYNTHIA. 1985. "Prospective Payment, Diagnosis Related Groups and Elders: A Challenge for Change." *Geriatric Nursing*, 6(5):260–263.

Identifies the nurse's role in alleviating concerns of older consumers regarding the Medicare prospective payment system. The author suggests that nursing organizations cooperate with consumer groups of the elderly to address the issues of health care accessibility and cost.

649   CLARK, PHILLIP G. 1985. "The Social Allocation of Health Care Resources: Ethical Dilemmas in Age-Group Competition." *Gerontologist*, 25(2):119–125.

Argues that allocation of health care resources to the aged involves both factual and value dimensions. The facts include the increasing expense of medical care for the elderly and the growing size of the aged population. The value dimension involves the allocation principles used. The author argues that the elderly have a claim "to each according to his [sic] need" based on past social contributions rather than on future economic potential. This approach uses a life-span frame of reference when evaluating the issue of distributional justice.

650   CRYSTAL, STEPHEN. 1990. "Health Economics, Old-Age Politics, and the Catastrophic Medicare Debate." *Journal of Gerontological Social Work*, 15(3–4):21–31.

Describes debate on catastrophic insurance and repeal of the Medicare Catastrophic Coverage Act of 1988. The bill divided the aging community and underscored the wide range of economic interests and health care concerns of the elderly. Lack of consensus among the elderly regarding health care and negative perceptions of the health care system make it difficult to develop effective legislation.

651 CURLEY, ANN, and CARLSON, ELLIOT. 1985. "Now You See It: Now You Don't." *Modern Maturity,* 28(2):32–36.

Examines a home health care program being run by the Minneapolis Age and Opportunity Center. It is an innovative, cost-effective program that provides medical and social services directed at preventing unnecessary institutionalization. The authors discuss Medicare and Medicaid coverage inadequacies as related to home health care.

652 DAVIS, KAREN. 1985. "Health Care Policies and the Aged: Observations from the United States." In *Handbook of Aging and the Social Sciences* (2nd ed.), edited by Robert H. Binstock and Ethel Shanas, 727–744. New York: Van Nostrand.

Reviews rationales for involving public policy in the health care of the aged, including maintaining minimum standards of decency, repaying past contributions of the aged, and correcting market failures. The author reviews the health needs of the elderly and current health policies, concluding with principles for a national health care policy.

653 ———. 1986. "Paying the Health-Care Bills of an Aging Population." In *Our Aging Society: Paradox and Promise*, edited by Alan Pifer and Lydia Bronte, 299–318. New York: Norton.

Finds that few mechanisms exist for controlling the amount spent on health care. Davis suggests that there should be greater emphasis on preventive health care measures. Medicare legislation in 1983 establishing prospective payment has helped to control costs, but it is limited and needs improvement.

654 DEMKOVICH, LINDA E. 1984. "Congress Eyes Limits on Doctors' Fees to Remedy Runaway Medicare Costs." *National Journal*, April 7:652–656.

Discusses the reluctance of Congress to confront physicians in an effort to cut back on spiraling Medicare costs. The author notes that physicians' fees rose 9.4 percent compared with an overall inflation rate of 8.6 percent for the years 1977–1983. She discusses various programs, such as freezing fees and forcing doctors to accept assignment of Medicare payments. She also reports the reaction of the American Medical Association.

655 ———. 1987. "Fight for Your Rights." *Modern Maturity*, 30(2):33–35+.

Enumerates the rights of hospitalized patients. The author discusses the impact of consumer groups and patients on access to medical records and the right to informed consent. The article includes the American Hospital Association's bill of rights for patients.

656 EISDORFER, CARL. 1976. "Issues in Health Planning for the Aged." *Gerontologist*, 16(1):12–16.

Summary of the political problems that affect health care services

for the elderly. These include fragmentation of social and health services, health promotion versus care, the tendency for specific care areas
to follow the funding dollar, and declining support for training programs.

657   EMLING, DIANE K. 1981. "Aging: Long-Term Care and the Fiscal State. A
Sociological Study of the Public Policy Process." Ph.D. dissertation,
Michigan State University. 142 pp.

Examines the causes of the continued dominance of the nursing
home care model long after the need for alternatives has been accepted.
Emling shows that nursing home dominance fits into the sectoral divisions of a capitalist economy and is reinforced by the role of the state in
stabilizing capitalism.

658   ESTES, CARROLL L. 1985. "Long-Term Care and Public Policy in an Era of
Austerity." *Journal of Public Health Policy*, 6(4):464–475.

Reviews data from two studies that document the shifts in government responsibility for the elderly and other needy individuals. Medicaid coverage and services were cut in the early 1980s and community
services were restructured. Decentralization has made programs for the
elderly vulnerable.

659   ———. 1988. "Cost Containment and the Elderly: Conflict or Challenge?" *Journal of the American Geriatrics Society*, 36(1):68–72.

Reviews the consequences of cost containment in health care, especially the focus on Medicare costs and the delegitimation of the federal role in health. The results have been to narrow the focus of health
problems to the detriment of supportive and social services and to shift
care out of hospitals and into the community.

660   ———. 1989. "Aging, Health, and Social Policy: Crisis and Crossroads."
Journal of Aging and Social Policy, 1(1/2):17–32.

Identifies seven turning points in the history of aging policy: the
Social Security Act, the Great Society, the federalization of Old Age Assistance, the enactment of comprehensive social services, Social Security enhancements, New Federalism, and medical cost-containment efforts. Future turning points will be framed by population aging,
increased longevity and disability, the link between health and income,
and the high proportion of women among the elderly. The key force,
however, will be politics.

661   ESTES, CARROLL L., and LEE, PHILIP R. 1981. "Policy Shifts and Their Impact
on Health Care for Elderly Persons." *Western Journal of Medicine*,
135(6):511–518.

Critiques the outcome for health care of the elderly that will result
from the governmental fiscal crisis and the resulting budget cuts, the

move to decentralize programs, and the increased emphasis on competition.

662 ESTES, CARROLL L., and BINNEY, ELIZABETH A. 1988. "Toward a Transformation of Health and Aging Policy." *International Journal of Health Services*, 18(1):69–82.

Reviews the inadequacies of current health care programs for the elderly, showing that out-of-pocket expenses of the aged are taking an increasing portion of their income. The authors describe elements that any national health plan must incorporate to meet the health needs of the aged.

663 ESTES, CARROLL L., and HARRINGTON, CHARLENE A. 1981. "Fiscal Crisis, Deinstitutionalization, and the Elderly." *American Behavioral Scientist*, 24(6):811–826.

Examines trends in the shifting of the aged from mental hospitals to nursing homes, and possible shifts out of nursing homes into the community. The authors argue that this trend has been caused in large part by the interests of the private, profit-making segment of the health care industry. The change is consonant with the needs of the market economy but not with the needs of the elderly.

664 FAMILIES USA (United for Senior Action). 1989. *Winners and Losers: The State-by-State Distributional Impact of Proposed Changes to the Medicare Catastrophic Act*. Washington, DC: Families USA. 31 pp.

Provides a state-by-state accounting of the consequences if Medicare Catastrophic Health Insurance is financed by a flat premium rather than a tax surcharge. The data show that the poor are the most adversely affected.

665 FEDER, JUDITH M. 1977. *Medicare: The Politics of Federal Hospital Insurance*. Lexington, MA: Lexington Books. 177 pp.

Often-cited book that examines the consequences of initially placing the medical program, Medicare, in a social insurance agency, the Social Security Administration. The author examines how and why decisions were made about hospital eligibility, utilization review, reimbursement, and cost control. She shows how the Social Security bureaucracy focused on efficient claims payment rather than on medical care costs and quality as a means to avoid controversy and simplify administration.

666 FEINGOLD, EUGENE. 1966. *Medicare: Policy and Politics*. San Francisco, CA: Chandler Publishing Co. 317 pp.

Presents the case for and against federal involvement in health care. Essays by the author and others provide a detailed history of the efforts to pass a national health insurance plan and the eventual passage of Medicare. The authors examine the roles of the American Medical

Association, labor, Congress, and the president in shaping the program. They review the important issues confronting the new system.

667 FERRARA, PETER J. 1989. "Catastrophic Health Benefits Translate into Catastrophic Taxes." *Consumers' Research Magazine*, 72(4):11–14.

Describes costs associated with the Medicare Catastrophic Coverage Act. A 15 percent surcharge on the income taxes of the elderly will make their marginal tax rate higher than the rate for other groups. Medicare premiums will increase and benefits provided will be inadequate. The author suggests that the surcharge be eliminated and financing be provided by increased co-payments.

668 FESSLER, PAMELA. 1981. "Soaring Health Care Costs for the Elderly: A Problem Growing Worse Every Year." *Congressional Quarterly Weekly Report*, 39(48):2337–2341.

Analyzes the political and economic implications of increasing health care costs for the growing elderly population. Tessler discusses the health care system's bias toward expensive, institutional care and government plans to address the problem.

669 FORMAN, ALLAN. 1974. "The Nursing Home Ombudsman Demonstration Program." *Health Services Reports*, 89(2):128–133.

Reviews the experience of the first two years of Health, Education, and Welfare's nursing home ombudsman demonstrations that attempted to provide nursing home care consumers with an effective voice in determining care practices. Fifty to sixty percent of complaints dealt with quality of care received, and over 80 percent were determined to be justified. Three models tested included mediating individual complaints, documenting and working to alleviate problems facing large numbers of nursing home patients, and increasing community involvement in defining and resolving problems.

670 FOX, DANIEL M. 1989. "Policy and Epidemiology: Financing Health Services for the Chronically Ill and Disabled, 1930–1990." *Milbank Quarterly*, 67(Suppl. 2, Pt. 2):257–287.

Provides a historical analysis of the accommodation of the health care financing system to the growth of chronic disease and disability. Fox argues that the growing incidence of chronic disease strongly influenced the perceived self-interest of such groups as physicians, insurers, and workers as well as their beliefs about the logic of the organization of health care. These beliefs shaped the struggles among those interest groups about government and private health insurance.

671 FOX, PATRICK. 1989. "From Senility to Alzheimer's Disease: The Rise of the Alzheimer's Disease Movement." *Milbank Quarterly*, 67(1):58–102.

See entry 309.

672 FRIES, JAMES F. 1980. "Aging, Natural Death, and the Compression of Morbidity." *New England Journal of Medicine*, 303:130–135.

Presents data to support the controversial theory that the average period of physical decline in the elderly will decrease as the population continues to age. Fries claims that advances in medical technology will dramatically change the characteristics of the average elderly individual and he questions the excessive use of technology at the end of the natural life-span, suggesting that humane care rather than heroics be utilized.

673 ———. 1984. "The Compression of Morbidity: Miscellaneous Comments about a Theme." *Gerontologist*, 24(4):354–359.

Reviews and rejects criticisms of the author's argument that the onset of significant morbidity may be postponed to coincide more closely with termination of the genetic life-span. Fries considers the efficacy of health promotion activities in light of limited resources available to deal with an increasingly elderly population.

674 FUCHS, VICTOR R. 1984. "Though Much is Taken—Reflections on Aging, Health, and Medical Care." *Milbank Memorial Fund Quarterly*, 62(2):143–166.

Uses the broad context of economic and social trends to examine the methodology of Medicare financing. The author analyzes unresolved health system structure deficiencies, retirement, and employment problems. The costs of care for the dying as a serious economic issue are addressed.

675 GEIGER, JACK H. 1980. "Elder Health and Social Policies: Prelude to a Decade of Disaster." *Generations*, 4(2):11–12, 52.

Blames pressures for federal programs and containment for creating "the probability that—in exact parallel to general social policy—medical cost containment, like general budget balancing, will take place on the back of the poor and the elderly." Geiger charges that ambulatory and preventive services will suffer while high-technology and other expensive health/social services are protected.

676 GIBSON, DONALD E. 1984. "Hospice: Morality and Economics." *Gerontologist*, 24(1):4–7.

Examines the moral issues presented by this style of health care. Gibson highlights the conflicting views presented by the hospice concept of alleged humanitarian superiority and the emphasis on cost efficiency. He draws on current literature and recent congressional legislation establishing Medicare hospice benefits.

677 GUCCIONE, ANDREW A. 1988. "Compliance and Patient Autonomy: Ethical and Legal Limits to Professional Dominance." *Topics in Geriatric Rehabilitation*, 3(3):62–73.

Reviews literature on the ethical, legal, and social problems of patient compliance. The author identifies four ethical principles in professional action: respect for autonomy, consideration of positive and negative consequences, fidelity, and justice. He considers the legal ramifications of informed consent and analyzes problems faced in informing patients without exerting subtle social control. He claims that asserting patient autonomy takes precedence over any obligation to promote good consequences.

678   HAAS, LAWRENCE J. 1989. "Fiscal Catastrophe." *National Journal*, 21(40):2453–2456.

Describes the political upheaval that followed the enactment of the 1988 catastrophic health care insurance law. Haas discusses the bill's failure to consider long-term health care, level of benefits, and financing.

679   HAMBOR, JOHN C. 1987. "Economic Policy, Intergenerational Equity, and the Social Security Fund Buildup." *Social Security Bulletin*, 50(10):13–18.

Reviews the economic consequences of the planned buildup of Social Security trust funds, expected to reach $12.5 trillion in 2030. Hambor shows how federal policy during the buildup will determine the economic impact of the fund, and how its disposition will affect future workers.

680   HARRINGTON, CHARLENE; ESTES, CARROLL L.; LEE, PHILIP R.; and NEWCOMER, ROBERT J. 1986. "Effects of State Medicaid Policies on the Aged." *Gerontologist*, 26(4):437–443.

Reviews trends from 1978–1982 in eight sample states and compares their relationship to national averages. The authors report that widely varying effects are caused by cost containment pressures. They did not find the anticipated curtailment of eligibility but did observe that constraints reduced service growths.

681   HARRINGTON, CHARLENE, and GRANT, LESLIE A. 1990. "The Delivery, Regulation, and Politics of Home Care: A California Case Study." *Gerontologist*, 30(4):451–461.

Describes seven different types of formal home care providers in California and the mixed levels of government oversight they face. Senior consumer groups reported that home health care is not a high priority issue. The authors found that increased regulation of unregulated types of care was supported by some provider and professional groups, but opposed by consumer groups of disabled because added costs would result in fewer services without making the services more consumer sensitive. There was little effort to rationalize the currently fragmented oversight of home care.

682   HARRIS, RAYMOND. 1975. "Breaking the Barriers to Better Health Care Delivery for the Aged: Medical Aspects." *Gerontologist*, 15(1):52–56.

Discusses problems arising from spiraling medical costs and gaps between Medicare and Medicaid coverage. Harris emphasizes the fragmentation and depersonalization of health and medical services as they affect the multiple chronic health problems of the elderly.

683　———. 1966. *A Sacred Trust*. New York: New American Library. 229 pp.

A detailed journalistic history of the role of the American Medical Association (AMA) in blocking compulsory government health insurance, beginning in 1912 and ending with Medicare in 1965. Harris focuses on the relationship between the AMA and Congress, the White House, and public opinion. The power of the AMA came from its organizational structure, which effectively eliminated dissent, its wealth, and the power of doctors over patients, hospitals, and other health professionals. He claims that its uncompromising position contributed to its eventual defeat.

684　HOLSTEIN, MARTHA, and MINKLER, MEREDITH. 1991. "The Short Life and Painful Death of the Medicare Catastrophic Coverage Act." In *Critical Perspectives on Aging*, edited by Meredith Minkler and Carroll L. Estes, 189–206. Amityville, NY: Baywood.

Argues that the rise and fall of Medicare's Catastrophic Health Insurance (CHI) is a result of the historical segregation of the aged by Medicare, the delegitimation of the elderly as a welfare state constituency, and the politics of austerity. CHI is described as the outcome of congressional and organizational efforts, with no solid grass-roots support. No public opinion data existed about the acceptability of new taxes on the aged to finance the program. Popular outcry forced its repeal, possibly further damaging the public view of the elderly as a deserving group.

685　JOO, SUNGSOO. 1987. "The Political Economy of Old-Age Policy: Health Care Financing for Aging in the Welfare State." Ph.D. dissertation, Northern Illinois University. 327 pp.

Examines health care spending in member countries of the Organization for Economic Cooperation and Development to determine the effect of aging populations on public policy. The author finds that the growing number and political power of the aged is more important than supply factors in explaining health care expenditure growth.

686　KATZ, MICHAEL B. 1984. "Poorhouses and the Origins of the Public Old Age Home." *Milbank Memorial Fund Quarterly/Health and Society*, 62(1):110–140.

Provides a concise history of poorhouses, beginning in the 1700s and ending when they became limited to the old and disabled as old-age homes. Katz shows that the elderly were considered to be deserving poor because their inability to work was presumed to be a result of their age. The function of poorhouses as temporary welfare for the poor and the negative public image of the facilities are explained.

687   KOSTERLITZ, JULIE. 1986. "Organized Medicine's United Front in Washington Is Showing More Cracks." *National Journal*, 18(2):82–86.

Addresses divisions within the ranks of physicians and hospitals as each tries to focus on its interests in ever-changing federal health care policy. The author shows that conflict between physicians who accept the Medicare fee assignment and those who charge more has created a rift. The AMA is criticized by many as being reluctant to change. An oversupply of hospitals and physicians is seen as a major factor in the competition.

688   ———. 1986. "Protecting the Elderly." *National Journal*, 18(21):1254–1258.

Reviews the growing burden of health care costs for the aged and its causes. Kosterlitz notes that the elderly poor pay the highest proportion of their income for health care. This situation has led Congress to avoid most proposals that would increase the amount paid by the aged under Medicare. The author describes congressional proposals to reduce medical inflation.

689   ———. 1987. "Health Focus." *National Journal*, 19(35):2187.

Briefly discusses pending federal legislation that attempts to provide long-term health care for the elderly.

690   LEE, PHILIP R., and ESTES, CARROLL L. 1983. "New Federalism and Health Policy." *Annals of the American Academy of Political and Social Science*, 468(July):88–102.

Explains the concept of federalism and summarizes four periods in U.S. history in which different forms of federalism have shaped health policy. The authors argue that New Federalism policies will result in cuts of health services rather than a redistribution of authority to the states.

691   LEE, PHILIP R.; ESTES, CARROLL L.; LEROY, LAUREN; and NEWCOMER, ROBERT L. 1982. "Health Policy and the Aged." In *Annual Review of Gerontology and Geriatrics*, vol. 3. New York: Springer. pp. 361–400.

Summarizes the major literature of the 1970s on aging and discusses the relevance of the findings for policymakers. In particular, the article reviews the problems of health personnel and health care costs and financing in the context of decentralization and fiscal crisis.

692   LIU, KORBIN; DOTY, PAMELA; and MANTON, KENNETH. 1990. "Medicaid Spend-Down in Nursing Homes." *Gerontologist*, 30(1):7–15.

Uses the 1985 National Nursing Home Survey to review the incidence and causes of Medicaid spend-down among the disabled elderly. The authors do not support the common belief that many nursing home patients spend all their savings and become Medicaid patients. They found that 90 percent of nursing home patients were either Medicaid patients at admission or never became Medicaid patients. They discuss the Medicare Catastrophic Coverage Act, private long-term care insurance, and debates surrounding long-term care financing.

693 LIN, ANDREW D. 1984. "Grandma Junkies." *Health*, 16(1):52–57.

Analyzes the problem of drug abuse in the elderly. The use of drugs as a form of social control is discussed. Efforts to disseminate information by private and public organizations are presented.

694 LONGMAN, PHILLIP. 1989. "Catastrophic Follies." *New Republic*, 201(8): 16–18.

Describes the Medicare Catastrophic Coverage Act and the reaction of the elderly community. Longman briefly discusses the origins, structure, provisions, and financing of the bill as well as the role of special interest groups in generating negative reaction to the proposal. He criticizes the affluent elderly for shifting health care costs to the poor elderly.

695 MARMOR, THEODORE R. 1973. *The Politics of Medicare*. Chicago: Aldine Publishing Co. 150 pp.

One of the most-cited books on the history of Medicare. Marmor reviews the history of the passage of Medicare, beginning with President Truman's 1951 tactical shift away from advocating a national health insurance plan and introducing the concept of covering only the elderly. The author attributes Medicare's slow passage to the lack of presidential support under Eisenhower and opposition by conservative members of the House Ways and Means committee after Kennedy became president. The power of the American Medical Association and the AFL-CIO was limited in blocking or promoting passage of Medicare, as was the power of public opinion. Elites had the major role in designing and passing Medicare, with interest groups limiting but not generating the agenda.

696 MCCONNELL, STEPHEN. 1990. "Who Cares about Long-term Care? A Review of National Opinion Surveys." *Generations*, 14(2):15–18.

Reviews public opinion polls from the 1980s to show that there is strong and widespread support for publicly funded long-term care. This was the most important issue listed by those age 45 and over, and the only issue other than homelessness for which a majority favor increased spending. Multiple polls show that all Americans favor a public program for long-term care and are willing to have taxes increased to pay for it. In-home care receives the strongest support, although most also support help with nursing home costs.

697 MELEMED, BRINA B. 1983. "Formulating a Public Policy for Long-Term Care: A Different View." *Perspective on Aging*, 12(3):4–5+.

Takes issue with the view that Medicare is the best vehicle for long-term care reform. The author suggests four alternatives for long-term care reform and questions whether "centralizing long-term care decision-making authority under the control of a physician—and by extension the medical establishment—will achieve the intended goals."

698 MENDELSON, MARY A., and HAPGOOD, DAVID. 1974. "The Political Economy of Nursing Homes." *Annals of the American Academy of Political and Social Sciences*, 415(September):95–105.
Describes the ways in which nursing homes maximize profits from government programs at the expense of patients and the taxpayer. While there are plenty of regulations they are poorly enforced because of the influence of the nursing home industry. The blame for the failure of regulation is the lack of effective countervailing public pressure.

699 MINKLER, MEREDITH. 1990. "Aging and Disability: Behind and beyond the Stereotypes." *Journal of Aging Studies*, 4(3):245–260.
Critiques the recent emphasis on "successful aging." The author argues that this perception perpetuates prejudices against disabled elders; she counters with an analysis of the social construction of aging and disability.

700 MORRISEY, MICHAEL; JENSEN, GAIL A.; and HENDERLITE, STEPHEN E. 1990. "Employer-Sponsored Health Insurance for Retired Americans." *Health Affairs*, 9(1):57–73.
Discusses the extent of retiree health benefits as a background for understanding the repeal of the Medicare Catastrophic Coverage Act of 1988 (MCCA). Health plans are analyzed in terms of coverage, vesting, and coordination rules. Five issues emerge as significant: number of retirees covered by employer plans, employer benefits verses Medigap coverage, utilization controls, conditions for obtaining coverage, and methods of receiving benefits. Approximately 30 percent of the elderly obtain health insurance from former employers. Benefits in these plans are superior to MCCA coverage. The authors suggest that this was the primary reason for opposition to MCCA from affluent elderly.

701 MOSES, STEPHEN A. 1990. "The Fallacy of Impoverishment." *Gerontologist*, 30(1):21–25.
Describes research questioning the belief that Medicaid requires impoverishment. Moses notes that although two-thirds of the elderly poor are not covered by Medicaid, many nursing home Medicaid recipients are retaining considerable assets, which pass on to their heirs. He discusses spousal impoverishment and long-term care financing.

702 NEUGARTEN, BERNICE L. 1972. "Social Implications of a Prolonged Life Span." *Gerontologist*, 12(4):323, 438–440.
Considers the effect of medical advancements on extending life expectancy. Neugarten points up the potential for intergenerational conflict and urges joint efforts by biological scientists, policymakers, jurists, and philosophers to address problem of social values versus economic values. She expresses concerns for the quality of life in old age.

703　PALMORE, ERDMAN B. 1976. "The Future Status of the Aged." *Gerontologist*, 16(4):297–302.

Summarizes census and national health survey data to review the status of the aged in comparison to younger age groups. Improvement in the key indicators, such as overall health and income, illustrate that gains have been made and many programs for the aged have had a beneficial effect. The author refutes the assertion that the status of the aged in modern society is declining.

704　————. 1986. "Trends in the Health of the Aged." *Gerontologist*, 26(3):298–302.

Utilizes data from 1961–1981 to illustrate health gains experienced by the elderly, suggesting that increased longevity is not necessarily accompanied by increased disability. Medicare and Medicaid are credited with some of the health gains.

705　PEPPER, CLAUDE. 1989. "Long-Term Care Insurance: The First Step towards Comprehensive Health Insurance." *Caring*, 8(4):4–8+.

Describes the basic provisions of Pepper's bill, which would provide Medicare coverage for long-term health care in the home. The bill is self-funded.

706　RATHBONE, ELOISE. 1985. "Health Needs and Social Policy." *Women and Health*, 10(2):17–27.

Identifies the Older Women's League as a leading health advocate working to increase awareness of the failure of current social policy to address the needs of older women. The League's major areas of concern are the vulnerability of women to inadequacies in the long-term care system, the role of women as caregivers and recipients of care, and the social and economic problems of widowhood.

707　RICE, THOMAS. 1989. *Older Americans and Their Health Coverage*. Research Bulletin R1389. Washington, DC: Health Insurance Association of America. 27 pp.

Analyzes data from 500 Medicare recipients about their knowledge and satisfaction with their health insurance. Rice found that in general satisfaction was high and knowledge low. Most respondents with Medigap insurance planned on renewing it despite the passage of the Medicare Catastrophic Coverage Act.

708　RICE, THOMAS; DESMOND, KATHERINE; and GABEL, JON. 1990. "Medicare Catastrophic Coverage Act: A Post-Mortem." *Health Affairs*, 9(3):75–87.

Presents the results of a survey of elderly individuals concerning their opinions of the Medicare catastrophic law before its repeal. The data show a low level of knowledge concerning the new law and a low level of support for the new tax it contained. Respondents continued to have a high level of concern over the remaining gaps in Medicare and were generally satisfied with their private supplemental policies. Most planned to keep their supplemental policies even after the catastrophic law was implemented. The authors suggest that a focus on long-term care coverage, which few elderly currently have, would generate more support from the aged.

709   ROBERTSON, ANN. 1991. "The Politics of Alzheimer's Disease: A Case Study in Apocalyptic Demography." In *Critical Perspectives on Aging*, edited by Meredith Minkler and Carroll L. Estes, 135–150. Amityville, NY: Baywood.

Examines how the biomedicalization of old age and the social construction of disease provided the context within which Alzheimer's became identified as a disease. Defining Alzheimer's as a disease benefits institutions and professions, even though diagnosis is problematic and the etiology is unknown.

710   ROBINSION, MICHELE L. 1989. "Backlash Forces Rewrite of Catastrophic Law." *Hospitals*, 63(18):28–29.

Brief review of the pressure put on Congress by middle-class and wealthy elderly against the Catastrophic Health Insurance taxes. The author outlines a House compromise proposal on funding.

711   ROOSEVELT, JAMES. 1988. "Congress Misleads Seniors: Catastrophic Care Bill Offers Little." *Journal of Public Health Policy*, 9(4):453–455.

Brief editorial by the Chairman of the National Committee to Preserve Social Security and Medicare explaining that the Catastrophic Coverage Act costs the elderly too much and provides too little, especially for long-term care.

712   ROTHMAN, DAVID J. 1971. *The Discovery of the Asylum*. Boston, MA: Little, Brown. 376 pp.

Often-cited history of the development of institutions for criminals, the insane, poor, orphaned, homeless, and aged. Rothman argues that their development resulted from an attempt to maintain social order in a changing society, not simply from scientific progress, the needs of capitalism, or increasing rationalism. He details the high hopes present during the founding of these institutions and their subsequent decline.

713   ROVNER, JULIE. 1988. "Long-Term Care Bill Derailed—For Now." *Congressional Quarterly Weekly Report*, 46(24):1604–1605.

Briefly discusses rejection of a bill to expand Medicare coverage to include long-term home care. Rovner describes Claude Pepper's sponsorship of the bill and the lukewarm support of the American Association of Retired Persons.

714   SARAH SHUPTRINE AND ASSOCIATES. 1989. *State Implementation of the Low Income Protection Provisions of the Medicare Catastrophic Coverage Act of 1988.* Columbia, SC: Sarah Shuptrine and Associates. 29 pp.

Findings from a 50-state survey in January 1989 about the implementation of the new Medicare law that has Medicaid paying for the

Medicare Part B premiums of low-income persons. Authors found that few states were exceeding the minimum requirements of the act.

715 SAVITT, HARRY L. 1969. "Persons Insured under Medicare, July 1, 1967." *Social Security Bulletin*, 32(3):15–21.

Presents data on number of persons in each state insured under the Social Security Act Hospital Insurance (HI) and supplementary medical insurance (SMI.) Savitt describes changes that occurred in the first year of the program and explains variation in year-to-year and geographic categories of enrollment.

716 SCHREIBER, E. M., and MARSDEN, LORNA R. 1972. "Age and Opinions on a Government Program of Medical Aid." *Journal of Gerontology*, 27(1):95–101.

Examines Survey Research Center Election Studies from 1956, 1960, 1964, and 1968 to determine whether there are age differences in public support for government involvement in helping people obtain medical care. The authors find that support rises modestly with age but that the relationship disappears when income and/or occupation are controlled in the analysis. This finding agrees with the interpretation that support for government intervention is a function of economic self-interest rather than age-related beliefs.

717 SCHRIMPER, RONALD, and CLARK, ROBERT. 1985. "Health Expenditures and Elderly Adults." *Journal of Gerontology*, 40(2):235–243.

Examines data on household expenditures for five groups of elderly. Reductions in food, housing, and transportation expenses are related to out-of-pocket direct health expenditures by the elderly. These direct expenditures are caused by rising health costs and Medicare cost sharing.

718 SCULL, ANDREW T. 1977. *Decarceration, Community Treatment and the Deviant—A Radical View*. Englewood Cliffs, NJ: Prentice-Hall. 184 pp.

Examination of the movement to deinstitutionalize criminals and the mentally ill. Scull argues that the ultimate cause of the shift is not improved treatment or beneficence but the state's need to reduce the costs of social control.

719 SHORE, HERBERT. 1972. "The Current Social Revolution and its Impact on Jewish Nursing Homes." *Gerontologist*, 12(2):178–180.

Explores ways of coping with the social changes of the 1960s, including the black consciousness movement, on patient care in nursing homes. Many employees are from minority groups while patients are white. The needs of residents for safety and care must be balanced with employee frustration, anger, confusion, and fear.

720 SINNING, KATHLEEN E. 1989. "Minimizing the Tax Effect of the Supplemental Medicare Premium." *Taxes*, 67(5):275–280.

Suggests ways that the middle-class and upper-income elderly can reduce the tax surcharge they would pay under the Medicare Catastrophic Coverage Act.

721 SOMERS, ANNE R. 1983. "Medicare and Long-Term Care." *Perspective on Aging*, 12(2):5–8+.

Expounds on a 1981 proposal to increase Medicare responsiveness to the long-term care needs of the elderly. Proposes elimination of prohibitions on custodial care, establishment of "reasonable, non-deterrent" patient cost-sharing formulas, and use of prospective payment for all Medicare services.

722 SOMERS, ANNE R., and SOMERS, HERMAN M. 1967. *Medicare and the Hospitals: Issues and Prospects*. Washington, DC: Brookings Institution. 303 pp.

Early evaluation of the effects of Medicare on the U.S. medical care system, especially hospitals. The authors describe the legislative and administrative background of the program, and discuss major issues that will face the program. Their focus is administrative issues and hospital industry responses.

723 STARR, PAUL. 1982. *The Social Transformation of American Medicine*. New York: Basic Books. 514 pp.

Pulitzer Prize-winning book on the history of medical care in the United States. Starr focuses on the shifting power and status of allopathic medicine and hospitals. He traces the rise of private and public health insurance, emphasizing the role of institutionalized interests in shaping the medical care system. He describes the elderly as providing the legitimacy needed to pass Medicare after national health plans had been unsuccessful politically for 60 years.

724 SUNDQUIST, JAMES L. 1968. "For the Old, Health Care." In *Politics and Policy: The Eisenhower, Kennedy, and Johnson Years*. Washington, DC: Brookings Institution. pp. 287–321.

See entry 147.

725 THOMAS, WILLIAM C. 1969. *Nursing Homes and Public Policy: Drift and Decision in New York State*. Ithaca, NY: Cornell University Press. 287 pp.

Case study of the development of the for-profit nursing home industry in New York from the 1930s to the 1960s. Thomas chronicles the development of proprietary homes as a response to public policies in other areas, such as efforts to eliminate almshouses and the underpayment for care in voluntary homes. The nursing home industry was loosely regulated until the 1950s. Most public policy toward nursing homes was reactive, often in response to scandals and crises, rather than planning oriented. The result was a gradual broadening of government oversight of the industry.

726 TORRES-GIL, FERNANDO. 1989. "Politics of Catastrophic and Long-Term Care Coverage." *Journal of Aging and Social Policy*, 1(1–2):61–86.

Discusses the political impact of the passage of the Medicare Catastrophic Coverage Act. The author considers the historical background, policy, interest groups, and political actors involved in the debate surrounding the bill. The defeated Pepper-Roybal Bill, which attempted to provide long-term home care coverage, is described. A review of the political climate surrounding both bills indicates public acceptance of the current federal role in health care policy.

727 ———. 1990. "Seniors React to the Medicare Catastrophic Bill: Equity or Selfishness?" *Journal of Aging and Social Policy*, 2(1):1–8.

Editorial that reviews the negative reaction to Medicare's Catastrophic Coverage Act. The author suggests that the bill provided needed benefits to the poor but was opposed by the wealthier elderly because of the new taxes. If long-term care (LTC) had been the issue the reaction might have been less negative. The author calls on the elderly to declare their willingness to accept higher taxes for LTC insurance.

728 TORRES-GIL, FERNANDO, and PYNOOS, JON. 1986. "Long-Term Care Policy and Interest Group Struggles." *Gerontologist*, 26(5):488–495.

Traces the history of the struggles to reform California's long-term care system. The authors describe the conflict that occurred between the disabled and the elderly during the planning and legislative process. Differences in goals and political organization of the two groups caused heated debate in passage of California Assembly Bill 2226.

729 U.S. GENERAL ACCOUNTING OFFICE. 1989. *Medicare Catastrophic Act: Estimated Effects of Repeal on Medigap Premiums and Medicaid Costs.* Fact Sheet for the Chairman, Subcommittee on Health, House Committee on Ways and Means. 9 pp.

Summarizes preliminary data on the increases in private Medigap premiums as a result of the repeal of the Medicare Catastrophic Act. The fact sheet estimates the costs to Medicaid of the loss of Medicare benefits.

730 ———. 1990. *Medigap Insurance: Expected 1990 Premiums after Repeals of the Medicare Catastrophic Coverage Act and 1988 Loss Ratio Data.* Washington, DC: U.S. Government Printing Office.

Survey of 50 insurance companies to determine that Medigap premiums will rise 20 percent to 34 percent, in part because of the increased coverage companies will have to provide after the repeal of the Medicare Catastrophic Coverage Act. The survey shows that many private insurance companies fail to meet standards for minimum returns on premiums paid.

731 VLADECK, BRUCE C. 1980. *Unloving Care.* New York: Basic Books. 305 pp.

Influential book on the problems of nursing homes and how public policy contributes to those problems. The author examines the history of public policy for nursing homes, policies that led to the dominance of for-profit homes, and problems of quality. He describes the politics of nursing home regulation and reimbursement, noting that nursing homes would be more politically powerful if they were not so politically fragmented. He notes that consumers and advocates are even weaker, and he attributes many problems to Americans' antigovernment values and limited concern for nursing home residents.

732 WALLIS, CLAUDIA. 1986. "Welcome to the 'No-Care Zone.'" *Time*, 127(12):68.

Reports on a three-year study in 32 communities in eight states alleging that frail elderly are being discharged "sicker and quicker" since the advent of Medicare's diagnosis-related group (DRG) system.

733 WATLINGTON, AMANDA G. 1985. "AARP Confronts Health Care Costs." *Health Care Strategic Management*, 3(8):23–25.

An interview with Cyril F. Brickfield, executive director of the American Association of Retired Persons (AARP). The author states that AARP advocates a prospective payment system for health care for all patients and suggests home and community-based care as alternatives to institutional care.

734 WOOD, JUANITA B.; HUGHES, ROBERT G.; and ESTES, CARROLL L. 1986. "Community Health Centers and the Elderly: A Potential New Alliance." *Journal of Community Health*, 11(2):137–146.

Analyzes data from community health centers (CHCs) nationally to determine how policy changes have affected their targeting of the elderly. The new emphasis on attracting paying clients makes Medicare patients more attractive, and CHCs reported increased number of older patients in 1984.

735 WYDEN, RON. 1977. "Public Regulation of Private Supplements to Medicare and Medicaid in Oregon." *Connecticut Law Review*, 9(3):450–461.

Describes the successful efforts of a coalition of senior citizens in Oregon to force the state to improve its regulation of Medigap policies. Wyden details the public pressure placed on the Commissioner of Insurance, the role of the media, and the strategy pursued by the coalition.

Ageism

736 • 1926. "Hiring and Separation Methods in American Factories." *Monthly Labor Review*, 35(5):1005–1017.

Reviews reports of the Bureau of Labor Statistics on employment methods. The article includes methods of recruiting labor, use of physical examinations, and use of age limits in hiring. It provides a historical perspective in showing a strong tendency against hiring older men.

737 ABRAMS, ALBERT J. 1952. "Barriers to the Employment of Older Workers." *Annals of the American Academy of Political and Social Science*, 279(Jan.):62–71.

Reviews age discrimination in the work force and describes a variety of causes including cultural barriers, lack of skills, inaccurate perceptions of the elderly by employers, and union practices. Abrams summarizes educational programs to overcome these problems conducted by a variety of public and voluntary groups.

738 ACHENBAUM, W. ANDREW. 1974. "The Obsolescence of Old Age in America, 1865–1914." *Journal of Social History*, 8:48–62.

A summary of how old age was presented in popular and other writing between the Civil War and World War II. In the earlier period the aged were idealized as survivors of the fittest. This changed to an emphasis on physical deterioration and the lack of societal contributions made by the elderly. The shift was caused by the growing proportion of elderly in society, changing medical views of old age, the effort of big business to retire workers arbitrarily at age 65, and the development of a youth culture.

739 ———. 1985. "Societal Perceptions of the Aging and the Aged." In *Handbook of Aging and the Social Sciences* (2nd ed.), edited by Robert H. Binstock and Ethel Shanas, 129–148. New York: Van Nostrand.

Assesses the work of historians and other humanistic scholars on perceptions of aging. The author summarizes the diversity of perceptions of aging in ancient Hebraic culture, early Christian times, Graeco-Roman culture, and the Middle Ages. He then examines the consequences of modernization and industrialization for the elderly, noting that the aged were among the last age group to be affected. Inaccurate perceptions of the aged are presented as a current problem.

740 BARRON, MILTON L. 1953. "Minority Group Characteristics of the Aged in American Society." *Journal of Gerontology*, 8(4):477–482.

One of the first analyses of the elderly as an emerging quasi-minority group. Barron states that the social psychology of older people resembles that of ethnic minority groups. He examines discriminatory behavior against the aged noting that the elderly exhibit the reactions of a minority group. He discusses legislation against age discrimination.

741 BINSTOCK, ROBERT H. 1983. "The Aged as Scapegoat." *Gerontologist*, 23(2):136–143.

Posits the view that an era of "compassionate stereotypes" defining the elderly as poor and frail and deserving of advocacy and federal support has ended, to be replaced by erroneous assertions that the elderly have obtained unfair public policy advantage. Binstock recommends a

need-based focus by advocates and policymakers, urging gerontologists
to focus on the heterogeneity of the elderly.

742   ———. 1984. "Reframing the Agenda of Policies on Aging." In *Readings
in the Political Economy of Aging*, edited by Meredith Minkler and Carroll L. Estes, 157–167. Farmingdale, NY: Baywood.

Critiques the assumptions made since the late 1970s about the elderly by policymakers. The author argues that all aged are not well off,
that many remain in or near poverty. He challenges the belief that seniors are a potent, self-interested political force, charging that it is incorrect to assume that demographic aging will place an unmanageable burden on the economy. The author reviews three ways that scholars and
others distort facts to attack the elderly.

743   ———. 1985. "The Oldest Old: A Fresh Perspective of Compassionate
Ageism Revisited." *Milbank Memorial Fund Quarterly*, 63(2):420–451.

Critiques the "compassionate ageism" of stereotypes about the elderly and warns of new stereotypes and misinformation emerging about
those age 85 and over. The author describes a variety of metaphors and
categories that are used to distort the reality of aging as a varied process, including the poorly documented assertion that the elderly vote as
a cohesive group. He argues that need should be the criterion for public
programs regardless of age. In acute care the major distinctions are
based on ability to pay rather than age, while in long-term care family
issues are also important.

744   BUTLER, ROBERT N. 1969. "Age-ism: Another Form of Bigotry." *Gerontologist*, 9(4):243–246.

Examines resident resistance to establishment of a federally assisted housing project for the elderly. The author coins the term *ageism,* which he defines as "a deep-seated uneasiness on the part of the
young and the middle-aged" to their own aging process and their concerns over what they view as age-related powerlessness. He criticizes
Medicare, Social Security, and public housing as "examples of token-
ism."

745   CAMERON, PAUL. 1973. "Which Generation Is Believed to Be Intellectually
Superior and Which Generation Believes Itself Intellectually Superior?"
International Journal of Aging and Human Development, 4(3):257–
270.

Analyzes the beliefs about intelligence reported by 317 randomly
selected young, middle-aged, and older adults in Detroit. The data show
that all age groups believe that the middle-aged have the greatest problem-solving abilities, while the young desire and receive the most intellectual stimulation. The aged have the lowest desire and the fewest opportunities for intellectual stimulation.

746 CARMICHAEL, CHARLES. 1978. "No More Apologies." *Generations*, 3(2):6–7.

Stresses the need for television media administrators and program sponsors to be more responsive to programming for the elderly. Carmichael notes the potential power of numbers and dollars that the older generation control. He cites the activities of the Gray Panther's "Media Watch" group as having had substantial impact on some media administrators.

747 CHUDACOFF, HOWARD P. 1989. *How Old Are You? Age Consciousness in American Culture*. Princeton, NJ: Princeton University Press. 232 pp.

Social history of old-age group consciousness as expressed in popular culture, public policy, and social organizations. The author shows how an awareness of age groups arose in the late 1800s with the institutionalization of age grading of the young in schools and medical practice, and of the elderly in the workplace. He examines the use of age as a criterion for social programs and concludes that age consciousness has peaked.

748 COE, RODNEY M. 1967. "Professional Perspectives on the Aged." *Gerontologist*, 7(Part 1):114–119.

Describes the views about aging and the aged of a small sample of health care professionals. Coe claims that all types of professionals view aging as a deteriorative process, with the focus varying from physical to mental changes based on the profession. They also view the elderly as slow to respond to treatment and benefiting primarily from palliative treatment. This attitude impairs the ability of the elderly to obtain adequate medical treatment.

749 COHEN, ELIAS S., and KURSCHWITZ, ANNA L. 1990. "Old Age in America Represented in Nineteenth and Twentieth Century Popular Sheet Music." *Gerontologist*, 30(3):345–353.

Examines American popular sheet music between 1830 and 1980 in an attempt to understand prevailing feelings about aging and old age. The authors find that persistent negative themes appear throughout the period. Fear of poverty, loneliness, and death as well as concern about the physical changes of aging were common themes.

750 COLE, THOMAS R. 1991. "The Specter of Old Age: History, Politics, and Culture in an Aging America." In *Growing Old in America*, edited by Beth B. Hess and Elizabeth W. Markson, 23–37. New Brunswick, NJ: Transaction.

Examines the lack of valued meaning in old age in society, and how that undervaluing has evolved historically. Before 1800, religious and communal values emphasized both the losses as well as the redemption of old age. Liberal individualism eliminated the duality, and in order to legitimize their work, the helping professions promoted a view of the aged as sick and needy. Current efforts to counter ageism rely on the same dichotomies and emphasize unrealistic levels of universal health and self-control. The author calls for new meanings for age that accept its strengths and weaknesses.

751   COWGILL, DONALD O. 1972. "Aging in American Society." In *Aging and Modernization,* edited by Donald Cowgill and Lowell D. Holmes, 243–262. New York: Appleton-Century-Crofts.
    Posits that American society, being highly modernized and individualistic, fails to utilize the older person as an instructor and arbiter of tradition. A fundamental ambivalence toward aging, even among the aged, results in inconsistent policies and limited privileges for the elderly. The author views retirement as an unhappy outcome for many.

752   ———. 1974. "The Aging of Populations and Societies." *Annals of the American Academy of Political and Social Sciences,* 415(September):1–18.
    Argues that modernization has decreased the status of the aged while providing the technology to increase life spans. Recently, institutions and cultures in advanced nations have begun to take the needs and interests of the aged into account again, in large part because the aged segment of the electorate is expanding.

753   ———. 1978. "Residential Segregation by Age in American Metropolitan Areas." *Journal of Gerontology,* 33(3):446–453.
    Examines patterns of age segregation in cities based on census data for 1940 to 1970. Generally higher concentrations of elderly are found in the center of urban areas; as distance from urban centers decreases, the number of elderly declines. Factors contributing to the level of segregation are growth rate of the total population, proportion of elderly in the population, size of the metropolitan area, proportion of minorities in the population, and percentage of the elderly living in institutions.

754   FISCHER, DAVID HACKETT. 1977. *Growing Old in America.* New York: Oxford University Press. 242 pp.
    See entry 11.

755   FLINT, JERRY. 1980. "The Old Folks." *Forbes.* 125(February 18):51–56.
    Argues that most elderly are well off and that the public view of the elderly as living in poverty has been perpetuated by government bureaucrats who want social programs to continue to grow. Flint claims that earlier retirement and longer lives will contribute to a crisis in Social Security financing. He discusses some limitations of private pensions, including the lack of indexing and unfunded liabilities. He is critical of government spending on the aged.

756   FREED, MAYER G., and DOWELL, EDWINA. 1972. "Age Discrimination in the Employment Act of 1967." *Clearinghouse Review,* 6(4–5):196–202.
    Discusses the coverage and definition of terms in the Age Discrimination Employment Act of 1967. The authors list the basic prohibitions,

exceptions, and judicial interpretations of the Act. They describe principles of proof, prerequisites for enforcement proceedings, and procedures for enforcement and relief. They question limiting the provisions of the Act to persons aged 40 to 65.

757   GRUMAN, GERALD J. 1978. "Cultural Origins of Present-Day 'Age-ism': The Modernization of the Life Cycle." In *Aging and the Elderly: Humanistic Perspectives in Gerontology*, edited by Stuart F. Spicker, Kathleen M. Woodard, and David Van Tassel, 359–387. Atlantic Highlands, NJ: Humanities Press.

Analyzes the roots of ageism in American society by drawing on philosophers and other writers from throughout Western history. Gruman reviews the "discovery" of ageism and discusses causes of ageism present since the 1890s, including the closing of the frontier and the rise of evolutionary positivism. He claims that disengagement theory developed from those forces. He outlines an alternative modernization perspective that supports an active role for the elderly in society.

758   HARRIS, FRED. 1974. "Old People Power: Fighting Ageism." *The New Republic*, 179(2):10–11.

Speculates that age discrimination will decrease as elderly become organized and gain political power.

759   HOLSTEIN, MARTHA. 1989. "Business and Aging: What's the Concern?" *Generations*, 13(3):61–64.

Discusses the problems of profit-making enterprises marketing health care and other products to the elderly. To the extent that business targets the well-to-do elder, others in society develop the false impression that all elderly are wealthy. This perception decreases the political legitimacy of the unmet needs of other elders.

760   HUDSON, ROBERT B. 1978. "Emerging Pressures on Public Policies for the Aging." *Society*, 15(5):30–33.

Describes two sets of pressures on the policy system that have resulted in financial benefits for the elderly. Taxpayers are becoming more aware and resentful of the fiscal burden created by old-age policies. Different groups of the elderly are demanding continued social participation and the benefits of early retirement. The rising costs of old-age policies have created a backlash against the aging, hurting the very old more than other elderly.

761   KALISH, RICHARD A. 1979. "The New Ageism and the Failure Models: A Polemic." *Gerontologist*, 19(4):398–402.

Defines a new concept of ageism that perceives all older people as helpless and dependent on agencies and organizations, encourages the development of services without adequate concern for quality and delivery of services, and criticizes society for mistreatment of the elderly. This new ageism results in the generic classification of all elderly and perpetuates an advocacy system focusing on dependency and need at the experience of more positive qualities of the elderly.

762 KENT, DONALD P. 1965. "Aging—Fact and Fancy." *Gerontologist*, 5(2): 51–56, 111.

The then director of the United States Office on Aging reflects on the gaps that exist between perceptions of aging and the facts. He asserts that adherence to false assumptions regarding aging and the needs of the aged has led to mismatching in public program objectives.

763 KUBEY, ROBERT W. 1980. "Television and Aging: Past, Present, and Future." *Gerontologist*, 20(1):16–35.

Extensive review of the literature on the TV-viewing habits of the aged, the image of the elderly in TV programs, the potential impact of TV on the lives of the aged, and the future of programming oriented toward the elderly. The author sees both the content and impact as having the potential for serving the elderly well.

764 LAWTON, M. POWELL, and HOFFMAN, CHRISTINE. 1984. "Neighborhood Reactions to Elderly Housing." *Journal of Housing for the Elderly*, 2(2):41–53.

Discusses the bases for negative reactions to elderly housing for five federally assisted housing projects. Examines the projects 12 years after construction to evaluate their effect on the community. Bases for negative reactions are described as ageism, tendency to associate the elderly with stigma-related services, loss of predictability in the community, and increase in density of housing projects.

765 LEVIN, JACK, and LEVIN, WILLIAM C. 1980. *Ageism: Prejudice and Discrimination against the Elderly*. Belmont, CA: Wadsworth. 153 pp.

Reviews the literature on aging to show the dominant focus on decline. The authors argue that this blames the victim, addressing symptoms rather than causes and show how the aged can be analyzed as a stigmatized minority group. They review the actions of the Gray Panthers to combat social prejudices.

766 LUBOMUDROV, SLAVA. 1987. "Congressional Perceptions of the Elderly: The Use of Stereotypes in Legislative Process." *Gerontologist*, 27(1):77–81.

Provides a content analysis of 893 congressional speeches concerning President Reagan's Social Security proposals. The author finds that less than one-third of the speeches were free of stereotypes and overgeneralizations. Most of the debate used compassionate stereotypes (e.g., the elderly are all poor and need help) similar to those found in general population surveys. Experience with aging issues from committee work led to fewer stereotypes.

767 MANGUM, WILEY P. 1985. "But Not in My Neighborhood; Community Resistance to Housing for the Elderly." *Journal of Housing for the Elderly*, 3(3/4):101–119.

Examines community opposition to two proposals to build housing for the elderly in Tampa, Florida. Mangum analyzes demographic characteristics of individuals who oppose housing for the elderly and the reasons given for this opposition. His findings suggest that negative feelings toward senior housing may be impossible to change, that resistance may be based on reaction to group housing rather than ageism, and that the greatest resistance to housing for the elderly can be expected in single-family home residential areas.

768 ———. 1988. "Community Resistance to Planned Housing for the Elderly: Ageism or General Antipathy to Group Housing?" *Gerontologist*, 28(3):325–329.

Analyzes a survey of 139 single-family housing residents in two south Florida communities to determine how much they would object if senior and other group housing were placed in their neighborhoods. Senior housing was least objectionable, with a general apartment complex being in the middle of the continuum of objection, and juvenile delinquent housing being the most strongly resisted. Resistance to group housing in general was the only significant predictor of resistance to senior housing. Ageism had no effect.

769 MITCHELL, JACK, and GREVE, FRANK. 1987. "Age Bias: The Uphill Battle." *Fifty Plus*, 27(3):32–36+.

Addresses age discrimination in the workplace. The authors note that early retirement incentives have become very sophisticated and frequently make subsequent employment difficult. While age discrimination is often hard to prove, elders should be aware of their rights and take appropriate legal action promptly. The authors claim that investigations conducted by the Equal Employment Opportunity Commission (EEOC) move very slowly, and they recommend that an attorney with expertise in age discrimination law might prove more effective than the EEOC if a case has sufficient merit.

770 NAVARRO, VICENTE. 1984. "The Political Economy of Government Cuts for the Elderly." In *Readings in the Political Economy of Aging*, edited by Meredith Minkler and Carroll L. Estes, 37–46. Farmingdale, NY: Baywood.

Argues that cuts in programs for the elderly in the early 1980s occurred despite general public support for helping the aged. The cause is thus not ageism but the resistance of the capitalist class to aid those no longer in the work force. The author argues that the issues need to be redefined around human needs rather than the needs of capitalism.

771   NILSEN, ALLEEN P. 1978. "Old Blondes Just Dye Away: Relationships between Sexism and Ageism." *Language Arts*, 55(2):175–179.

Presents an overview of how popular culture and language are biased against older women more than older men. The author analyzes data to show the relationship between ageism and sexism and concludes with suggestions teachers can use to combat some of the stereotypes.

772   NUESSEL, FRANK H. 1982. "The Language of Ageism." *Gerontologist*, 22(3):273–276.

Defines derogatory and demeaning terms used to describe the elderly. Nuessel asserts that many terms are both ageist and sexist, dehumanizing the elderly. He describes actions by the American Association of Retired Persons, the National Council on Aging, and especially the Gray Panthers to monitor the use of ageist language in the media. The author recommends a voluntary set of guidelines for language usage in the media.

773   PALMORE, ERDMAN B. 1978. "Are the Aged a Minority Group?" *Journal of the American Geriatrics Society*, 26(5):214–217.

Argues that the elderly are like a minority because they suffer from prejudice, discrimination, and deprivation. They are different in that they are not born into the group and have little group identity or political unity. The author predicts the society will become "age-irrelevant," decreasing the minority status of the aged.

774   PALMORE, ERDMAN B., and MANTON, KENNETH. 1973. "Ageism Compared to Racism and Sexism." *Journal of Gerontology*, 28(3):363–369.

Compares inequality among race, sex, and age groups for income, occupation, weeks worked, and education. The authors find that age produces more income inequality than race, with the inequality of each status being additive. Nonwhites made progress in all areas between 1950 and 1970 while the aged lost ground in income and education. Losses were due to cohort differences, militancy and organization of each group, and differences in programs to overcome inequality for each.

775   PERRY, RALPH B. 1942. *Plea for an Age Movement*. New York: Vanguard. 23 pp.

See entry 206.

776   RANGE, JANE, and VINOVSKIS, MARIS A. 1981. "Images of Elderly in Popular Magazines." *Social Science History*, 5(2):123–170.

Examines how the elderly were portrayed in nineteenth-century short fiction, based on an analysis of one magazine. The authors find that elders were less likely to be portrayed as important characters, but that characterizations of the elderly were not becoming increasingly negative. The elderly were generally depicted as healthy, sane, economically independent, and mostly treated with respect. Elderly characters did not provide guidance to the young. The authors conclude that while images of older people may not reflect the reality of the period, they probably influenced readers' perceptions of them.

777 RODIN, JUDITH, and LANGER, ELLEN. 1980. "Aging Labels: The Decline of Control and the Fall of Self-Esteem." *Journal of Social Issues*, 36(2):12–29.

Reviews existing experimental studies to show how negative labeling of the aged lowers self-concepts and leads to more sick-role behavior. The authors found that changing labels increased self-benefiting behavior for some elderly as their experience of control grew.

778 ROSENCRANZ, HOWARD A., and MCNEVIN, TONY E. 1969. "A Factor Analysis of Attitudes toward the Aged." *Gerontologist*, 9(1):55–59.

Data from 200 college-age students found they held stereotypes about the elderly as being ineffective, dependent, and unfriendly. Respondents with regular contact with older persons judged the aged more favorably.

779 ROSENFELT, ROSALIE H. 1965. "The Elderly Mystique." *Journal of Social Issues*, 21(4):37–43.

Describes the core of ideas and attitudes held about the elderly in terms of the feminist concepts of women described by Betty Friedan in *The Feminine Mystique*. Rosenfelt states that the perception of the elderly as poor, dependent, and incapable emerged with major social and technological changes following World War II. She cites the beliefs and attitudes that make up this perspective. She also references research that disputes these stereotypes. The author briefly discusses the negative implications of this bias toward the elderly.

780 SCHONFIELD, DAVID. 1982. "Who Is Stereotyping Whom and Why?" *Gerontologist*, 22(3):267–272.

Presents evidence challenging the assertion that a negative attitude toward the elderly pervades American society. Part of the difficulty lies in terminological confusion. Data include questions in which respondents were asked their opinions on the number of exceptions to generalizations frequently made about the elderly. The author concludes that careless use of language has led to erroneous conclusions.

781 SELTZER, MILDRED M. 1971. "The Concept of Old: Changing Attitudes and Stereotypes." *Gerontologist*, 11(Part 1):226–230.

Analyzes the descriptions of old people and old objects compared with young people and objects in 40 books of children's literature from 1870 to 1960. The aged were viewed less positively than the young, but little change in the difference between the age groups was found over the years. The literature was generally less ageist than had been expected.

782 THOMAS, WILLIAM C. 1981. "The Expectation Gap and the Stereotype of the Stereotype: Images of Old People." *Gerontologist*, 21(4):402–407.

Explores misconceptions about the elderly and the aging process

by examining previous work on loneliness studies and alienation of the
elderly. The presence or absence of loneliness in an elderly individual's
life is determined not only by social contacts but also by the person's
subjective frame of reference. Survey results show that elderly report
experiencing fewer serious problems than is assumed by both the general public and other elderly.

783   TUCKMAN, JACOB, and LORGE, IRVING. 1953. "Attitudes toward Old Peo-
      ple." *Journal of Social Psychology*, 37(2nd half):249–260.
          Investigates the attitudes of 147 graduate students, age 20 to 51,
      toward old age. The survey addresses commonly held stereotypes in the
      following areas: personality characteristics, physical change, adjust-
      ment, conservatism, activities, and family relationships. No significant
      differences in attitude could be identified based on age or sex of respon-
      dents, although some attitudinal variations based on these factors are
      apparent. The authors conclude that substantial misconceptions exist
      about the elderly because of a lack of knowledge about the aging pro-
      cess. This misinformation creates a negative social climate for the el-
      derly.

784   U.S. COMMISSION ON CIVIL RIGHTS. 1977. *The Age Discrimination Study*.
      Washington, DC: U.S. Government Printing Office. 55 pp.
          Reviews ten major federal programs to determine the extent to
      which the elderly are not receiving their share of services. The report
      concludes that age discrimination against children and the aged exists
      to some extent in each program and that it adversely affects those
      groups.

785   ———. 1979. *The Age Discrimination Study. Part II*. Washington, DC:
      U.S. Government Printing Office. 298 pp.
          Provides a detailed description of the methodology and programs
      examined in the age discrimination study (1977). The report summa-
      rizes the interviews and testimony concerning each program.

Intergenerational Conflict

786   BINNEY, ELIZABETH A., and ESTES, CARROLL L. 1988. "The Retreat of the
      State and Its Transfer of Responsibility: The Intergenerational War." *In-
      ternational Journal of Health Services*, 18(1):83–96.
          Challenges the validity of the widely discussed conflict of interests
      between the generations. The authors present evidence that the use of
      demographic trends to support claims of intergenerational conflict is
      faulty and shifts attention away from broader social issues. Health care
      financing and caregiving are two issues within which a false conflict is
      being fostered by some groups.

787   CALLAHAN, DANIEL. 1985. "What Do Children Owe Elderly Parents?" *Hastings Center Report*, 15(2):32–37.
      Examines traditional views on moral obligations of children to their aging parents. Callahan discusses the impact of state legislation under consideration that may require children to pay a portion of Medicaid costs for their parents' care.

788   CAMERON, PAUL, and CROMER, ARTHUR. 1974. "Generational Homophyly." *Journal of Gerontology*, 29(2):232–236.
      Analyzes the reported association preferences of 317 randomly selected young, middle-aged, and older adults in Detroit. The data show that the middle-aged and old desire to associate with the next younger generation; the elderly represent the least popular target of association overall.

789   CHAKRAVARTY, SUBRATA, with WEISMAN, KATHERINE. 1988. "Consuming Our Children?" *Forbes*, 142(November 14):222–232.
      Argues that the old are getting richer as the young are getting poorer. Social security and Medicare help the elderly keep their wealth by taxing working people. The authors attribute the programs to the voting power and organizations of the aged. They advocate reducing entitlements given to the nonpoor.

790   CLARK, PHILLIP G. 1985. "The Social Allocation of Health Care Resources: Ethical Dilemmas in Age-Group Competition." *Gerontologist*, 25(2):119–125.
      See entry 649.

791   COLE, THOMAS R. 1989. "Generational Equity in America: A Cultural Historian's Perspective." *Social Science and Medicine*, 29(3):377–383.
      Presents historical information to argue that intergenerational conflict results from the U.S. military and economic decline, the legitimation crisis of the state, and population aging. Generational equity requires the distribution of valued social roles and meanings to the aged, a shift that in turn will lead to a new generational compact that could eliminate competition over other resources.

792   COOK, FAY LOMAX. 1979. *Who Should Be Helped? Public Support for Social Services.* Beverly Hills: Sage Publications. 227 pp.
      Reports a survey of a cross-section of Chicagoans in 1976–77 to ascertain opinions regarding welfare decisions in a context of increasing scarcity and conflict. The results reveal that expenditures for the elderly are favored over those for children, and programs for children are preferred over those for adults under 65. The author concludes that the public is not opposed to public spending in the welfare domain, even during a tax-cutting period.

793   ———. 1979. "The Disabled and the Poor Elderly: Preferred Groups for Public Support?" *Gerontologist*, 19(4):344–353.
      Analyzes data from 384 Chicago residents concerning their relative

support for services for the elderly and other groups. The author finds that support for poor elderly and disabled elderly is greater than for other age and income groups. Support was higher for children only for education. The ranking was similar by race, income, age, sex, and education of respondent.

794   COWGILL, DONALD O. 1979. "The Revolution of Age." In *The Age of Aging: A Reader in Social Gerontology*, edited by Abraham Monk, 62–72. Buffalo, NY: Prometheus.

Disputes the argument that greater public policy attention to aging will produce a severe burden on younger generations. Cowgill cites a study of 82 countries noting that a rise in the proportion of elderly inevitably is accompanied by a decline in the ratio of the young. He cautions about the dangers of pressures for early retirement.

795   DANIEL YANKELOVICH, INC. 1969. *Generations Apart*. New York: Columbia Broadcasting System. 84 pp.

National survey results from 1,340 youth aged 17 to 23 and 663 of their parents examining differences in values, political orientations, and social alienation. The results show attitudinal gaps between children and parents for both radical as well as conservative youth. The primary focus of the survey is on the youth movement.

796   DANIELS, NORMAN. 1983. "Justice between Age Groups: Am I My Parent's Keeper?" *Milbank Memorial Fund Quarterly*, 61(3):489–522.

Addresses moral questions raised by the practice of rationing health care, questioning whether distributive schemes are fair or age biased. The author discusses the concept of age bias in public policy and the distributive problem posed by different age groups. He suggests competition between age groups be approached from an institutional perspective; this will provide a means for expressing preferences and transferring resources from one life stage to another. Two strategies for accomplishing this are (1) relying on market mechanisms and (2) designing social institutions to address relevant problems. He argues that rationing may not be morally objectionable if it is carried out by a just institution under nearly ideal conditions.

797   DAVIS, KINGSLEY, and VAN DEN OEVER, PIETRONELLA. 1981. "Age Relations and Public Policy in Advanced Industrial Societies." *Population and Development Review*, 7(1):1–18.

Examines intergenerational conflict in industrial societies. Historically there has been little friction between age groups. Intergenerational conflict has increased as the populations of industrial societies have aged and economic support for them has become institutionalized. Public policy, based on the assumption that most elderly are poor and incapacitated, has increased the incomes of the elderly faster than those of other age groups. This shift has increased the burden on younger workers, who must support a growing elderly population that is retiring at an earlier age. The authors conclude that policy should emphasize the needs of younger workers rather than the nonworking elderly in order to maximize productivity during times of scarcity.

798 DONNELLY, HARRISON. 1981. "Percentage of Aged to Grow Sharply as Baby Boom Generation Turns Gray." *Congressional Quarterly Weekly Report*, 39(48):2330–2331.

Brief consideration of the increasing proportion of elderly as a percentage of total population. The author lists selected demographics of the older population.

799 DOWD, JAMES J. 1980. "Exchange Rates and Old People." *Journal of Gerontology*, 35(4):596–602.

Analyzes developments in the conceptualization of social exchange theory and explores methods in which these concepts explain social behavior in old age. Dowd addresses the issues of status characteristics and exchange and the rule of distributive justice. He also discusses cross-age interaction. The author suggests that as future cohorts, who are in better health and are better educated, test the boundaries of the exchange rate, age conflict is likely.

800 DYCHTWALD, KEN, and FLOWER, JOE. 1989. "Calling a Truce in the Age Wars." *State Government News*, 32(3):7–9.

Describes the aging of the baby boom as placing strains on old-age programs designed for a smaller aged population. The authors suggest providing benefits only to those in need.

801 FENGLER, ALFRED P., and WOOD, VIVIAN. 1972. "The Generation Gap: An Analysis of Attitudes on Contemporary Issues." *Gerontologist*, 12(Summer):124–128.

Examines the attitudinal differences over a variety of concerns among three generations in 73 families. Age provides the most consistent explanation of different attitudes, even when education, religion, and urban-rural residence are controlled in the analysis. The young (college students) are the most liberal, parents less liberal, and grandparents least liberal.

802 FEUER, LEWIS S. 1969. *The Conflict of Generations*. New York: Basic Books. 543 pp.

Analysis of U.S. and foreign student movements as the combination of idealistic altruism and generational conflict. The author finds the pre-1960s absence of mass U.S. student movements a consequence of an earlier "generational equilibrium," when no generation felt its energies and intelligence frustrated by the others. He describes the small incidence of student conflicts prior to that era.

803   GILBERT, NEIL, and SPECHT, HARRY. 1982. "A 'Fair Share' for the Aged:
      Title XX Allocation Patterns, 1976–1980." *Research on Aging*, 4(1):71–
      86.
          Analyzes Title XX allocations to determine whether the elderly re-
      ceived a fair share of services. The authors analyzed and ranked Com-
      prehensive Annual Service Plans for all states and Washington, D.C., and
      concluded that the elderly do receive a fair share of services in all but a
      few states, if the following assumptions are correct: what constitutes a
      fair share is roughly proportional to the number of elderly in the pop-
      ulation, 1975–1980 trends are stable, state plans indicate actual expendi-
      tures, and state patterns for allocations are similar to national patterns.

804   HACKETT, DAVID H. 1978. "Putting Our Heads to the 'Problem' of Old
      Age." In *The New Old: Struggling for Decent Aging*, edited by Ronald
      Gross, Beatrice Gross, and Sylvia Seidman, 58–62. Garden City, NY: An-
      chor.
          Reviews the historical conflict of the young as victims of the old and
      the old as victims of the young. Hackett recommends a public policy
      that would provide adequately for all without age discrimination. Social
      Security is criticized for placing a regressive burden on the younger gen-
      eration.

805   HAYES-BAUTISTA, DAVID E.; SCHINK, WERNER O.; and CHAPA, JORGE. 1988.
      The Burden of Support: Young Latinos in an Aging Society. Stanford:
      Stanford University Press. 196 pp.
          Presents demographic projections for California to show the
      possibility of intergenerational conflict between a young working-poor
      Latino population and an older, wealthier, retired Anglo population.
      The authors suggest ways to avoid this conflict.

806   HELCO, HUGH. 1988. "Generational Politics." In *The Vulnerable*, edited
      by John L. Palmer, Timothy Smeeding, and Barbara Boyle Torrey, 381–
      411. Washington, DC: Urban Institute Press.
          Argues that social policies did not evolve from children versus el-
      derly debates. In recent years the means of consumption have become
      increasingly politicized. Helco does not see intergeneration conflict
      over Social Security even a possibility until the baby-boom workers re-
      tire and costs rise. He discusses the prospects for changes in public sup-
      port for both children and the aged.

807   HUDSON, ROBERT B. 1978. "Political and Budgetary Consequences of an
      Aging Population." *National Journal*, 10(42):1699–1705.
          Describes the federal budgetary pressures being created by the
      growing number of elderly. Hudson notes that the improved economic
      and health situation of the aged may erode public support for programs.
      Other groups, like poor children, will demand increasing support. Ris-
      ing costs of existing programs for the aged will constrain future pro-
      grams.

808 KALISH, RICHARD A. 1969. "The Old and the New as Generation Gap Allies." *Gerontologist*, 9(1):83–89.

An essay that describes the different values of the young and the old as consequences of their life experiences. The author argues that both age groups share similar concerns and should work together to their mutual advantage.

809 KAYE, LENARD W. 1988. "Generational Equity: Pitting Young against Old." *New England Journal of Human Services*, 8(1):8–11.

Takes issue with advocates of the generational equity policy framework. Americans for Generational Equity (AGE) assert that the elderly receive a disproportionate share of social welfare funds at the expense of the young. The author recommends that advocates for the elderly work with the young to counteract the misunderstandings and misinformation that abound.

810 KIESTER, EDWIN, JR. 1986. "Young vs. Old: The War We Must Never Allow to Happen." *Fifty-Plus*, 26(8):40–42+.

Confronts news reports of predicted intergenerational conflict surrounding shrinking fiscal resources. The difference in viewpoint between Americans for Generational Equity (AGE) and the Gray Panthers and members of the American Association of Retired Persons is presented. The author suggests that the issue is clouded by many myths and that both sides must work together for an equitable solution.

811 KINGSON, ERIC R. 1988. "Generational Equity: An Unexpected Opportunity to Broaden the Politics of Aging." *Gerontologist*, 28(6):765–772.

Summarizes different views of generational equity including those presented in the Gerontological Society of America's 1986 report *Ties That Bind*. Policy recommendations that address the issues of justice in resource distribution between rich and poor and the inadequacy of a pluralist approach to politics in accomplishing this goal are presented. The author suggests that interest groups for the aging should become involved in developing a multigenerational agenda to assure justice between rich and poor and advocacy for all age groups.

812 ———. 1989. "Misconceptions Distort Social Security Policy Discussions." *Social Work*, 34(4):357–362.

Discusses the misconceptions about Social Security that have recently been popularized by those who wish to pit the old against the young. Kingson explains how the system assures adequacy as well as individual equity, and how it serves well both minorities and the young.

813 KINGSON, ERIC R.; HIRSHORN, BARBARA A.; and CORNMAN, JOHN M. 1986. *Ties That Bind: The Interdependence of Generations*. Washington, DC: Seven Locks Press. 195 pp.

Report commissioned by the Gerontological Society of America that discusses the challenges of an aging society. The authors empha-

size the interrelationships between generations and explain why conflict need not occur. They discuss family caregiving, social security, research, public policy, and the stake that the elderly have in child policy.
They argue that proponents of the intergenerational conflict perspective rely on a series of misunderstandings.

814   LAMM, RICHARD D. 1987. "Ethical Health Care for the Elderly: Are We
      Cheating Our Children?" In *Should Medical Care Be Rationed by Age?*,
      edited by Timothy Smeeding, xi–xv. Totowa, NJ: Rowman & Littlefield.
          Claims we are taking resources from children to provide unneeded
      benefits for the elderly. Lamm argues that well-to-do persons should not
      receive Social Security and that we should not prioritize medical care for
      those with a poor quality of life.

815   LAUFER, ROBERT S., and BENGTSON, VERN L. 1974. "Generations, Aging and
      Social Stratification: On the Development of Generational Units." *Jour-
      nal of Social Issues*, 30(3):181–205.
          Suggests that generational analysis to date has ignored the issue of
      how superordinate and subordinate class groupings influence the expe-
      rience of age-cohort membership. Four types of generational units
      among youth are defined: radicalism, freakism, communalism, and re-
      vivalism. The possibility of existence and functioning of such genera-
      tional units among the elderly is discussed.

816   LONGMAN, PHILLIP. 1985. "Justice between Generations." *Atlantic
      Monthly*, June: 73–81.
          Argues that the price of Social Security and Medicare for the cur-
      rent and baby-boom elderly will unfairly burden today's youth when
      they reach adulthood. The author presents a view of most elderly as well
      off. He claims that the forecasts that public programs can meet their
      obligations in the future rest on unrealistic economic assumptions. He
      suggests that economic growth and reduced benefits for the elderly are
      needed to balance the needs of the young and old.

817   ———. 1986. "Age Wars: The Coming Battle between Young and Old."
      The Futurist, January-February:8–11.
          Argues that federal budget deficits are mortgaging the future of the
      young for the benefit of today's elderly.

818   ———. 1987. *Born to Pay: The New Politics of Aging in America*. Bos-
      ton: Houghton Mifflin. 308 pp.
          Argues that the elderly in society are receiving benefits at the ex-
      pense of the young. The elderly benefit more than they deserve in the
      areas of housing, medical care, social security, consumer consumption,
      and taxation. The author critiques the concept that social benefits
      should be provided solely on the basis of age rather than need. Because
      senior advocacy groups work to protect age-based programs like Social

Security, a large number of wealthy elderly continue to obtain unneeded social benefits that could better be targeted to children.

819 MINKLER, MEREDITH. 1986. "'Generational Equity' and the New Victim Blaming: An Emerging Public Policy Issue." *International Journal of Health Services*, 16(4):539–551.

Analyzes policy discussions on "intergenerational equity." Minkler asserts that assumptions of the elderly as a homogeneous, financially secure population are erroneous. Census data and national opinion poll data are cited to demonstrate that multiple generations and ethnic groups depend on Social Security and Medicare. The author suggests that reexamination of the issue of income equity for all in our society would provide a truer framework for policy analysis.

820 ———. 1986. "The Politics of Generational Equity." *Social Policy*, September:48–52.

Critiques the claims that the elderly are receiving more than their fair share and argues that the maldistribution of political and economic resources is the real problem.

821 ORIOL, WILLIAM E. 1970. "Social Policy Priorities: Age vs. Youth—The Federal Government." *Gerontologist*, 10(3):207–210.

Presents the argument by Oroil, a former Secretary of Health, Education and Welfare, that expenditures for the elderly were excessive during the 1960s when compared to spending for the young. The fragmentation of congressional authority is viewed as central to the problems.

822 PALMORE, ERDMAN B., and WHITTINGTON, FRANK. 1971. "Trends in the Relative Status of the Aged." *Social Forces*, 50(1):84–91.

Argues that the status of the aged has declined with industrialization and that the aged are becoming more like a minority group. Trend analysis from census and health statistics for 1940–1969 shows that the elderly are poorer, work in lower-status occupations, have poorer health, and are residentially concentrated in rural areas and central cities. The authors note that most gaps increased over the period of study.

823 PONZA, MICHAEL; DUNCAN, GREG J.; CORCORAN, MARY; and GROSKIND, FRED. 1988. "The Guns of Autumn? Age Differences in Support for Income Transfers to the Young and Old." *Public Opinion Quarterly*, 52(4):441–466.

Analyzes 1973 and 1986 national survey data that show elderly people do not favor spending on poor older women more than on poor young families with children. Income was more important than age in predicting support for public programs for the poor. The authors suggest that public programs for the aged are a result of universal support for such benefits.

824   PRESTON, SAMUEL H. 1984. "Children and the Elderly: Divergent Paths for
      America's Dependents." *Demography*, 21(4):435–457.
          Examines the consequences of changing demography for children
      and elderly. Even weakened, the family system is the primary support
      for children while government has become the primary source of up-
      keep for the elderly. Support for public programs for the elderly comes
      from the aged, family members who would have to provide mainte-
      nance for their elders, lacking public programs, and adults who are con-
      cerned about their own old age. Children have only the aid of their fam-
      ilies. Changing demography reduces the base of political support for
      children while increasing it for the elderly. The changing favor of child
      education versus health care for the aged demonstrates the disadvan-
      taged status of children.

825   PRESTON, SAMUEL H. 1984. "Children and the Elderly in the U.S." *Scien-
      tific American*, 251(6):44–49.
          Often-cited article that argues that the elderly have benefited more
      than children from social policies since the 1960s. Preston examines
      poverty rates, health indicators, education, and federal spending and
      claims that political support for the elderly comes from more sources
      than for children, a position reinforced by the growing number of el-
      derly in society. This shift disproportionately benefits the aged as poli-
      tics is now based more on self-interest than collective needs.

826   QUADAGNO, JILL S. 1989. "Generational Equity and the Politics of the Wel-
      fare State." *Politics and Society*, 17(3):353–376.
          See entry 131.

827   RAGAN, PAULINE K. 1977. "Another Look at the Politicizing of Old Age:
      Can We Expect a Backlash Effect?" *Urban and Social Change Review*,
      10:6–13.
          Identifies the limited instances of political backlash against the el-
      derly and describes the constraints on the mobilization of the elderly
      that would limit the development of such negative opinion. The author
      notes that backlashes generally occur during troubled economic times
      and are often a reaction to only a perceived injustice.

828   RUGGLES, PATRICIA, and MOON, MARILYN. 1985. "The Impact of Recent
      Legislative Changes in Benefit Programs for the Elderly." *Gerontologist*,
      25(2):153–160.
          Reviews the impact of federal budget cuts made between 1981 and
      1983 on programs for the elderly. Households with elderly members
      were found to have lost a smaller share of their benefits than house-
      holds without elderly members. Since Supplemental Security Income
      benefits increased, the overall benefit reductions for the elderly were
      concentrated among families with incomes above the poverty line.

829 SAMUELSON, ROBERT J. 1978. "Busting the U.S. Budget—The Costs of an Aging America." *National Journal* (February):256–260.

Argues that the increasing costs of programs for the elderly will challenge the ability of the federal government to pay for them. Government spending will shift from local areas that focus on schools and programs for the young to the federal government where spending is concentrated on the elderly. The author reviews major federal programs for the elderly.

830 SCHIFFRES, MANUEL. 1984. "Next: Young vs. Old?" *U.S. News and World Report*, November 5:94.

Claims that Social Security benefits should be cut to balance the budget. The author argues that the politically powerful elderly protect the program that transfers wealth from struggling youth to comfortable elderly.

831 SMITH, LEE. 1987. "The War between the Generations." *Fortune*, July 20:78–82.

Argues that changing demographics will make it impossible for the baby-boom generation to enjoy the same levels of Social Security benefits that current elders do. Smith suggests reducing future benefits so as not to burden younger adults.

832 STEWART, DOUGLAS J. 1970. "The Lesson of California—Disenfranchise the Old." *The New Republic*, 163(8–9):20–22.

Describes the changing culture of California and the effect of the large number of persons retiring there. Stewart charges that the elderly have no stake in the future of the state and should lose the right to vote at retirement.

833 TAYLOR, PAUL. 1986. "The Coming Conflict as We Soak the Young to Enrich the Old." *Washington Post*, January 5:D1, D4.

Claims that the elderly are being enriched at the expense of the young, primarily through Social Security. The statistics presented show the economic situation of the elderly as better than that of children, with the economic condition of the middle aged declining. The power of the elderly vote is seen as protecting Social Security from the types of cuts other programs have suffered.

834 TOBIN, JAMES. 1987. "An Exchange on Social Security." *The New Republic*, 196(20):20–23.

Critiques *The New Republic*'s (*TNR*) articles attacking Social Security. Tobin argues that Social Security does not contribute to the federal deficit, is not regressive, will not burden the young in the next century, and involves a social contract between the aged and society. *TNR* editors defend their articles.

835 U.S. PRESIDENT'S SCIENCE ADVISORY COMMITTEE. 1973. "Background: History of Age Grouping in America." In *Youth: Transition to Adulthood*,

9–29. Report of the Panel on Youth. Washington, DC: U.S. Government Printing Office.

Describes how industrialization and urbanization have changed age groupings of youth from broad, integrated groups in the family, school, and work to narrow age ranges in each. The report suggests that there was no Golden Age in intergenerational relationships between youth and older adults given tensions present even in the earlier groupings.

836   WARREN, EARL. 1951. "California's Biggest Headache." In *The Politics of California*, edited by David Farrelly and Ivan Hinderaker, 3–12. New York: Ronald.

Outlines migration to California between 1940 and 1950 and the resulting civic problems. Warren speculates on the reasons for California's popularity, especially among the retired. He discusses problems associated with large populations and urban development in the postwar era.

837   WYNNE, EDWARD. 1991. "Will the Young Support the Old." In *Growing Old in America* (4th ed.), edited by Beth B. Hess and Elizabeth W. Markson, 507–524. New Brunswick, NJ: Transaction.

Argues that the elderly must move away from claiming rights to asking for reciprocity as the basis for government benefits. Wynne explains that the young need to be socialized to expect reciprocity; the elderly need to make their past and present contributions evident so the young will be willing to support the growing number of elderly.

The Law and the Legal System

838   • 1963–64. "The Disguised Oppression of Involuntary Guardianship: Have the Elderly Freedom to Spend?" *Yale Law Journal*, 73(4):676–692.

Examines legal procedures that allow the imposition of involuntary guardianship on the elderly and the lack of adequate legal protection for them. Involuntary guardianship imposes limits on the freedom of older people to spend income since nonconservative spending patterns may be interpreted as incompetence. The article explains the legal and historical basis of involuntary guardianship and the relationship between perceptions of mental incompetence and loss of personal and property rights. Evidence of mental disability in the elderly is more likely to result in loss of rights. The article suggests appointing two guardians, one to care for the individual and one for the individual's property, to reduce conflicts of interest.

839   • 1989. "Law of the Elderly Poor: 1988." *Clearinghouse Review*, 22(8):954–965.

Summarizes 1988 litigation and legislation that will have an impact on poor elderly. Medicare Catastrophic Coverage Act improves Medicare benefits, but does not cover long-term or community-based care. The article describes new Medicaid rules affecting transfer of assets as well as significant reforms dealing with federal nursing home law. Other important legislation includes the Older Americans Act Amendments of 1987 and proposed IRS regulations affecting pensions and health benefits.

840 BRICKFIELD, CYRIL F. 1975. "A Legal Advocate for the Aged Looks at Their Legislative Problems." In *Legal Problems of Older Americans*, edited by Dorothy Heyman, 24–27. Durham, NC: Center for the Study of Aging and Human Development, Duke University.

Describes the political strategy in Congress and states of the American Association for Retired Persons and the National Retired Teachers Association and summarizes the issues they are concerned with.

841 CAIN, LEONARD D, 1974 "Political Factors in the Emerging Legal Age Status of the Elderly." *Annals of the American Academy of Political and Social Sciences*, 415(September):70–79.

Reviews legal history to show that the elderly have developed a distinct legal status. Earlier law focused on distinguishing children from adults. Legal status is based on formal chronological definitions of age, although it is often justified on the functional status of the elderly. Cain predicts that the courts will be called on to decide whether formal and/or functional definitions of old age are constitutional.

842 ———. 1974. "The Growing Importance of Legal Age in Determining the Status of the Elderly." *Gerontologist*, 14(April):167–174.

Examines the historical roots of according the elderly a separate legal status based on age rather than functional status or need. The author notes the paradox in advocates who want to eliminate restrictions on the elderly based on age but who continue to advocate special programs for the elderly based primarily on age. He also notes that gerontological theory is not reflected in laws that target the elderly. Laws that are based solely on age are seen as fundamentally flawed.

843 ———. 1976. "Aging and the Law." In *Handbook of Aging and the Social Sciences*, edited by Robert H. Binstock and Ethel Shanas, 342–368. New York: Van Nostrand.

Examines the use of age in law throughout history to show that the major concern has been to distinguish between pre-adults and adults. Concern with old age versus younger adults is confined mostly to the post-eighteenth century. The law uses chronological age as a determinant and assumes that the elderly are unable to provide for their own basic needs.

844 COHEN, ELIAS S. 1974. "Legal Research Issues on Aging." *Gerontologist*, 14(3):263–267.

Reviews the limited literature on aging and the law, which focuses mostly on substantive issues. Cohen found little on frameworks, such as ways of looking at the impact of legal age on the status of the elderly. The author provides a research agenda.

845 COPPELMAN, PETER DAVID. 1972. "Legal Challenges to Relative Responsibility in Old Age Security Programs: Establishing the Right to Grow Old with Dignity." *Clearinghouse Review*, 6(4–5):212–219.

Criticizes relative responsibility laws because they act as a tax on the relatives of poor elderly. Coppelman discusses the enforcement of relative responsibility laws against adult children of elderly receiving Old Age Assistance. If welfare reforms similar to those in California are implemented at the federal level, relative responsibility will increase in both extent and liability. The author advocates legal challenges of relative responsibility laws and outlines the legal basis for such suits under equal protection and privacy laws.

846 EGLIT, HOWARD. 1985. "Age and the Law." In *Handbook of Aging and the Social Sciences* (2nd ed.), edited by Robert H. Binstock and Ethel Shanas, 528–553. New York: Van Nostrand.

Reviews significant legal developments against age discrimination. Eglit examines the reasons that courts have not considered age discrimination as significant as racial and sex discrimination, why discrimination against the aged has recently become an issue, conditions when age is an appropriate category, and whether the anti-ageism movement can be sustained without also eliminating the privilege of old age. The author concludes that the rejection of age discrimination is largely a result of the broader societal rejection of race and sex discrimination.

847 FAHR, SAMUEL H. 1983. "Legal Problems of Older People." In *Hoffman's Daily Needs and Interests of Older People*, edited by Woodrow Morris, Iva Bader, and Adeline Hoffman, 66–80. Springfield, IL: Charles C Thomas.

Addresses legal problems relating to Social Security benefits, Medicare, Medicaid, incompetency, and age discrimination in employment as well as the private issues of wills, trusts, and guardianships.

848 GILFIX, MICHAEL. 1986. "Advising Aging Clients." *California Lawyer*, 6(9):50–54, 80–81.

Discusses how to advise older clients about the law in ways to empower them to take full advantage of public programs. The author reviews strategies concerning MediCal and other public benefits, and discusses durable power of attorney.

849 GILFIX, MICHAEL, and STRAUS, PETER J. 1988. "New Age Estate Planning: The Emergence of Elder Law." *Trusts and Estates*, 124(4):14–30.

Explains how the cost of long-term health care and other problems associated with aging have established the need for elder law. The authors describe steps attorneys can take to make legal consultation easier for elderly clients. They stress the importance for lawyers of understanding the aging process. They discuss the role of aging networks, services, and support groups in elder law and outline the major issues in this area.

850   GOLDSMITH, JACK. 1977. "Criminal Victimization of Older Persons: Problems and Programs." *Connecticut Law Review*, 9(3):435–449.
Examines the issues and problems in the conceptualization and implementation of programs to reduce the impact of crime on the aged; discusses policy implications.

851   HACKLER, EUGENE T. 1977. "Expansion of Health Care Providers' Liability: An Application of *Darling* to Long-Term Health Care Facilities." *Connecticut Law Review*, 9(3):462–481.
Reviews the potential for using accreditation and licensing standards in negligence litigation against long-term care facilities.

852   HEALTH LAW PROJECT, UNIVERSITY OF PENNSYLVANIA LAW SCHOOL. 1972. "Legal Problems Inherent in Organizing Nursing Home Occupants." *Clearinghouse Review*, 6(4–5):203–211.
See entry 187.

853   KELLER, OLIVER J., and VEDDER, CLYDE B. 1968. "The Crimes That Old Persons Commit." *Gerontologist*, 8(1):43–50.
Examines the 1964 uniform crime reports on arrests by age group. The authors repeat that the most common offenses for all age groups involved drunkenness, disorderly conduct, and drunk driving. Older offenders are less likely to be arrested for crimes involving violence, burglary, or homicide, but are more likely to be arrested for vagrancy, embezzlement, fraud, and sexual offenses (excluding forcible rape).

854   LEVINE, MARTIN. 1980. "Four Models for Age/Work Policy Research." *Gerontologist*, 20(5):561–574.
Reviews how exclusions of the elderly from the work force are explained by theories of employer rationality, rivalry, time preference, stereotyping, and a psychoanalytic ambivalence toward the aged. The author relates these theories to legal trends in using age as an employment criterion, suggesting that case law is based on the first three theories.

855   ———. 1980. "Research in Law and Aging." *Gerontologist*, 20(2):163–167.
Reviews the basic issues in the study of aging and the law. At the heart of the field is the question of whether the law should take chronological age into account or whether doing so is a type of discrimination.

856   NATHANSON, PAUL S. 1975. "Legal Services Resources: Pensions and Other Concerns." In *Legal Problems of Older Americans*, edited by

Dorothy Heyman. Durham, NC: Center for the Study of Aging and Human Development, Duke University. pp. 16–22.

Discusses how lawyers can serve as advocates and advisers for the aged, especially in the area of private pensions. The author reviews funding sources for legal services for the aged and describes several legal cases against private pension plan rules that created difficulties for employees in qualifying for the pension.

857   SAPER, MICHAEL S. 1988. "To Move or Not to Move?" *Trusts and Estates*, 124(4):31–36.

Advice column directed at convincing lawyers and trust officers to help their elderly clients make sensible decisions about housing changes. Saper provides basic information on community services and housing options.

4

Resources for Research and Advocacy

Reference Works

858 AMERICAN ASSOCIATION FOR INTERNATIONAL AGING. 1989. *U.S. Directory and Sourcebook on Aging, 1989–1990*. Silver Spring, MD: Business Publishers.

Profiles hundreds of organizations involved in the study of and planning for the aged. The directory includes public, business, voluntary, community, and mass membership groups. It describes the constituency, mission, issues of concern, types of activity, publications, organization and structure, staffing, and finances. The entries are organized by state.

859 BUREK, DEBORAH M. 1990. *Encyclopedia of Associations–1991*. (25th ed.). Detroit: Gale Research. 3 vols.

Comprehensive listing of virtually all national and regional voluntary associations in the United States, updated yearly. The work includes addresses and phone numbers as well as information on organization staff, budget, membership size, activities and mission, and publications.

860 CAIN, LEONARD D., JR. 1959. "The Sociology of Aging: A Trend Report and Bibliography." *Current Sociology*, 8(2):57–133.

Discusses the development of sociology of aging as a field of study. Cain considers its role in society and distinguishes between social gerontology as a social movement and the disciplines of sociology of aging and sociology of old age. A lengthy annotated bibliography is included.

861 COBERLY, SALLY; ESTES, CARROLL L.; and CUTLER, NEAL E. 1990. Brief Bibliography: Aging and Public Policy. Washington, DC: Association for Gerontology in Higher Education. 9 pp.

Succinct annotated bibliography of articles and books appropriate for teaching a class on aging and public policy.

862   U.S. DEPARTMENT OF HEALTH, EDUCATION, AND WELFARE. 1960. *Handbook of National Organizations with Delegate Status at the White House Conference on Aging*. Washington, DC: U.S. Government Printing Office. 117 pp.

      Lists several hundred organizations involved in services for and with the aged, including information on their memberships, affiliates, purpose of organization, programs and services for the aging, plans for future programs, official policy positions, and cooperative work with other organizations.

863   U.S. NATIONAL INSTITUTE ON AGING. 1989. *Resource Directory for Older People*. Washington, DC: U.S. Government Printing Office. 224 pp.

      Directory of organizations and government agencies that deal primarily with older persons and their families. Provides addresses, phone numbers, missions, services, and publications.

Appendix: Addresses and Missions of Advocacy Organizations

Leadership Council on Aging—Advocacy Organizations

AFL-CIO
815 16th Street, N.W., Suite 306
Washington, DC 20006
Karen Ignagni, Director of Employee Benefits
(202) 637-5204
Margaret Seminario, Director, Occupational Safety, Health and Social Security
(202) 637-5366

AFSCME Retiree Program
1625 "L" Street, N.W.
Washington, DC 20036
Steve Regenstreif, Director of Retiree Program
(202) 429-1000

American Association for International Aging
1511 "K" Street, N.W., Suite 443
Washington, DC 20005
Dr. Helen K. Kerschner, Executive Director
(202) 638-6815

American Association of Retired Persons
1909 "K" Street, N.W.
Washington, DC 20049
Horace Deets, Executive Director
(202) 728-4200
Mission: The American Association of Retired Persons (AARP) is a consumer organization that seeks to improve the quality of life for older people.

American Association of Homes for the Aging
901 "E" Street, N.W., Suite 500
Washington, DC 20005
Sheldon Goldberg, President
(202) 296–5960
Mission: The American Association of Homes for the Aging (AAHA) is a professional organization of nonprofit nursing homes, independent housing facilities, continuing care communities, and community service agencies.

American Baptist Churches, USA
P.O. Box 851
Valley Forge, PA 19482–0851
Dr. Carol S. Pierskalla, Chairman
(215) 768–2395

American Society on Aging
833 Market Street, Room 512
San Francisco, CA 94103
Gloria Cavanaugh, Executive Director
(415) 543–2617
Mission: The American Society on Aging is a nonprofit, membership organization that informs the public and health professionals about issues that affect the quality of life for older persons and promotes innovative approaches to meeting the needs of these individuals.

American Society on Aging
600 Maryland Ave., S.W., West Wing 100
Washington, DC 20024
William Oriol (Washington Representative)
(202) 479–6977

Arthritis in Aging
1363 Kalmia Rd., N.W.
Washington, DC 20012
Dr. Josephine H. Kyles
(202) 723–2472

Association for Gerontology in Higher Education
600 Maryland Ave., S.W., Suite 204 West Wing
Washington, DC 20024
Elizabeth B. Douglass, Executive Director
(202) 484–7505
Mission: The Association of Gerontology in Higher Education (AGHE) is a professional organization that includes colleges, universities, and other educational institutions that offer training in the field of gerontology (the study of the biological, clinical, economic, and psychosocial aspects of aging).

Associacion Nacional Pro Personas Mayores
3325 Wilshire Blvd., Suite 800
Los Angeles, CA 90010
Carmela G. Lacayo, CEO
(213) 487–1922

Catholic Golden Age
1012 14th Street, N.W., Suite 1008
Washington, DC 20005
Joseph Leary, President
(202) 737–0321
Mission: Catholic Golden Age sponsors charitable work and offers religious worship opportunities for older individuals.

Charities of Santa Clara County
100 N. Winchester Blvd., Suite 262
Santa Clara, CA 95050
Dee Wischmann, Executive Director
(408) 243–3001

Eating Together in Baltimore
118 N. Howard Street
Baltimore, MD 21202
Colleen Pierre, Nutrition Program Director
(301) 396–1631

Families USA
1334 "G" Street, N.W., Suite 3
Washington, DC 20005
Ronald Pollack, Executive Director
(202) 737–6340

Gray Panthers
1424 16th Street, N.W., Suite 607
Washington, DC 20036
Gary Christopherson, Executive Director
(202) 296–8130
Mission: The Gray Panthers is an advocacy group that works to eliminate age-ism, discrimination against older people on the basis of chronologic age.

Gray Panthers of Metropolitan Washington
711 5th Street
Washington, DC 20001
Esther Weisser (Washington Representative)
(202) 347–9541

National Association of State Units on Aging
2033 "K" Street, N.W., Suite 304
Washington, DC 20006
Daniel A. Quirk, Executive Director
(202) 785–0707

National Association for Older Persons
2025 "I" Street, N.W., Suite 219
Washington, DC 20006
Mario Diaz (Washington Representative)
(202) 293–9329

National Association of Foster Grandparents
195 E. San Fernando Street
San Jose, CA 95112
Betty Pate Manley, Director of FPG
(408) 280–5553

National Association of Retired Federal Employees
1533 New Hampshire Ave., N.W.
Washington, DC 20036
Hal Price, President
(202) 234–0832

National Association of Area Agencies on Aging
1112 16th Street, N.W., Suite 100
Washington, DC 20036
Johnathon D. Linkous, Executive Director
(202) 296–8130
Mission: The National Association of Area Agencies on Aging (NAAAA) represents
the interests of approximately 650 Area Agencies on Aging across the country.

National Association of RSVP Directors, Inc.
703 Maine Street
Paterson, NJ 07503
Maureen Milligan, President
(201) 881–6536

National Association of Meals Programs
204 "E" Street, N.E.
Washington, DC 20002
Gail Martin, Executive Director
(202) 547–6157

National Association of Older American Volunteers
11481 Bingham Terrace
Reston, VA 22091
Fran Butler, Program Director, Washington Representative
(703) 860–9570

National Caucus and Center on Black Aged, Inc.
1424 "K" Street, N.W., Suite 500
Washington, DC 20005
Samuel J. Simmons, President
(202) 537–8400
Mission: The National Caucus and Center on Black Aged is a nonprofit organization that works to improve the quality of life for older black Americans.

National Council of Senior Citizens
925 15th Street, N.W.
Washington, DC 20005
Lawrence Smedley, Executive Director
(202) 347–8800
Mission: The National Council of Senior Citizens, a nonprofit association of clubs, councils, and other community groups, works as an advocate on behalf of older Americans.

National Council on the Aging
600 Maryland Ave., S.W., West Wing 100
Washington, DC 20024
Daniel Thursz, President
(202) 479–1200
Mission: The National Council on the Aging (NCOA), a nonprofit, membership organization for professionals and volunteers, serves as a national resource for information, technical assistance, training, and research relating to the field of aging

National Interfaith Coalition on Aging
600 Maryland Ave., West Wing 100
Washington, DC 20024
Rev. John F. Evans, Program Manager
(202) 479–6689
Mission: The National Interfaith Coalition on Aging (NICA), whose members belong to Roman Catholic, Protestant, Jewish, and Greek Orthodox faiths, supports research on aging and provides technical assistance and advice to religious groups that serve older people.

National Pacific/Asian Resource Center on Aging
1511 3rd Avenue, Suite 914
Seattle, WA 98101
Louise M. Kamikawa, Director
(206) 624–1221
Mission: The National Pacific/Asian Resource Center on Aging is a private organization that works to improve the delivery of health care and social services to older members of the Pacific/Asian community.

National Senior Citizens Law Center
1815 "H" Street, N.W.
Washington, DC 20006
Burton Fretz, Executive Director
(202) 887–5280
Mission: The National Senior Citizens Law Center (NSCLC) is a public interest law firm that specializes in the legal problems of older people.

Older Women's League
730 11th Street, N.W., Suite 300
Washington, DC 20001
Joan Kuriansky, Executive Director
(202) 783–6686

Mission: The Older Women's League (OWL) seeks to educate the public about the problems and issues of concern to middle-aged and older women.

The Gerontological Society of America
1275 "K" Street, N.W., Suite 350
Washington, DC 20005–4006
Jack Cornman, Executive Director
(202) 842–1275
Mission: The Gerontological Society of America (GSA) is a professional organization that promotes the scientific study of aging in the biological and social sciences.

United Auto Workers/Retired & Older Workers Department
8731 E. Jefferson Avenue
Detroit, MI 48214
Tim Foley, Director
(313) 926–5231

University of Wisconsin Center for Health Sciences
610 Walnut Street, 707 WARS Bldg.
Madison, WI 53705
James T. Sykes, Chair of Public Policy Committee
(608) 263–1946

Other Advocacy Organizations

American Health Care Association
1201 "L" Street N.W.
Washington, DC 20005
(202) 842–4444
Mission: The American Health Care Association (AHCA) is a professional organization that represents the interests of licensed nursing homes and long-term care facilities to Congress, federal regulatory agencies, and other professional groups. The Association also provides leadership in dealing with long-term care issues.

Concerned Relatives of Nursing Home Patients
3130 Mayfield Road
Cleveland, OH 44118
(216) 321–0403
Mission: Concerned Relatives of Nursing Home Patients is a consumer group made up of persons who have had, currently have, or soon will have a family member or friend in a nursing home. The goals of this group are to maintain quality care and improve services of all nursing home residents.

Federal Council on Aging
330 Independence Ave., S.W., Room 4545 HHS-N
Washington, DC 20201
(202) 245–2451

Mission: The Federal Council on Aging, an advisory group authorized by the Older Americans Act of 1965, is selected by the president and the Congress. The 15 members represent a cross-section of rural and urban older Americans, national organizations with an interest in aging, business, labor, and the general public.

Health Insurance Association of America
1025 Connecticut Ave., N.W., Suite 1200, Washington, DC 20036
(202) 223–7780
Mission: The Health Insurance Association of America offers information to the public about all aspects of health and disability insurance.

Legal Services for the Elderly
132 W. 43rd St., 3rd Floor
New York, NY 10036
(212) 391–0120
Mission: Legal Services for the Elderly (LSE) is an advisory center for lawyers who specialize in the legal problems of older persons.

National Action Forum for Midlife and Older Women
c/o Dr. Jane Porcino, P.O. Box 816
Stony Brook, NY 11790–0609
Mission: The National Action Forum for Midlife and Older Women (NAFOW) serves as a clearinghouse of information dealing with issues of special concern to middle-aged and older women.

National Alliance of Senior Citizens
1700 18th Street, N.W., Suite 401
Washington, DC 20009
(202) 986–0117
Mission: The National Alliance of Senior Citizens is a consumer group that advocates policies and programs to enhance the lives of senior citizens.

National Association of Area Agencies on Aging
600 Maryland Ave., S.W., Suite 208
Washington, DC 20024
(202) 484–7520
Mission: The National Association of Area Agencies on Aging (NAAAA) represents the interests of approximately 650 Area Agencies on Aging across the country.

National Association for Hispanic Elderly/Associacion Nacional Pro Personas Mayores
2727 W. Sixth St., Suite 270
Los Angeles, CA 90057
(213) 487–1922
Mission: The National Association for Hispanic Elderly works to ensure that older Hispanic citizens are included in all social service programs for older Americans.

National Association for Home Care
519 "C" St., N.E.
Washington, DC 20002
(202) 547–7424
Mission: The National Association for Home Care (NAHC) is a professional organization that represents a variety of agencies that provide home care services, including home health agencies, hospice programs, and home-maker/home health aid agencies.

National Citizens Coalition for Nursing Home Reform
1424 16th St., N.W., Suite L2
Washington, DC 2005
(202) 797–0657
Mission: The National Citizens Coalition for Nursing Home Reform works to improve the quality of life for nursing home and boarding home residents and to ensure that consumers have a voice in the long-term care system.

National Committee to Preserve Social Security and Medicare
2000 "K" Street N.W., Suite 800
Washington, DC 20006
(202) 822–7848
Mission: The National Committee to Preserve Social Security and Medicare lobbies to protect the benefits provided by those programs and to further the interests of the elderly.

National Foundation for Long-Term Health Care
1200 - 15th St., N.W., Suite 402
Washington, DC 20005
(202) 659–3148
Mission: The National Foundation for Long-Term Health Care is a private, nonprofit organization that works on behalf of professionals who provide long-term care to older people and chronically ill individuals.

National Hispanic Council on Aging
2713 Ontario Rd., N.W.
Washington, DC 20009
(202) 265–1288
Mission: The National Hispanic Council on Aging is a private, nonprofit orga-nization that works to promote the well-being of older Hispanic individuals.

National Hospice Organization
1901 North Fort Myer Dr., Suite 307
Arlington, VA 22209
(703) 243–5900
Mission: The National Hospice Organization (NHO) promotes quality care for terminally ill patients and provides information about hospice services avail-able in the United States. Hospices provide medical care for dying patients as well as counseling and supportive services for the patient and family members.

National Indian Council on Aging

P.O. Box 2088
Albuquerque, NM 87103
(505) 242–9505
Mission: The National Indian Council on Aging, a nonprofit organization
funded by the Administration on Aging, works to ensure that older Indian
and Alaskan Native Americans have equal access to quality, comprehensive
health care, legal assistance, and social services.

Pride Long-Term Home Health Care Institute

153 W. 11th St.
New York, NY 10011
(212) 790–8864
Mission: The Pride Institute is a private organization that works to coordinate
research and policy development in the field of long-term home health care
for older persons.

Save Our Security

1201 16th Street NW, Suite 222
Washington, DC 20036
(202) 822–7848
Mission: Save Our Security (SOS) is a coalition of organizations devoted to
protecting and expanding Social Security.

Index of Authors

187

Index of Subjects